THE
JAPANESE
MATERIAL CULTURE

HOUSE
IN THE MODERN HOME

inge daniels

with photography by susan andrews

Routledge
Taylor & Francis Group

LONDON AND NEW YORK

First published 2010 by berg publishers

Published 2020 by Routledge
2 Park Square, Milton Park, Abingdon, Oxon OX14 4RN
605 Third Avenue, New York, NY 10017

Routledge is an imprint of the Taylor & Francis Group, an informa business

Library of Congress Cataloging-in-Publication Data

A catalogue record for this book is available from the Library of Congress.

British Library Cataloguing-in-Publication Data

A catalogue record for this book is available from the British Library.

ISBN13: 978-1-8452-0517-1 (pbk)

Typeset by JS Typesetting Ltd, Porthcawl, Mid Glamorgan

CONTENTS

ACKNOWLEDGEMENTS

Many individuals have contributed to this project, but my gratitude beyond expression goes to Shaun, my husband, who has been a tremendous companion throughout. Not only has he sacrificed much of his own time assisting me with copy-editing, selecting visuals and producing layouts, he has also offered relentless encouragement, patience and his rather unique brand of humour.

The book would not have been possible without the hospitality and long-term assistance of numerous friends in Japan, including the Kadonaga, Kuwahara, Nakao, Nishiki, Sakai, and Yano families. However, I would like to pay special tribute to the following people who over the years have become like family to me; to Noriko, Yutaka and Shigeko Kagemori for their genuine support and concern as well as their lavish parties with delicacies from all over the globe (many prepared by Fujii-san, a family friend), always accompanied by generous quantities of wine and sake. Seiichi, Chiyuki, Yasuko and Yuko Takahashi have been a continuous source of inspiration and comfort. They welcomed me into their warm family home, repeatedly sharing their delicious meals, stories and passions well into the night with me. Miyako-san, my long-standing friend, has never faltered in assisting, although I am sure she must have become tired of my relentless questions and calls for help. Not only has she introduced me to many participants in the project, she has also taken me on regular expeditions to unusual, local cafés, restaurants and sites. Finally, for her intellectual stimulus and enthusiasm I would also like to thank Kema-san (Kemake); without her advice on many parts of the book as well as her continuous stream of letters and packages this study would have been considerably poorer.

Many individual scholars have provided insightful comments and suggestions upon which I have drawn. However, I am especially grateful to Professor Daniel Miller, who has been an excellent mentor and critic and, above all, a great friend. I should also like to express my gratitude to Professor Senda Minoru for his unceasing support over the last fifteen years for rather unconventional research projects, whether as a timid graduate student at Nara Women's University or as post-doctoral fellow at the International Research Center for Japanese Studies. Finally, special thanks go to participants of the EASA conference in Vienna in September 2004, and anthropology seminars at the University of Sussex, UCL, SOAS and Oxford University. Portions of this book have grown out of papers published in the journals *Home Cultures* and *The Journal of Material Culture* as well as two edited volumes entitled *Religion and Material Culture* and *Time, Consumption, and Everyday Life*. I would like to thank the anonymous reviewers and the editors of these publications for their helpful comments.

I have been fortunate to receive several grants that provided financial support. In 2002–3 I was granted a one-year post-doctoral fellowship from The Japanese Society for the Promotion of Science to conduct the fieldwork this book is based on. A small grant from the British Academy has enabled me, and the photographer Susan Andrews, to travel to Japan in 2006. And a generous contribution from the John Fell OUP Research Fund has made it possible to print this publication in full-colour.

Finally, I gratefully acknowledge the generous support and collaboration of Susan Andrews. I should like to thank her for keeping up with my harrowing regime of home visits in Japan, for spending numerous sessions discussing and selecting her fascinating photographs, and for perfecting each image to the highest, possible standard. Special thanks also go to Tomo Morisawa, Go Sugimoto and Jump Studios for offering their expertise and invaluable visual assistance.

NOTE TO READERS

In the text I have followed the Japanese convention for using names, which is family name followed by first name. I have only created pseudonyms for a small minority of participants in this project who preferred to remain anonymous. British pounds equivalents have been calculated at the exchange rate during my fieldwork in 2003, which was approximately ¥200 per £1.

Dr Inge Daniels
University Lecturer in Material and Visual Culture
Institute of Social and Cultural Anthropology
University of Oxford

INTRODUCTION

THE JAPANESE HOUSE?

> Does the Japanese house as we know it actually exist? The Western architect who goes to Japan can spend his whole time hunting feverishly for it in vain – what he is searching for is … something firmly fixed in the secondary and tertiary environments (of the media and one's imagination) … he could find it more easily in any library … A coffee-table reverie … exploited by the JAL advert and embassy literature. (Fawcett 1980: 12– 14)

These words, written by a British architect in 1980, pinpoint one of the central questions guiding this publication; How, when and why did the fascination with the abstract, idealized category of 'The Japanese House', and by extension Japan, develop, and what is its persistent, worldwide appeal? It is fitting to start with the musings of a foreign architect as architects were among the first to carry out extensive research about Japanese dwellings, and they have played an active role in the conceptualization and dissemination of the stereotype of 'the Japanese house' abroad and in Japan.

During the Meiji period (1868–1911) European and US architects, as well as many other professionals, were invited by the Japanese government to participate in cross-cultural exchange programmes as part of a nationwide modernization project. Within this context the American scientist Edward Morse took up a post as a visiting lecturer in Zoology at the University of Tokyo, and during his four-year stay in Japan he conducted the first comprehensive study of urban, middle-class Japanese dwellings in English. To date, Morse's book entitled *Japanese Homes and Their Surroundings* (1886), illustrated with more than 300 of his meticulous sketches, remains one of the finest sources of information on premodern domestic architecture. It not only offers scholarly

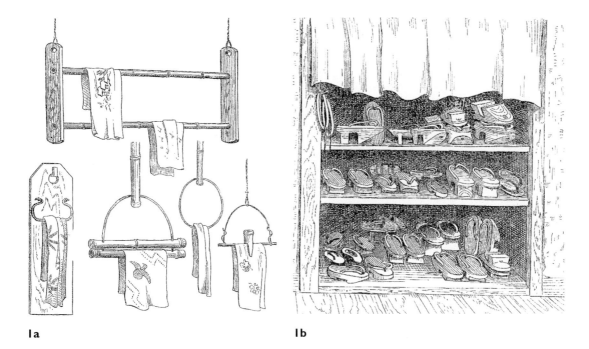

1a   1b

descriptions of construction techniques, interior decoration and gardening but also pays minute attention to the material culture of everyday, domestic life, discussing and depicting objects such as towel racks (fig. 1a), lamps, shoe closets (fig. 1b) and toilets. As the following two quotations illustrate, Morse was eager to approach his object of study objectively. He frequently drew a comparison with domestic architecture in the USA, and he acknowledged both the strengths and weaknesses of Japanese homes:

> The first sight of a Japanese house is disappointing; it is unsubstantial in appearance, and there is a meagerness of color … An American finds it difficult to consider such a structure as a dwelling, when so many features are absent that go to make up a dwelling at home, – no door or windows; no attic or cellar; no chimneys, and within no fireplace, and of course no customary mantle; no permanently enclose rooms; and as for furniture, no beds or tables, chairs …

> A severe, Quaker-like simplicity is really one of the great charms of a Japanese room. Absolute cleanliness and refinement, with very few objects in sight upon which the eye may rest, are the main features in household adornment. (Morse 1886: 6–7, 309)

Morse's intentions aside, during the 1930s the Modernist Movement hijacked his work in their attempt to elevate the Japanese House to an aesthetic ideal characterized by the simplicity of form and harmony of its empty interiors. The German architect Bruno Taut (1880–1938) played a key role in propagating this stereotype.[1] The fact that his milestone publication about Japanese domestic aesthetics from 1938 (*Houses and People of Japan*) continues to inspire contemporary readers attests to his unique insight into everyday life in Japan at the beginning of the twentieth century. However, this work can also be read as a conservative treaty for the promotion of traditional values and 'good taste'. Indeed, the text is peppered with negative remarks about the tacky homes of 'normal' Japanese who 'lack culture' and whose houses thus fail to live up to Taut's idealized notion of what Japanese homes should look like. For example:

> I feel simply incapable of describing the 'normal' townsman's apartments. As to taste, they vary exceedingly. From … perfect achievements we pass to cases not exactly showing bad taste and thence to those where a lack of culture manifests itself in trash or in misunderstood imported articles, and where the feeling for the significance of Japanese tradition, for instance, the tokonoma, is lost. In such places Japanese floral art is mixed with European; or a wireless, a gramophone, golf-clubs, a chest of drawers, even a piano are introduced. (Taut 1938: 176)

Throughout the remainder of the twentieth century this traditionalist attitude towards the aesthetics of Japanese private dwellings has prevailed in the growing numbers of publications on the topic in both English and Japanese. Interestingly, the majority of this literature has 'Japanese House' (Ishimoto 1963) in the title supplemented with a range of revealing adjectives such as 'essential' (Ito 1967), 'elegant' (Ito 1969) and 'modern' (Sasaki 1970; Pollock 2005). One notable exception within this genre is Heinrich Engel's *The Japanese House – A Tradition for Contemporary Architecture* (Engel 1964). Although parts of this hefty volume are written in a rather pompous style (and one can detect a purist streak throughout), many of Engel's discussions are highly original and thought-provoking, which professes to his high standard of scholarship.

We have to wait until the 1980s for an architectural publication that directly challenges the stereotype of the minimal Japanese house. In *The New Japanese House* (1980) Fawcett draws on Japanese domestic rituals in order to demonstrate that the private arena is always dynamic and multifaceted. Throughout the book he engages in poetic and philosophical explorations of private dwellings designed during the 1960s and 1970s by Japanese architects who drew inspiration for their designs from domestic, ritual practices. With this work Fawcett has firmly shifted the focus of the research agenda within architecture to 'contemporary' Japanese homes. However, by concentrating on concept houses inhabited – if at all – by an urban elite, and by stressing the uniqueness of these designs 'inaccessible to the architect in the West' (Fawcett 1980: 16), he might inadvertently have contributed to mythologizing the 'Japanese House' (even if his is a modern version) for a whole new generation of architects, designers and lay people alike. The fact that so many subsequent volumes published on contemporary Japanese domestic architecture focus on the production and design of homes that are empty of people and their possessions seems to confirm this (Black and Murata 2000; Brown and Cali 2001; Pollock 2005).

Since the 1980s, the academic literature about modern Japanese minimalism has played a key role in disseminating information about Japanese homes to the general public in Europe and the USA because it has successfully crossed over into the DIY/design literature for the mass market. Books with titles such as *A Japanese Touch for your Home* (Yagi 1992) or *Space: Japanese Design Solutions* (Freeman 2004) are churned out in ever greater numbers. These popular publications, as well as countless newspaper and magazine articles, TV programmes and films, thrive on the relentless fascination with Japan as the quintessential, exotic 'other' which is commonly articulated in two equally biased ways. First, there is an admiration for some of kind of Ur-Japanese aesthetic philosophy expressed through traditional arts such as flower arranging and tea ceremonies, which is thought to resonate in all aspect of modern Japanese life ranging from fashion and food to design and architecture. Second, there is a relentless obsession with what I call 'the weird and the

'wacky' depicted as normal. Examples include dirty underwear dispensers, high school prostitutes and sadistic game shows.[2] I aim to question this unrelenting fantasy using ethnography to confront the de-contextualized, ahistorical stereotype of 'the Japanese house' with the contradictions and complexities of everyday life behind closed doors.

ETHNOGRAPHIES OF THE HOME: ANTHROPOLOGY OF THE EVERYDAY

'Ethnography' refers to an assortment of research techniques employed by anthropologists (and also many other researchers) to study the complexity of human life. Typically it involves spending a substantial period of time with the people one studies in order to gather original data through observation and participation. Until the second half of the twentieth century ethnographies of domestic architecture and the material culture of the home have remained marginal within anthropology. During the 1960s and 1970s structural anthropologists changed this by drawing attention to the private sphere as a meaningful context for understanding the social organization of particular societies. Pierre Bourdieu's much-cited analysis of the Kabyle house in Algeria, first published in 1970, is firmly grounded in this structuralist research tradition. He argues that the house is an inverted microcosm organized according to a series of structural oppositions (high–low, male–female, light–dark) that are common in Kabyle society at large.[3] During the 1980s, this kind of approach has come under attack as it implies that the material aspects of the dwelling are merely expressive of larger, underlying principles that guide social life.[4] Moreover, by focusing on the visual, spatial divisions of the home instead of examining how people actually live in these spaces, structuralists have reproduced binary social categories and overlooked the 'fluidity and ambiguity which characterizes much social life' (Helliwell 1996: 141–5).

Bourdieu's study of the Kabyle house has also invited this kind of critique, but it is often overlooked that during his long career, in accordance with his shifting interpretation of the relationship between human actors and the social structures in which they are embedded (*habitus*), he has repeatedly reworked this essay.[5] Indeed, his definition of the *habitus* has gradually changed from 'an (unconscious) system of structuring structures based on past experiences' and routinized through bodily actions (Bourdieu [1972] 1979) to a more dynamic, context dependent *habitus* that 'is durable but not eternal' (Bourdieu [1980] 1990: 113) as it 'changes constantly in response to new experiences' (Bourdieu [1997] 2000: 161). Thus, in his later work subjects (such as the inhabitants of the Kabyle house) are thought to be able to act creatively within particular constraints.[6]

In recent years, a number of social scientists (Sangren 2000; Farquhar 2002; Hillier and Rooks 2002) have revisited Bourdieu's notion of the *habitus*.[7] In their view it remains one of the most powerful conceptual tools to study human life because it 'is neither culture nor psychological structure, role, or national character. It may vary by class, region, community, or family, but it cannot be reduced to either individual or collective behavior' (Farquhar 2002: 9). I have been particularly drawn to Sangren's work (2000) as he uses Chinese ethnographic examples in order to fine-tune Bourdieu's *habitus* by stressing the significance of individual desire. He argues that although the people he studied reproduce the social system, they are also driven by individual motives that are not necessary structurally defined (Sangren ibid.: 6–9). Through an analysis of ongoing, ordinary dynamics of everyday life behind closed doors, this book similarly aims to explore the paradoxes and tensions between individual actions and social obligations in contemporary Japan.

Finally, Bourdieu's *oeuvre* also warrants special attention because he has been a pivotal figure in the development of consumption studies and the renewed interest in material culture within British anthropology since the 1980s (Miller 1987; 1988; 1994). This new research strand has, in turn, been influential in the establishment of the home as a significant research topic.[8] Since the mid-1990s it has produced a large body of literature that interprets the home as an ongoing, changing process, giving similar importance to material and social practices while highlighting the contradictions and conflicts inherent in everyday life (Chevalier 1998; 1999; Buchli 1999; Attfield 2000; Miller 2001; Clarke 2002; Daniels 2003).[9] This publication is firmly embedded in the material culture research about the domestic (Daniels 2001b) but it also references the large body of literature that specifically deals with Japanese homes. I will turn to this next.

JAPANESE PIONEERS IN THE STUDY OF DOMESTIC MATERIAL CULTURE

The Japanese house and home has been a major topic of investigation for more than eighty years for a diverse range of Japanese and foreign scholars. I have already mentioned some important architectural studies above, but the bulk of the research about Japanese domestic life has been carried out by historians (Koizumi 1980; 1995; 2002; Uchida 2002; Uchida, Ogawa and Fujiya 2002). Topics that have been studied recently and are of interest for my work include the sociability of food consumption (Cwiertca 1999), the hybridity of Western and Japanese style elements in the home (Teasley 2001) and the gendered consumption of domestic spaces (Inoue 2003). Throughout this book, I will repeatedly engage with these rich historical materials in order to clarify specific practices I encountered during my fieldwork. Jordan Sand's (2003) historical study of processes that led to the creation of the modern Japanese dwelling deserves a special mentioning as it could be read as a complementary introduction to this book which starts where he left off.

A second, important body of research about the Japanese domestic sphere has been produced by social scientists (Funo 1997; Yamashita 2003) who work on topics such as the relationship between home and work (Allison 1994), the role of the housewife (Imamura 1987) and changing inter-family relationships (Fujiwara 2003). Although this work has led to important new insights into the changing social relationships and the underlying ideologies in the domestic, it has completely ignored the material and spatial qualities of the home. My aim is to approach contemporary Japanese homes more holistically by reconnecting these various research strands.

By far the most innovative studies about Japanese homes have been published in Japanese; bridging the gap between this research and the literature in the English language will be another important contribution of my book to the field. Indeed, there is a long indigenous tradition of conducting fieldwork inside homes. Collaborative projects carried out in rural dwellings during the 1920s and 1930s by folklorists such as Yanagita Kunio ([1940] 1962) have been well documented. However, it is less well known that during the same period Japanese ethnographers were also conducting meticulous research into the material culture of everyday urban life. A key example is Kon Wajirô (1888–1973) who led a number of seminal research projects about everyday urban life in Tokyo during the 1920s. Topics studied range from the aesthetics of barracks built by those made homeless after the 1923 earthquake and fashion trends in Tokyo's main shopping venue, Ginza, to urban hairstyles and complex typologies of fences, lanterns and rain pipes.

In 1930 Kon compiled and published a series of essays together with his trademark sketches in a book entitled *Modernologio* (*kôgengaku*) that promoted his innovative methods for studying objects in a contemporary urban context.[10] Three essays examined interiors of dwellings: a room in a rural traditional inn, a student's dormitory room, and, most interesting for my own work, the house of a newly married couple in Tokyo. Kon not only recorded furniture, fixtures and ornaments but also made detailed sketches of the contents of closets and storage rooms, and supplied a complete inventory of the kitchen. Subsequently, some of Kon's students successfully applied the Modernologio methodology. Between 1935 and 1938 Kobayashi Keiko, for example, conducted a study of her family home using meticulous sketches of mundane items of domestic material culture such as lights, electrical appliances and the whole content of her wardrobe (Nitta, Tanaka and Koyama 2003: 80–1).

In this context it is also worth mentioning Nishiyama Uzo (1911–94), a Japanese architect whose impressive career spans more than six decades but whose seminal research about urban dwellings remains largely unknown outside Japan. During the 1930s, for example, Nishiyama visited and studied more than 3,600 homes in the Kansai region. He was a socially engaged visionary focusing on a wide range of issues such as barracks, company housing and slum living, and like Kon he made detailed drawings of the material culture of everyday life. Some of his publications, such as *Dwelling Problems* (1942) and *Housing From Now On* (1947), directly influenced the state-led

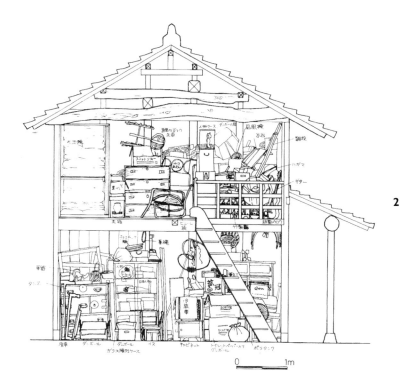

2

housing reforms of the post-war period, while in later life he became actively engaged in the preservation of old buildings.

Groundbreaking Japanese research inside urban dwellings continues until today. Particularly, noteworthy is a large-scale project conducted since the 1970s by two Japanese research institutes, the Consumer Goods Research Institute (CORE) and the Communication and Design Institute (CDI). Researchers affiliated with both institutions draw on questionnaires as well as an impressive collection of visual representations such as photographs, sketches, architectural plans and advertising in order to catalogue the changing material culture of Japanese homes (CDI 1980; 1983; 1993). Moreover, a number of Japanese researchers trained in the ethnology/folklore studies tradition continue to deliver research of the highest academic standards into the mundane aspects of domestic life. Hashidate Masumi, for example, uses detailed sketches to examine the content of hidden domestic spaces such as storehouses or closets (Hashidate 1990) (fig. 2), and she cleverly analyses commercial pamphlets in order to discuss the consumption of innovative products during ritual events (Hashidate 2002).

Taken together, the studies introduced above offer an in-depth account of everyday urban life in Japan since the 1920s. Although most researchers employ a range of methods, all demonstrate the insights that may be gained by giving more primacy to visual methods such as photography or drawing. Still, as I have already mentioned, this body of research remains largely unnoticed in the international research community. The fact that the majority of the work is only published in Japanese is a factor, but another significant flaw is that many studies fail to engage with larger debates and theories. This might also explain why so many Japanese anthropologists tend to dismiss this literature. Although I agree that the lack of sustained analysis and critical engagement is a problem, in order to highlight the potential of this kind of research, I should like to end this section with a brief discussion of a recent project about the material culture of the Japanese home that combines the long native research into domestic material culture with current anthropological thinking about objects.

Seoul Style 2002 was the title of an exhibition curated by the anthropologist Sato Koji for the National Museum of Ethnology in Osaka in 2002. The display drew on Sato's study of the whole content of one Seoul apartment belonging to the Lee family. For the exhibition, the family's possessions were all carefully documented, wrapped and shipped to Japan. In two books Sato (Sato and Asakura 2002; Sato and Yamashita 2002) describes this process and its impact on the family. Throughout, he discusses current themes in the anthropological study of the material culture of the home such as: (1) the discrepancy between ideal and everyday lived in homes; (2) the dialectical relationship between people and things, or, in his words, 'the home and its material culture creates people' (Sato 2002b: 7); (3) the importance of the storage and disposal of things. Importantly, Sato does not aim to produce a display that represents the essence of 'Korean culture', but throughout he stresses the similarity of everyday urban life in both Japan and Korea. Likewise, in this publication I will refrain from making grand statements about 'Japanese culture'. By contrast, by focusing on mundane, familiar practices in Japanese homes I hope to counteract at least some of the persistent yearnings for a weird and wonderful Japan.

THE FIELDWORK SETTING: 'JAPAN IS NOT TOKYO'

This is the first publication of its kind that is based on long-term anthropological fieldwork inside urban Japanese homes. I will draw on multiple ethnographic encounters I have had with Japan since 1995 (see Daniels 1996; 2001a; 2003). However, the specific data presented in this volume was collected during fieldwork carried out over a one-year period (2002–3) in thirty homes in the Kansai region (fig. 3) (Spread 1).[11] Most ethnographies of urban life in Japan conducted since 1945 have focused on the Tokyo area.[12] One type of urban ethnography explores the delicate relationship between tradition and social change from the point of view of those with strong local roots.[13] Examples range from Dore's groundbreaking 1950s study of a Tokyo ward (1958) to the Tokyo neighbourhood studies of Bestor (1989) and Thang (2001) and Robertson's (1991) research in a Tokyo suburb. As Clammer (1997) has rightly pointed out, since the late 1970s the majority of the Japanese have not create communities tied together by locality. Social networks are constructed around work, school and friendship, and consumption practices such a travel, eating and shopping play a central role in consolidating these new type of communities. The anthropological literature about Japanese consumption has only really taken off since the mid-1990s (Moeran 1996; Clammer 1997; 2000; Goldstein-Gidoni 1997; Robertson 1998; McVeigh 2000; Spielvogel 2003; Aoyagi 2005). Some of these studies have opted for a multi-sited approach (Hendry 2000; Bestor 2004; Allison 2006), but Tokyo seems to remain by far the preferred area of investigation.[14] My fieldwork, conducted in the area around Osaka, will therefore add much needed regional variation to anthropological studies about Japan. It will also complicate the current research about Japanese consumption by highlighting the specificity and complexity of domestic consumption practices.

Japan is a modern nation-state with a central administration located in Tokyo, where twenty-six per cent of the population lives. Highly efficient media networks and state of the art transport systems have made the same goods, services and information available anywhere in Japan.

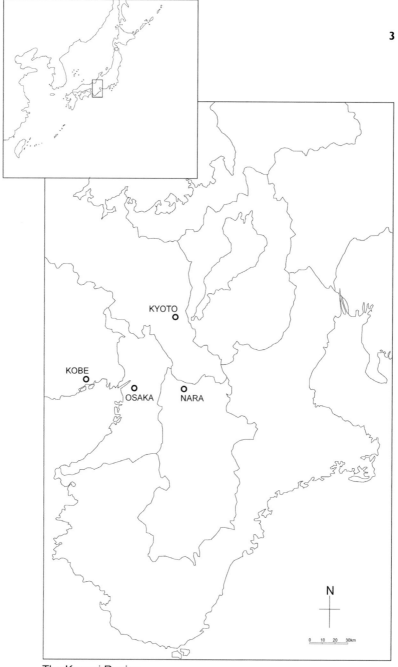

3

The Kansai Region

Moreover, commodification and standardization of all aspects of life have led to the consolidation of a strong notion of a homogeneous Japanese identity. Still, historically rooted regional differences have survived in the form of strong antagonisms between the regions. The rivalry between the

Kansai and the Kanto region (the urban sprawl around Tokyo) remains particularly vivid and is primarily played out in the cultural arenas of food and language (Daniels 1994).[15] Interestingly, one particular, post-war commodity that embodies this complex relationship between the regional and national is the modern Japanese house. Indeed, mass-produced houses have facilitated the creation of a unified, 'mainstream' Japanese identity while continuing to display subtle regional characteristics.

During the Second World War the housing stock in all major Japanese cities was almost completely destroyed. The government built some temporary houses and invested in social housing, but the scope of these schemes was limited and the accommodation provided came nowhere near the estimated 4 million homes that were needed (Uchida, Ogawa and Fujiya 2002: 120–1). Moreover, post-war economic growth meant that large numbers of young people migrated to urban areas in search of work.[16] Both developments led to a ceaseless demand for affordable, urban accommodation that ensued during the 1960s with the development of large national construction companies. These businesses primarily traded in ready-built (*tate-uri*) homes on developed plots,

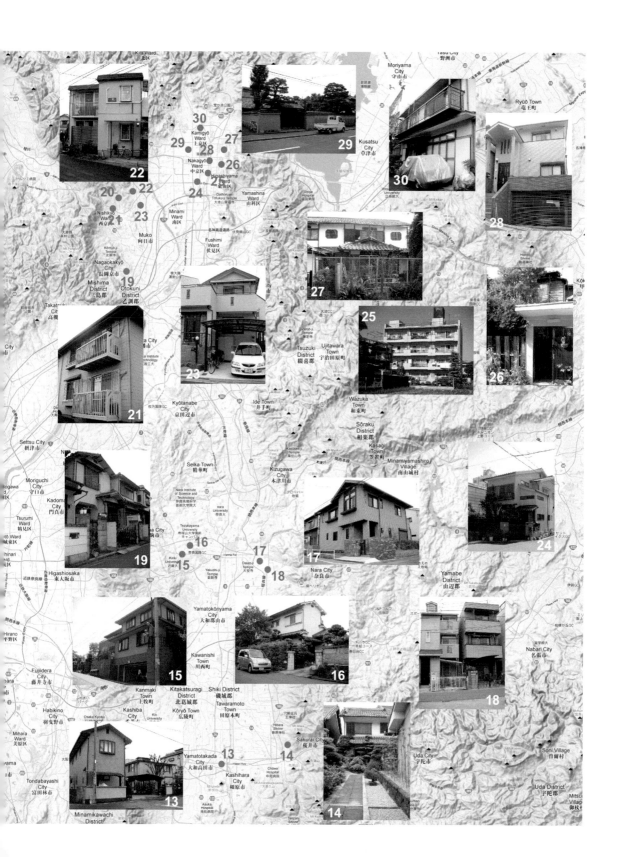

where customers would either buy a detached house (*ikkodate*) or an apartment (*manshon*). Over time many of these national construction companies have amalgamated into gigantic home-building conglomerates such as Misawa, Mitsui, Sekisui, Daiwa and Panasonic that continue to dominate the contemporary housing market. The success of these giant, home-building companies resulted in the continued industrialization of building techniques and the standardization of the exterior and interior features of Japanese homes. This is the reason why today all domestic layouts are based on a central living area (consisting of either a dining-kitchen or a living-dining-kitchen) with a number of private rooms. Although designs are similar across producers, the construction method each company uses differs. Mitsui, for example, is famous for its two-by-four system, while Sekisui uses a lightweight steel structure and Misawa introduced a panel-construction system (fig. 4a/fig. 4b).

The majority of people in large cities live in apartments (*shûgô jûtaku*, literally collective housing), but my data suggests that for many the detached house (*ikkodate jûtaku*) remains the ideal housing form. Most housing companies sell both made-to-order houses (*chûmon jûtaku*) and prefabricated houses on a developed plot (*tate-uri jûtaku*). The former are more desirable than the latter, but they are considerable more expensive, and the less well-off and first-time buyers tend to choose the second option (Suzuki 2002b). Prospective buyers are given the opportunity to visit model homes, either constructed on site or in a 'model house park', where they can inspect a potential home before they make a purchase. Moreover, all customers can also personalize their future homes by using catalogues to select particular features such as the colour of the kitchen,

4a   4b

bathroom and toilet fittings, or the size and material used for doors, windows, gates and fences. The immense variations in style that are offered in accordance with a particular budget exemplify how through everyday consumption contemporary Japanese may express subtle differences within the overall ideal of sameness (see Chapter 2).

A small percentage of contemporary home construction is carried out by regional family businesses consisting of anything from a licensed carpenter with a dozen of craftsmen up to medium-sized contractors with up to 100 employees (Brown and Cali 2001: 67-8). The home-building giants discussed above target potential customers through nationwide advertising campaigns. Moreover, their sales representatives frequent companies in order to entice employees to subscribe to their loans with special deals. Smaller businesses, by contrast, tend to team up with local architects and estate agents as they target people with strong roots in a particular locality. Although the designs of these companies also reflect the overall standardization of the industry, many have retained some local flavour through the types of building materials but also the tatami sizes used.[17]

Whatever the scale of the company concerned, all have to reckon with the regional characteristics of climate and natural landscape. In Hokkaido, the most northern island of Japan, for example, sturdier roofs are necessary to deal with the severe winters, while in the Tokyo area all buildings have to be able to withstand regular tremors. Interestingly, Suzuki (2002a) has compiled a list of eight types of contemporary prefabricated houses grouped around an urban core that broadly correspond with both the major climatic and the administrative regions of Japan (fig. 5). These are from the top right to the bottom left: (1) Hokkaido (Sapporo), (2) Tohoku Nanbu (Sendai), (3) Hokuriku (Kanazawa), (4) Tokyo-en (Chiba), (5) Tokai (Nagoya), (6) Osaka-en (Osaka), (7) Sanin (Hiroshima), (8) Kitakyushu (Fukuoka). The description of the Osaka-type house reads as follows:

> Many of these houses, built on narrow plots, are typical three-storied (even if the law only allows two-storied dwellings) with a garage on the ground floor. In Osaka city it is common to find a Japanese-style sitting room adjacent to a western-style room. Shutters, a fence, a western-style exterior, a toilet on the first floor are some of the other characteristics of these homes. (Suzuki 2002a: 24)

A second, small player in the housing markets, situated at the opposite end of the spectrum, is the urban architectural studio consisting of a relatively small number of architects and designers. These businesses target a niche market willing to pay extra for customized solutions to specific housing problems such as a lack of space or special needs associated with old age and disability. These companies do not generally deliver the innovative features associated with celebrity architects such as Ando or Ito, but their personalized products are very expensive and therefore only attainable for the more affluent strata of the population.[18]

THE PARTICIPANTS: FAMILY, CLASS AND HOMEOWNERSHIP

Most participants in my research claimed they did not want to live in a designed house both because it was too expensive but also because it would set them apart from their neighbours. Like some ninety per cent of the country's population (Taira 1993: 169), they considered themselves to belong to a broadly defined and generally undifferentiated middle stratum, referred to by the term *chûryû*. Social scientists, Japanese and other, generally equate this word with 'middle class',

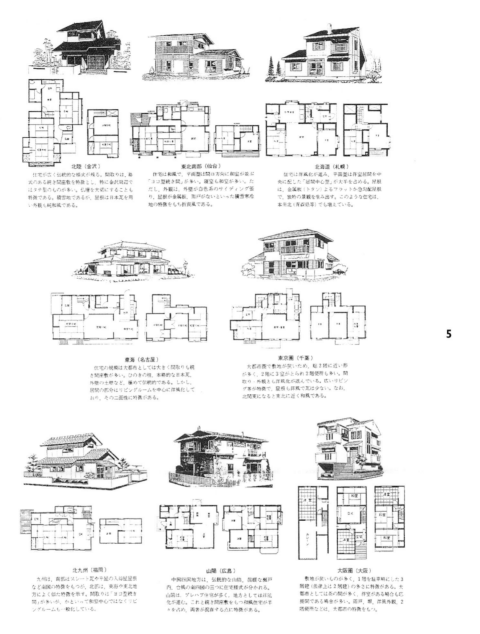

5

but 'mainstream' seems a more appropriate, emic translation. This distinction is important because the notion of class refers to difference based on socio-economic status linked with occupation and education while 'mainstream' actually denotes social inclusiveness.[19] In spite of social differences, the Japanese mainstream identity developed during the 1960s and has remained hegemonic for more than four decades. Kelly (2002) has demonstrated that this ideological construct gained such a strong hold on society because it is deeply embedded in public discourses and is socially grounded in institutions that frame people's everyday experiences, namely family, work and education (ibid.: 234–5).

Although statistics show that the number of single-person households and homes without children are increasing,[20] in 2003 the nuclear family with one or two children remained the ideal social unit for the majority of Japanese. The ideal life of a 'mainstream' citizen would probably unfold as follows. As a child she or he would grow up in a nuclear family and enrol at the age of seven for twelve years in compulsory, high quality state education. In the case of male children this schooling would automatically lead to life-time employment as a white-collar worker (*sarariimen*) in a large cooperation. As sole providers, men would work long hours, while women would have a complimentary domestic role as full-time housewives with sole responsibility for the home. The 'mainstream' married woman would be 100 per cent devoted to housework, the education of children and the care of elderly relatives. By the time the first child was born the couple should be able to buy a detached house (*ikkodate*) with a garden and a garage, preferably located in a newly developed suburb. Once their children were grown up, parents might build a new house on the same spot, but they would generally be expected to remain in the same locality until one of them passed away.

By 2003 many cracks had appeared in this perfect picture of domestic bliss, but one aspect of the 'mainstream' family ideology that remains unchallenged, and is particularly important for my study, is the ideal of home ownership. Twenty-four of the thirty participating units in my study were homeowners. Of these, sixteen lived in two-storey detached houses and eight owned apartments in city centres. Only six units, three students, two recently married couples, and one single woman in her forties, lived in rented accommodation, but all saw this as a temporary solution and expected to purchase their own home as they progressed through life. Indeed, according to a 1998 nationwide survey, 60.3 per cent of all Japanese homes were owned. The lowest percentage of homeowners is found in Tokyo (41.5 per cent) and Osaka (49.6 per cent) where land is very expensive. However, in three other urban areas where I conducted fieldwork these figures are much higher; in Nara home owners amount for 71 per cent, in Kobe for 60.9 per cent and in Kyoto for 59.4 per cent of the population (AS 2002: 191).

Interestingly, before 1945 the majority of *urban* homes were rented. In 1934, for example, ninety per cent of the housing stock in Osaka and seventy per cent of that in Tokyo were rented properties (Miyawaki 1998: 225). Miyawaki explicitly links the increased popularity of home ownership since the 1950s to the rise of rural to urban migrants who had their roots in the Japanese countryside and had a strong desire to own land, preferably with a detached house on top (ibid.: 234). However, Ronald (2004) has proposed a more complex explanation for the phenomenon based on the specific interplay between the state, the company and the family. In the post-war period the state consistently supported industry and business at the expense of improving social conditions. Thus, for example, large governmental investments were made in the coal and heavy industries instead of in providing social housing.

The prioritization of economic growth was warranted with the promise that this strategy would eventually result in financial and social benefits for all (Uchida, Ogawa and Fujiya 2002: 120–1). However, in reality, the state escaped its social responsibilities towards its citizens and was able to hide huge inequalities. In its place, private companies took on a welfare role by providing cheap 'company housing' as well as low-cost loans for employees. However, welfare continues to be almost explicitly provided through the family, organized around moral ideals of reciprocity and interdependence across the generations (Ronald 2004: 56–7). Thus, for Ronald, the privately owned family home is 'the symbolic basis by which reciprocal family obligations are defined, the

physical space were welfare services are exchanged, and, as the main financial commitment and reservoir of family wealth, the economic basis of household welfare' (ibid.: 57).

Contemporary Japanese homes, their physical structure and material contents, form the basis for the social and economic wellbeing of their inhabitants. However, my study aims to expose the tensions and frictions that occur at the intersection between domestic ideologies and practices. To achieve a happy home inhabitants need to balance the relationship between the individual and the collective (see Chapters 1 and 4), negotiate multiple connections between the home and outside networks (see Chapters 2 and 5) and create beneficial alignments with spirits and ancestors (Chapter 3) as well as with the material world (Chapter 6).

MATERIAL METHODOLOGIES: THERE IS MORE TO UNDERSTANDING THAN MEANING

> Research about social relations is made out of social relations, and these are as much created as they are found through the research process.
>
> Cook and Crang 2007: 59

Japanese homes are sheltered spaces. Most Japanese rarely visit each other's homes, while socializing with family, friends and colleagues takes place in public spaces. The search for volunteers willing to open up their homes to participate in my study has, therefore, been time-consuming and complex. Some of the well-documented strategies employed to conduct in-depth research into urban domestic settings such as targeting a particular location (for example, a street or an apartment block) with letters and/or door-to-door visits (Miller 1988; 1998b; Halle 1993), putting up posters on public notice boards or placing advertisements in newspapers and magazines (Cook and Crang

2007: 18) either failed or were considered too perilous to pursue. In the end, I was only able to embark on this project because I could draw on a variety of social networks built up while living in Japan for five years from 1992 until 1997. Most participants were recruited either through personal introductions by long-term friends or at face-to-face meetings with people attending public lectures and some rather esoteric seminars I gave about topics such as Belgian food and London design.

The difficulty involved in conducting long-term fieldwork in spaces usually considered off-limit to outsiders has meant that the bulk of social researchers studying the domestic arena have used unstructured, qualitative interviews as their main method of enquiry. One key weakness attributed to this narrative approach is its overemphasis on meaning and the agency of the individual. Indeed, interviews inside the home setting tend to encourage particular individuals, often the woman of the house, to create stories about themselves (and their families) (Hurdley 2006).[21] Specific domestic objects are mere props in these human life histories, and one thus loses sight of the fact that all homes are both social and material realities. I agree with Colloredo-Mansfeld that: 'in treating goods as signs … [we] have divorced objects of their most obvious property, their materiality. The weight, shape, flavor, odor, coarseness or fineness of things that require us to interact with them in specific ways' (Colloredo-Mansfeld 1998: 38). The material world is not just a context for the movement of human bodies; it also imposes certain socio-spatial configurations and '[material agents] prescribe programmes of action that schedule and monitor our day-to-day activities' (Olsen 2003: 97). In their everyday lives people engage with objects not only through critical reasoning but also through embodied interactions such as storing, placing, washing, eating, sitting, sleeping and disposing. Thus, the conceptualization and the material properties of objects and spaces are dialectically related and equal attention needs to be paid to both.

Some anthropologists studying the home have successfully transcended the limitations of the interview by adapting 'traditional' *in situ* fieldwork techniques to modern, urban conditions. By paying multiple follow-up visits to the same homes (Miller 2001; 2008), or by living for extended periods of time in the particular community studied, even if not inside the participants' homes, (Gregson 2007) one may build up a relationship of trust with the people studied and gain a more profound insight into the aspects of life behind closed doors that are taken for granted. In order to explore the minute details of everyday domestic life in Japan I have employed a two-level approach: I lived for between three and four weeks with each of five families and paid a series of research visits to the other twenty-five homes.[22]

Japanese homes are highly gendered. Women, whether or not they are full-time housewives, tend to have sole responsibility for managing daily domestic routines such as cleaning, providing and cooking food and taking care of children and elderly relatives. They also control the flow of goods in, through and out of the home. In other words, they decide what is displayed, what is stored away, what is recycled and what is disposed of. Although my gender initially put some constraints on the selection of my fieldwork sites, once I was inside the home it became an asset that enabled me to conduct extensive participant observation. For example, I assisted with everyday domestic chores and learned home crafts. Moreover, I was trusted to baby-sit, teach English to school-going children and socialize with the elderly. Not only did the *in situ* fieldwork enable me to transcend some of the methodological challenges associated with the perceived ordinariness of the home, but, through gaining access to the backstage areas of the domestic, I have also been able to problematize the well-rehearsed research into what I call the three Ds: display, design and DIY, which centre on issues such as aesthetic choice and domestic ideologies about order and hospitality.

6a

6b

The present volume propagates a much-needed expansion of this research agenda into less visible domains such as storage, displacement and disposal.

The rich data gathered through participant observation with the five families was supplemented with multiple, shorter visits to twenty-five homes. The majority (seventeen) of these homes were also inhabited by families, but the sample included different domestic set-ups such as university students in their mid-twenties (three), recently married couples (two), a single woman in her forties (one) and single elderly people living with an adult child (two). The main methodologies employed to study this second group of homes were informal, repeat interviews as well as visual methods. I decided to use these methods because they would allow for a more collaborative approach (Kuhlmann 1992).[23] Photographs provided by those studied as well as my own research images were employed in lengthy discussions, called photo-elicitations (Harper 2002), in order to gain a better understanding of emic perspectives on some of the key themes guiding this book. Moreover, some participants kept detailed photo-diaries of their daily routines as well as events linked to the domestic that occurred at a significant moment in time, such as New Year (fig. 6a) and graduation ceremonies (fig. 6b). This kind of data collecting was particularly popular with the younger generation. It thus enabled me to surpass the authority of the housewife and gain information about home life from different members of the same family. This research technique also provided me with invaluable data about seasonal events that occurred only once during my fieldwork.[24]

Apart from the ethnographic data collected in the thirty homes studied, the project also draws on formal interviews conducted with a range of professionals linked with the home, such as architects, managers and staff at prefab housing companies, producers of New Year decorations, department store employees and Shinto and Buddhist priests. Additionally, I collected a large amount of ephemeral printed materials such as newspaper articles, promotional material from housing companies and door-to-door advertising from furniture makers, household goods stores and supermarkets (Daniels 2009b). Finally, I also conducted intensive research of historical sources as well as rare Japanese-language materials in libraries, archives and museums in Osaka and Tokyo.

OTHER WAYS OF TELLING

> A book with too many pictures is a picture book. A classroom with too many images, entertainment. A world with too many images, popular and low brow.
>
> Bakewell 1998: 26

To my knowledge, there is only one English-language publication that explores the material culture of contemporary urban Japanese dwellings from the perspective of its inhabitants. In *Tokyo: A Certain Style* (1999) the Japanese writer–photographer Tsuzuki Kyoichi draws on more than 400 colour photographs of interiors in Tokyo to create a realistic portrayal of contemporary Japanese homes.[25] Tsuzuki directly critiques the avalanche of 'glossy' foreign-language publications that propagate the myth of 'the Japanese house', saying, 'Let's put an end to this media trickery, giving poor ignorant foreigners only images of the most beautiful Japanese apartments to drool over … I wanted to show you the real Tokyo style, the places we honest-and truly do spend our days. Call it pathetically overcrowded, call it hopelessly chaotic … hey, that's the reality' (Tsuzuki 1999: 9). Paradoxically, because of its strong reliance on visual materials, the reader might easily mistake this book for yet another 'coffee-table reverie'. However, the rich, detailed information contained in his 'messy' photographs differs from your typical glossy image, and through his creative use of montage and juxtaposition Tsuzuki provides a unique insight into how one particular section of the Japanese urban population (single, mobile, creative people) live.

This book, as well as a number of other innovative, visual research projects, has motivated me to question the rather unimaginative use of images in academic publications. I am particularly interested in the ethnographic monograph that remains the main representational form through which anthropological knowledge is disseminated. Targeted at an audience of anthropology scholars and students this is an academic work that characteristically contains only a few visuals (maps, graphs, and some black-and-white photographs) which serve to illustrate the text.[26] Although, since the 1970s, there has been a flourishing of rhetorical strategies to write up fieldwork data (Rabinow 1977; Clifford and Marcus 1986; Bennett 2000) influenced by debates about reflexivity,[27] apart from a handful of pioneers who have successfully employed film (Worth 1972) and photography (Danforth and Tsiaras 1982), experimentations with visual representations have been far less common. In my view, the main reason for the paucity of images in academic publication should be sought in deeply engrained assumptions about the inappropriateness of their use in scientific research.[28] Because of their subjective qualities, images are considered to be the antithesis of objective scholarship.[29] It is, thus, conveniently forgotten that, like texts, all images are constructed within a complex matrix of producers, consumers and their ideological frameworks, the agencies of the subjects photographed and the social and material trajectories of the (visual) object.

Only recently have growing numbers of anthropologists (McDougall 1998; 2005; Pink 2006; Schneider and Wright 2005) and sociologists (Chaplin 1994) argued that 'in social science, as in social life, there can be no fundamental categorical separation between words and images'(ibid.: 224). Thus, through their multi-vocality and their capacity for capturing phenomenological experiences, images are said not only to bridge subjective and objective understanding but also to stimulate new ways of thinking about social life across cultures. These arguments in favour of a more balanced approach between image and text are especially enticing for those studying material

7a   **7b**

culture who are accustomed to the limits of textual representations in exploring the multifaceted nature of objects. In Tilley's words,

> We cannot adequately capture or express the powers of things in texts. All we may conceivably hope to do is to evoke. This is why experimentation with other ways of telling, in particular with exploiting media which can more adequately convey the synaesthetic qualities of things, in particular the use of imagery and film, must become of increasing importance to the study of material forms in the future. (Tilley 2001: 268)

Drawing inspiration from these debates as well as from previous publications about the home that use visuals in innovative ways (McAllester and McAllester 1980; Tsuzuki 1999; Sato and Asakura 2002), this publication experiments with weaving together image and text. Apart from a small number of historical images and illustrations published in advertising pamphlets, the book contains the following three types of photographs:

Type 1: Photographs taken by the British photographer Susan Andrews who has previously conducted visual research about domestic interiors in the UK but visited Japan for the first time in 2006 in order to collaborate on this project (fig. 7a).[30]
Type 2: Research photographs that I took during my 2003 fieldwork supplemented with images I produced during repeated stays in Japan beginning in 1992.
Type 3: Photographs taken by the participants in my study that either already existed or were created as part of this project (fig. 7b).

Each type of photograph offers a different visual perspective on contemporary urban Japanese homes. Indeed, a UK-based photographer on her first visit to Japan will see everyday domestic life differently from a Belgian anthropologist who has lived and worked in Japan for more than seven years. These visual representations will in turn differ from how Japanese inhabitants see their own homes. One could argue that the three types of photographs used in this publication correspond with a top-down scale moving from an 'outsider' to an 'insider' view. However, although photographs taken by 'insiders' have enriched my understanding of how Japanese people envision their everyday lived worlds, I do not wish to propagate a hierarchy of viewing. Like explicit vocal statements, all photographs are subjectively constructed sources of information, and the fact that someone lives in a particular environment does not necessary mean that their photographic representations of these spaces are more truthful. Besides, in the domestic context, everyday, bodily routines might actually become 'invisible' to those enacting them (see also Miller 1998b), while 'outsiders' might see the banality of the mundane anew.

None of the images will be accompanied by captions. However, I have provided bibliographical, copyright and descriptive information in an extended list of illustrations. The logic behind this approach is to embrace the polysemic nature of visual representations instead of pinning their meanings down with text (Barthes 1964; Stasz 1979; Chaplin 1994). I agree with Chaplin that because the social sciences prioritize verbal discourse, a photograph is considered to depend on 'a caption and textual contextualization to give it authentic verbal and precise social scientific meaning' (ibid.: 207). Thus, uncaptioned photographs retain a degree of visual autonomy, and by pairing and sequencing visuals further attention is drawn to their material/visual qualities. Both strategies aim to encourage a more 'active looking' that may result in interpretations that differ from what the producers and/or authors intend. Still, because I consider image and text to be complementary, all visuals are carefully placed in the text to allow for their interaction with the ideas and information presented therein. Because I will make direct reference to Type 2 and Type 3 images they have been numbered throughout. Andrews's images, on the other hand, are not numbered, but I provide descriptive information in a list of all her images ordered by page number.

Finally, the book also includes ten spreads consisting of combinations of written and visual essays. Each spread explores a specific aspect of the domestic that has only been touched upon in the main text and merits further investigation. Topics range from the use of slippers and the creation of street gardens to the Dolls Festival and second-hand markets. Apart from Spread 1, which shows a map of the Kansai area with the approximate locations and exterior views of all thirty homes studied and is placed in the Introduction, the spreads occur at the end of each chapter. Spreads 2, 3, 4, 5 and 9 contain Andrews's photo-essays, while Spreads 6 and 10 depict sequences of my photographs. The visual essay in Spread 7 is a mixture of participants' wedding photos and Andrews's photographs of textiles, while Spread 8 contains a photographic diary by one of the participants. These visual experiments will undoubtedly leave my work vulnerable to criticism, but I believe it is a risk worth taking considering the potential for conveying my ideas more effectively and allowing a more varied, wider audience to engage with the material.

SYNOPSIS OF CHAPTERS

Chapter 1 explores ideal notions of house and home in contemporary Japan. It discusses historical processes that have resulted in the creation and dissemination of new ideas about domesticity modelled on European and American examples. Since the end of the nineteenth century, as part of a wide-scale modernization project, the state has promoted new forms of dwellings based on the separation of areas for sleeping and eating and the use of new consumer goods such as chairs and system kitchens. However, it was only during the 1960s that the modern Japanese home with a central living-dining-kitchen area and private bedrooms became a reality for the majority of the population. These new domestic spaces were furnished with material culture thought to enable intimate family sociality such as sofas, dining tables and double beds. However, the complex spatial, material and social practices enacted in Japanese homes cannot be reduced to processes of Westernization or modernization. Through everyday, embodied routines such as eating, sleeping and bathing contemporary Japanese families create and recreate themselves as an intimate entity. In other words, intimacy is not necessarily equated with privacy, and happy homes are those that achieve a delicate balance between family-oriented activities and individual yearnings for relaxation.

Whereas Chapter 1 focuses on how inter-family relationships are shaped inside the home, Chapter 2 examines the social and spatial connections between the inhabitants and their surrounding community. A large number of physical barriers such as gates, fences, balconies, barred windows and steel doors shield urban homes from the immediate world outside. Moreover, visitors are rarely entertained in the domestic setting, and socializing with friends, colleagues and family generally takes place in public spaces. At first sight these observations seem to substantiate the much-discussed inside-versus-outside Japanese categorization, but, in practice, boundaries are always fluid and open for negotiation. Mundane domestic activities such as gardening or garbage disposal cut across the inside–outside divide, while cooperative practices such as fire-fighting or caring for territorial guardian deities (re)produce links between individual homes and the local community. Moreover, 'inside' domestic relations constantly intertwine with networks of connections created in schools and the work place, whether or not these institutions are located in the close vicinity to the home. Examplifying this are mothers who are actively involved in their children's school activities or wives who are responsible for exchanging gifts with husbands' work colleagues (Chapter 5). Finally, local networks of relationships are increasingly based on shared interests and constructed around consumption practices such as travel or food. Overall, this chapter argues that personal relationships of friendship and sentiment are considered as important as kinship ties grounded in filial piety and obligation, and that both are not mutually exclusive.

Chapter 3 takes this exploration into spatial ties between homes and their surrounding community a step further by examining the complex domestic spiritual technology consisting of domestic altars, auspicious material culture and graves that is thought to protect the domestic against malevolent influences. Inhabitants aim to produce beneficial alignments with the spiritual world by enacting a number of domestic rituals at specific intervals throughout the year to invite good fortune. Moreover, ancestors are worshipped through offerings made at Buddhist home altars and family graves, while auspicious objects are strategically placed to counteract evil forces. These practices that link homes with specific religious centres are in tune with larger considerations such as seasonality, human and cosmic hierarchy and auspiciousness. Importantly, those held responsible for interacting with the divine on behalf of their families are primarily women. While this chapter ends with the consideration of a number of ways in which women try to negate the huge pressures wrought by the domestic, spiritual defence system, Chapter 4 will concentrate on how gender is actively negotiated on a day-to-day basis through domestic aesthetic practices.

In Chapter 4 I will dissect the stereotype of the minimal Japanese house typified by the following aesthetic elements: tatami flooring, rice-paper sliding doors (*shôji*) and decorative alcoves (*tokonoma*). The 1960s standardization of domestic interiors into a central Western-style living-dining-kitchen (LDK) area with a number of private rooms did not result in the disappearance of tatami rooms. However, as this chapter will reveal, the material culture placed inside these rooms, and the contemporary practices enacted on tatami mats are complex and varied. For some, tatami may indeed convey a certain taste and status linked with Japaneseness, but many tend to use them as efficient, multifunctional tools to combat the reality of cramped living situations. Furthermore, while designated display areas such as alcoves and hallways might to some extent adhere to 'native' aesthetic rules, spaces of everyday use are generally characterized by an 'eclectic aesthetic' consisting of a mixture of souvenirs, gifts and handmade objects. In both cases taste is not just based on individual aesthetic judgments but is also socially and materially constructed. Moreover, contemporary Japanese aesthetic practices are less oriented towards outsiders, as display, decoration and, perhaps less so, DIY, are activities through which Japanese women and men may challenge their expected gender roles.

In Chapter 5 I will pay attention to ordering practices in domestic spaces in everyday use, particularly highlighting the dialectic relations between display and storage. Those possessing an excess of goods used to circulate them either between the house and storehouse, or through informal sharing networks within the larger community. However, the excessive volume of things entering 'mainstream' homes since the 1970s has resulted in material surplus. Some have dealt with this problem by adding storage or moving into bigger homes, but others have no other option other than to stay put. Women who are over forty-five years old tend to employ bulky pieces of free-standing storage furniture that formed part of their dowry, while those who married after 1985 either jointly purchased furniture or surround themselves with hand-me-downs from family and friends. In the former case, maternal family ties across the generations are highly valued, while in the latter case relationships between the couple are considered more important.

Finally, in Chapter 6 I will examine anxieties regarding the disposal of large numbers of objects that are kept in storage and on display in Japanese homes, and that are referred to as 'things one would like to dispose of, but are difficult to throw away'. Most are unwanted or disliked gifts, and one obvious reason why people might hold onto these goods is because they value the relationship of exchange that they embody. However, once gifts have been reciprocated, they tend to become unused goods that over time morph with an unidentifiable mass of things that can no longer be reduced to people or social relationships. Although for special occasions such as births gifts 'that remain' are acceptable, regularly occurring events are best celebrated with ephemeral items that can be shared with others. These kinds of gifts not only allow the creation of new relationships through shared consumption, but because of their material qualities they will also need to be renewed regularly. The propensity for not throwing away unused things is associated with a strong concern about their wellbeing. This attitude, which grows out of a feeling of duty towards objects rather than emotional attachment, points at a more general awareness that people belong to extended networks of human and non-human agents that transcend space and time.

1
FEELING AT HOME

'A HAPPY FAMILY TOGETHER'

The illustration in figure 8 appeared in an advertisement pamphlet for new homes that was circulated through the post in October 2003 in the Kyoto area.[1] I have selected this image because it highlights four interior spaces that are at the base of the conceptualization of the ideal post-war Japanese home. The areas discussed are clockwise from the top right: (1) the dining-kitchen area: 'Of course we can install a popular front-facing kitchen system which enables you to talk with your family while preparing meals'; (2) the children's room: 'One would like to give one's children a room where they can study in peace'; (3) the master bedroom: 'Anyone would like a bedroom just like this to relieve the fatigue of the day'; and (4) the living room: 'Why not try to gather the whole family in the living room to exchange opinions?'

During much of the twentieth century the Japanese dream family home was a two-storey detached house with a central dining-kitchen and an adjacent living area, preferably a Japanese-style room. The living-dining-kitchen (or LDK) area is envisioned as a communal space where family members socialize while sharing meals, debating and exchanging opinions or playing board games. There also are a number of private rooms: a toilet and a bathroom on the ground floor and several bedrooms on the first floor.[2] Ideally one bedroom should be provided for the parents and one for each child. The expectation is that the former will enable the couple to spend some intimate moments together, while the latter will allow children to study independently in a calm atmosphere.

This ideal notion of home draws heavily on the ideology of the 'mainstream' happy family (see Introduction), and both are the outcome of complex historical processes.

京都市
WHITE TOWN
伏見
Professional Eye
プロとしての視線で

第1期〜第5期完売
第6期分譲開始

リビングルーム
家族の集まるリビングは家族みんな
の意見を取り入れてみては?

主寝室
1日の疲れを癒す寝室こそこだわりが
ほしいですね。

8

At the end of the nineteenth century the Meiji government (1868–1912) aspired to modernize Japan along Western lines.[3] A key objective was to replace the patriarchal family unit (*ie*), grounded in the Confucian notion of filial piety, with a new type of domesticity based on the nuclear family and 'Western' ideas such as conjugal love and the private individual. A popular women's magazine from 1892 defined this new family model, literally called 'the happy family together' (*ikka danran*), as follows: (1) the man and woman love each other, (2) their relationship is monogamous, (3) the family is nuclear, (4) the man is a salaried worker and (5) the woman is a full-time housewife (see Cwiertka 1999). The Taishô leaders (1912–26) further developed and disseminated this new family model through popular media such as magazines, newspapers and exhibitions. Moreover, they also ratified a number of policies that aimed to redesign the outlook of the Japanese dwelling based on a shift from guest-centred to family-centred and from tatami-based to chair-based living.

The houses belonging to the pre-modern elite were fitted with tatami mats throughout and divided into front and back areas. The front, facing south, contained at least one large formal guest room (*yashiki*) overlooking an ornamental garden.[4] The back areas in the darker, northern part of the dwelling, on the other hand, were reserved for everyday use and contained family rooms, the

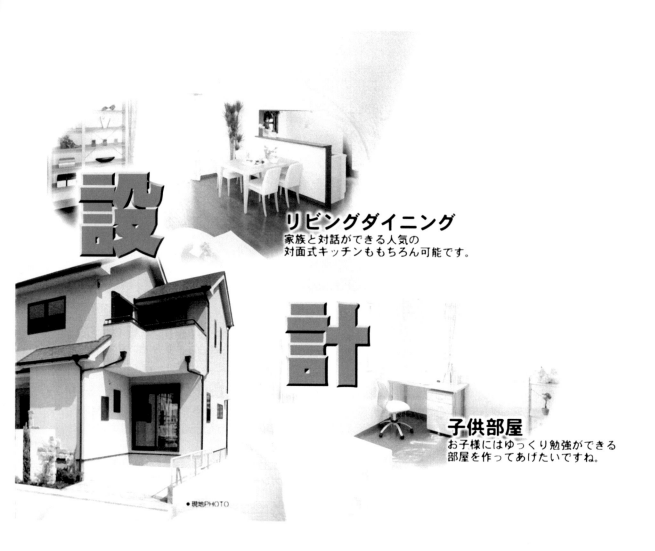

リビングダイニング
家族と対話ができる人気の
対面式キッチンももちろん可能です。

子供部屋
お子様にはゆっくり勉強ができる
部屋を作ってあげたいですね。

● 現地PHOTO

maids' quarters, the kitchen, the bath and toilet. This layout gave prime location to spacious guest rooms where the male household head would entertain guests as a representative of the extended family unit. This space also doubled as the patriarch's private study and sleeping area, while the rest of the family lived and slept in one or more multifunctional rooms in the back. These rooms could be closed off with paper sliding doors, but because there was no central corridor, one had to walk through one room to reach another. The absence of private rooms suggests that the privacy of individuals was not a major concern. This is consistent with native perceptions of the self that viewed the identity of each family member as inseparable from the larger family unit.

FROM TATAMI-BASED TO CHAIR-BASED LIVING

During the 1920s the government launched a number of propaganda campaigns that aimed to encourage people to create a more family-centred home. Figure 9 shows one of a series of posters produced for a Ministry of Education exhibition held in Tokyo during the 1920s. It is accompanied by the slogan 'A Happy Family Together Is More Important Than Dabbling With Antiques' and

9   10

aims to promote the abolition of the time-consuming custom of receiving formal guests in special Japanese-style rooms. The poster successfully brings across it message by juxtaposing two different domestic scenes. The frame on the right depicts a male family head entertaining a male guest in a spacious, sparsely decorated Japanese-style guest room. The second frame, by contrast, shows a husband/father who prioritizes spending time with his wife and children in a Western-style living room. As Figure 10 demonstrates, in 1934 the modern Japanese family is expected to relax 'happily together' in an informal, chair-based space.

Throughout the twentieth century, similar public propaganda campaigns were at the base of state-led modernization projects in other cultural contexts. During the 1980s the Vietnamese state, for example, employed billboards to spread a new domestic ideology that centred on the nuclear family instead of the communist individual (Drummond 2000). The emphasis was on the productive and reproductive role of women because the 'happy Vietnamese family' was thought to be achievable through strict family planning (ibid.: 2385–6). However, other examples demonstrate that in order to change radically social structures that are firmly entrenched in everyday practices more drastic measures might be necessary. The anthropologist Victor Buchli, for example, has shown how during the 1920s the Russian state tried to break up the bourgeois, patriarchal family unit and restructure traditional gender roles by re-housing the population in apartment blocks with modern furniture and communal spaces such as kitchens, dining halls and crèches (Buchli 1999). Similarly, during the 1920s, the Japanese state introduced a range of intrusive measures that aimed to enforce chair-based living. These reforms were part of a larger policy to rationalize everyday life by encouraging the adoption of 'Western' forms of clothing, food and dwelling.

From the turn of the century chairs were brought into use in most public spaces such as schools, offices and restaurants, and through work and study men and children became familiar with new spatial and corporeal practices associated with this type of furniture (Teasley 2001: 54–6). However, the incorporation of chairs into the home proved more of a challenge. Prolonged consultations with architects and urban planners, many of whom had spend time abroad, led to the design of a number of innovative floor plans that challenged the previous front–back layout and promoted the transition from tatami to chairs. Two layouts were particularly popular. The first, the *chûroka* style, is characterized by a central corridor (fig. 11a). Although this plan kept a guest room in the front, the family's living quarters were located adjacent to this room while the kitchen, servants' rooms and toilet remained in the back. The second of the floor plans, called the *imachûshin*-style, also retained a guest room but the design was more revolutionary because it had a large central dining-kitchen room with a table and chairs (fig. 11b). These innovations were introduced to the general public through so-called cultural houses (*bunka jûtaku*),[5] first displayed at the cultural village open-air exhibition in Osaka in 1922.[6]

Neither the new house plans nor the housing reforms they were part of achieved the wished for effect. In reality, only a small minority of the population, such as rich intellectuals or artists, could afford the modern homes that prioritized harmonious family life over the entertainment of guests (Uchida 2002: 57).[7] Paradoxically, just as guest rooms began to disappear in the houses of the elite, knowledge about the proper treatment of guests became a marker of social distinction for other strata of the population. As a result, formal guest rooms were given the prime location in the homes of the aspiring classes in post-war Japan (Sand 2003: 46–7).[8] The family-centred dining-kitchen area with living room and chair-based living only spread among the masses during the 1960s.

THE POST-WAR 'LDK HOME'

During the Second World War the Japanese urban housing stock was almost completely destroyed, and the government's decision to prioritize the rebuilding of the national economy over the construction of affordable houses resulted in a housing crisis that continued for more than a decade. Only during the mid-1950s, as the economy recovered, did the state begin to fund the development of suburban housing blocks of up to four to five storeys in height (*danchi*). Each *danchi* apartment was about 40 m[2] and consisted of a central dining-kitchen area with two tatami rooms (one living room (fig. 12) and one multi-functional bedroom), a bathroom and a toilet.[9] The three main innovations introduced through the *danchi* were the separation between spaces for eating and relaxing, the creation of a hybrid Western–Japanese lifestyle and the conversion to using private bathrooms instead of visiting public baths.[10] The core interior features of the *danchi* flats were borrowed from the interiors of the so-called dependants housing built by the American occupation army just after the war.[11] Inside these houses meals were prepared with modern appliances in a Western-style dining-kitchen and then shared while sitting on chairs at a dining table. Adjacent was a living room with a sofa set, a coffee table, a bookcase and a radio.[12]

Although the family-centred, Western-style dining-kitchen area with living room had already been part of some of the plans from before the Second World War, it was the *danchi* apartments that spread this new type of layout to the masses. From the mid-1960s onwards, the living-dining-kitchen (LDK) layout became standard in all urban homes, whether detached houses or apartments (Funo 1997: 68).[13] Moreover, new items of material culture such as sofas, dining tables and double beds were supposed to play a pivotal role in enabling family solidarity in the modern LDK home. Practical knowledge about the use of these pieces of furniture was disseminated in the post-war years through American TV dramas and comics. However, as the Japanese sociologist Miyawaki (2000) has demonstrated, for the majority of the Japanese, family members gathering to socialize in a living room with a sofa, or a husband and wife sleeping together in a double bed remained alien practices. Next, we will see how living rooms and bedrooms and the items of material culture associated with these spaces were adapted to Japanese needs.[14]

child's room

entrance

closet

bath

kitchen

maid's room

guest reception room (Japanese)

living room

six-mat room

guest reception room (western)

eight-mat room

study

veranda

IIa

The Chūroka-style

bedroom

pergola

kitchen

dining room

living room

maid's room

bath

hall

study

entrance

IIb

The Imachūshin-style

12

SOFAS AND DINING TABLES

The LDK layout did not allocate a special room for the reception of guests. Instead, a Western-style living room with a sofa set (one settee and two armchairs) was supposed to function both as a meeting space for the whole family and a guest room. In post-war Japan, the sofa was often the first piece of Western-style furniture that Japanese couples acquired for their home. Western-style living rooms remained popular until the late 1980s, and five families in my sample, all living in detached houses built before 1990, possessed a living room with a sofa. However, in practice this space was rarely used. The notion, grounded in American ideas of equality,[15] of a central communal space where the whole family meets, talks, plays and entertains guests on an equal basis never caught on in Japan (Miyawaki 2000: 26–8). This might also explain why a recent study among Japanese families living in the UK in houses with separate living rooms, found that they barely used them (Ozaki and Rees Lewis 2006).

In 2003, all families participating in my study preferred the central dining-kitchen set-up without a living room. The Matsuis, a couple in their late thirties, lived with their four-year-old daughter Nao in a newly built two-storey detached house in Nara. They did not like the initial architectural plan for their house because it was based on the 'traditional' layout with the kitchen located in the darkest part of the house. Instead, they choose a large open-plan LDK space situated in the sunny front of the house. Towards the rear they created an office with dark space for Mr Matsui, who is a professional photographer. This decision was primarily based on information Mrs

Matsui received from friends who told her that 'when children are small they spend most of their time with their mother in the kitchen and the living room is not used at all'.

Housewives used to prepare food isolated in the dark areas of the home, but my data with regards to the choices of contemporary women suggest that they do not like to be isolated from the rest of the family. Mrs Kuwahara, a fifty-year-old high schoolteacher who lives with her husband and their two daughters, Keiko and Yoshiko, in Itami, for example, claimed that, when they rebuilt their house after the 1995 Kobe earthquake, 'the main thing I asked my husband for was this kind of kitchen (a system kitchen in an open-plan dining-kitchen area). I do not want to be in a space that is separate from the rest of family, but other people like this because one cannot see the dirty dishes.'

Homes fitted with system kitchen rose from 28.2 per cent in 1995 to 46 per cent in 2003 (AS 2004: 181). Staff at the Yamaha home showrooms in Osaka pointed out that in 2003 their best-selling system kitchen was a model that enabled those preparing and cooking food to face other people in the room. The head of design further revealed that the kitchen is the most expensive purchase for the home. Indeed, the modern system kitchen – as well as the high-tech bathroom, which I will turn to later – has become a status symbol. Suzuki, for example, claims that staff in a Japanese funeral company where he conducted fieldwork could estimate the social status of their clients based not only on the size and the location of the house, but also on the modernity and cleanliness of the kitchen and bathroom (Suzuki 2000: 75).

During successive periods of fieldwork in Japan since 1995, I have observed a major shift in attitudes towards the kitchen. While I was conducting research about kitchen utensils in 1995, for example, few people allowed me into their kitchens because they considered these spaces to be 'dirty' (*kitanai*) (Daniels 1996). Many of the homes I visited were built during the 1970s and 1980s when the front–back layout was still very common. By contrast, during my 2003 fieldwork I was generally invited to sit at the dining table in a modern dining-kitchen area. The few people in my sample who had not modernized their kitchen were contrite about its condition. The Ebaras, a family of four living in Nagaoka Tenjin, a commuter town between Kyoto and Osaka, exemplify this attitude. Their dining-kitchen, separated from a Western-style living room with a sliding door, dated back to 1980. Bright orange floor tiles and white and blue coloured kitchen units exposed the fact that the space had remained unchanged for more than twenty years. On the one occasion that I was invited to enjoy a meal with the family in this space, Mrs Ebara repeatedly apologized, saying, 'as you can see the place is rather shabby (*dorodoro*). I would really like to change the kitchen but …'

Rather than the sofa set, it was the Western-style dining table, present in all the family homes studied, that played a central role in enabling smooth family relationships through food consumption. Interestingly, the predecessor of this table, a low table called *chabudai*, introduced by the reformers at the start of the twentieth century, had first encouraged the family group to eat together on an equal basis. Koizumi (2002) described how at the end of the nineteenth century, in the homes of all classes, family members would eat from individual meal trays (*zen*). The patriarch was given the largest tray and was served first followed by the first son, then the second son and so on and so forth. It was considered good manners to eat silently and finish fast. In other words, the domestic consumption of food was 'not about enjoying food together but about filling the body with energy' (ibid.: 155).

During the 1930s and 1940s the urban middle classes warmed to the *chabudai* and the sociality it enabled.[16] However, in rural areas, where patriarchal, vertical family relations remained strong, these new practices, which shifted the focus from discipline and hierarchy engrained in the notion of filial piety to the creation of harmonious, interpersonal relationships did not take root until after the Second World War. Still, this innovation was soon superseded by the Western-style dining table.[17] In 2003, this latter type of table epitomized 'happy' family life, but its ubiquitous presence was somewhat misleading. Indeed, busy work and study schedules meant that in many of the homes studied family members ate at different times of the day. It was common for housewives to either eat alone or with small children before warming up meals when their husbands or school-going children arrived home. This said, some families managed to have dinner together at least a few times a week. However, in most cases the mother was busy preparing and serving food while the others were eating. During meals, conversation was generally kept to a minimum and some families watched TV throughout. Still, there were exceptions such as the Kagemoris, a family of three in Osaka, whom I repeatedly observed cooking as well as enjoying their meals together, and the Takahashis, living with three-generations under one roof in Nara, who shared cooking responsibilities among the adult females in the household.

DOUBLE BEDS

The standardization of the LDK layout in post-war Japan has meant that houses have at least one private room. Ideally – based on the pre-war ideology of the happy nuclear family – this extra room should be turned into a bedroom for the married couple. Only six of the twenty-three married couples in my sample slept in the same room.[18] My data confirms suggestions made by Japanese researchers that, even if they have enough space not to, couples would prefer to sleep separately (Miyawaki 2000: 40). Among married couples specific sleeping arrangements varied. Mrs and Mr Kuwahara, in their fifties, for example, slept in single beds placed in private bedrooms. The Wadas, in their sixties, on the other hand, had different sleeping preferences; Mrs Wada slept in a Western-style room with a bed while her husband preferred to sleep on a futon in a Japanese-style room. In less spacious homes, the father would generally sleep on his own in one room, while the mother might share a room with her children. Of the six couples who slept in the same room, two were over sixty, while the four others were in their late twenties or thirties. The elderly Noguchis, and two couples in their thirties, the Nishikis junior and the Sawais, shared a double bed, while the others slept on futons. Three of the couples in their thirties shared their bedroom with children under ten years of age.

Until the 1960s it was common for families to sleep together in one or more Japanese-style rooms. Adults would each sleep on a futon and small children would share a futon with their parents or grandparents. This close bodily contact between parent and child was considered important in creating a sense of wellbeing. Anthropologists working in various cultural contexts have discussed co-sleeping. Ellen Pader, for example, explains how it remains common in Mexico for several individuals to share a bed because 'the warmth of other bodies in the bed, the sounds of breathing, the turnings and stirrings of others, are all reassuring' (Pader 1993: 126). Until fairly recently co-sleeping also remained widespread in China. Yan (2005), for example, discloses that the extended patrilineal family used to sleep together in a large, heated bed. The private bedroom for the married couple was an innovation that was only introduced during the 1980s to encourage the development of intimate conjugal bonds.[19]

In the ideal LDK home children possessed private bedrooms, and in those homes with an extra space priority was given to the creation of a children's room instead of a master's bedroom. Mr Togo, an architect in Kyoto born in 1952, explained that people of his generation who were children during the 1950s aspired to provide their own children with private rooms 'because it is something we could never have ourselves, because we were poor'. Indeed, the desire to provide children with a private room seemed strongest among those born in the immediate post-war years. Moreover, the fact that even those living in small 3DK apartments in city centres, such as the Terayamas, the Yamamotos and the Matsunagas, turned one of their two extra rooms into a private children's room illustrates that this space continues to engender powerful connotations among the aspiring classes.[20]

Most children sleep with their parents until they start attending elementary school, but sometimes this practice even continues until they reach puberty. When the Matsuis built their house in Nara in 2001 they created a Western-style children's room for their daughter on the first floor. However, in 2003 the whole family slept together on futons in a Japanese-style room. Mrs Matsui,

thirty-seven years old, told me that once four-year-old Nao was 'a bit older, probably when she starts elementary school, she will sleep on her own in a bed in the children's room'. When I visited the family in 2006, Nao had just started her second year in elementary school, but the family still slept in the same room. Mrs Matsui explained that she revised her opinion about private children's rooms because their social benefits had recently come under scrutiny. In her words, 'Until a few years ago it was considered good to have a children's room just like people in Europe. But recently, cases in which families cannot create smooth internal relationships have increased. That is why the view that it is good to be [sleep] together as a family is re-gaining popularity.'

It is difficult to verify whether parent–child co-sleeping is indeed on the increase in contemporary Japan, but my data suggests that it remains common. In other words, once children are born the personal bonds between parent (commonly the mother) and child tends to be prioritized. However, I would like to caution that my discussion about sleeping practices is not meant to fuel the assumption that affection (whether of a sexual nature or other) between Japanese couples is non-existent. As in other cultural contexts, degrees of conjugal intimacy vary, and some couples in my sample had warm personal relationships; they enjoyed each other's company and attached great importance to the reciprocity of love, care and kindness.

BATHING AND BELONGING

Like Western-style dining-kitchen areas and bedrooms, private bathrooms were an innovation introduced through the *danchi* apartments during the 1950s and 1960s (Aoki 2001: 18–9).

However, unlike the 'ideal' practices associated with the former two spaces, bathing was already widespread during the Tokugawa period (1603–1867). The elite possessed private bathtubs, but public baths were popular places for socializing and relaxing that were enjoyed by all strata of the population (Morse 1886: 203).

Shove has demonstrated that in Europe and North America the private bath is a fairly recent innovation influenced by the development of the middle-class home as a place of retreat. In her view, private bathing is associated with 'the positioning of self in society ... and the relation between pleasure and duty' (Shove 2003: 94). According to staff at the Yamaha store in central Osaka, baths are the second most expensive purchase for the Japanese middle-class home, only superseded by kitchens.[21] As the following texts used in 2003 advertisements for baths illustrate, bathing is primarily associated with relaxation:

1. This 1.6 metre by 1.6 metre bathroom enables you to relax and feel at ease (*yutori*).
2. Experience an invigorating (*sawayakana*) bath time.
3. Use this relaxing (*yuttari*) space and the tiredness of a whole day will be lifted from your shoulders (*iyashite kuremasu*; healing, removing pain).

These kinds of slogans target men. As my research confirms, choosing a bath is one of the only domestic decisions that they are eager to be actively involved in. Indeed, it is mainly male customers visiting the Yamaha store mentioned above who are tempted to take a bath in an in-store cubicle equipped with the latest bath technology before making a purchase.

Many men in my sample associated being at home with switching off after a long day at work. Bathing allows them to balance this individual desire for relaxation (pleasure) with the ideal of domestic sociality (duty). Indeed, the daily bath plays an important role in nurturing a sense of belonging among Japanese family members. In every home studied, in the evening family members would take turns in taking a bath.[22] After undressing in an adjacent room,[23] one may step into the bathroom, where the body is repeatedly cleansed with soap and thoroughly rinsed with water before entering the tub. The same water, which stays clean and is kept at the desired temperature with advanced heating technology,[24] is shared among family members.

Bathing is a mundane, taken-for granted practice that is not much talked about (Miller 1998a), and my questions about the sociality and intimacy of bathing were commonly met with general statements such as 'all Japanese like taking a bath' or 'bathing helps you to relax'. The importance of bathing in the production of the intimate family unit was brought home to me during an unrelated discussion I had in 2003 with Ms Kema, a long-time friend from Yokohama in her mid-forties. The previous year both her parents had passed away in quick succession and, among all the stress

and anxiety caused by the preparations for the funerals and the settling of their affairs, she had been delighted to be able to give her parents a final bath (*yûkan*). The bathing of the deceased used to be part of the final rites for the death that were conducted in the home by members of the immediate family. However, the commercialization of funerals after the Second World War has resulted in the loss of local, domestic knowledge about funeral rituals. It was only during the 1990s that the bathing ritual had been reinvented by funeral companies drawing on 'the sincere affection for the deceased' and the meanings associated with bathing such as 'relaxation after a long day at work, and also as a family activity, a time for nurturing the sense of belonging' (Suzuki 2000: 188–9).[25]

TATAMI MATS: MULTIFUNCTIONALITY AND NOSTALGIA

Those participating in my ethnography strongly associated the bath with domestic relaxation. Another area in the home associated with what is called 'feeling at ease' is the tatami room. Although

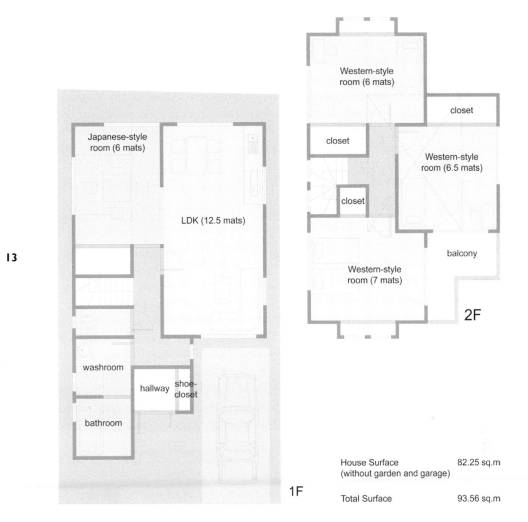

Japanese-style
room (6 mats)

LDK (12.5 mats)

washroom

hallway   shoe-
           closet

bathroom

1F

Western-style
room (6 mats)

closet

closet

closet

Western-style
room (6.5 mats)

balcony

Western-style
room (7 mats)

2F

House Surface   82.25 sq.m
(without garden and garage)

Total Surface   93.56 sq.m

13

the post-war urban interior has become standardized into a central Western-style, dining-kitchen area with a number of extra rooms (mostly bedrooms), tatami rooms and floor-based living has not disappeared. Twenty-six of the homes studied possessed at least one Japanese-style room, which raises questions: why do these rooms continue to be ubiquitous? And, what they are actually used for? The Japanese architectural planner Suzuki (2002a) distinguishes between the following three contemporary uses of Japanese-style rooms. First, they have a ritual function linked with seasonal change, religious celebrations and life-cycle events such as weddings and funerals. Second, they are used for display and the reception of guests, and are supposed to reflect the quality of the dwelling and the taste of its inhabitant (ibid.: 102). Third, they are spaces for relaxation, where members of the family 'read the newspaper, drink tea, or take a nap' (ibid.: 103). During my fieldwork I observed tatami rooms being used in all three ways. The two first functions pertain to the widespread stereotype of the minimal Japanese-style room, and although I will occasionally touch upon these uses, they will be dealt with in more detail in Chapters 3 and 4. Here, I would like to concentrate on the use of tatami rooms as a place for inhabitants to relax.

Most advertisements for new homes depict a layout with at least one Japanese-style room located in the centre of the home, often adjacent to the dining-kitchen area (fig. 13). This central location suggests that the room is supposed to be family-centred, and one could argue that it replaces the unpopular Western-style living room. Although this centrally located Japanese-style room has become part of the imagination about the ideal home, only one family, the Kuwaharas in Itami, actually possessed such a room. In 2003 they used this space for relaxation, but the practices enacted inside diverged from the ideal family sociality proposed in the literature. In the evening, all three female family members liked to sit on the tatami mats around a low table. Keiko and Yoshiki, their two daughters, enjoyed reading magazines or engaged in handiworks, while Mrs Kuwahara read the newspaper or watched television. Mr Kuwahara, a 55-year-old pharmacist, in contrast, preferred to retreat into his own room on the first floor either to work or to read novels. According to Mrs Kuwahara, the tatami mats hurts his back, and a low rattan chair placed on a carpet in one corner of the room references his absence.

Ideally, tatami rooms might be spaces to relax in, but my ethnography provides plenty of evidence for the fact that tatami mats embody a range of different things for different people. For contemporary Japanese living in small homes, tatami mats are primarily efficient tools to fight cramped living conditions (Enders 1987). Indeed, the majority of those participating in my study used tatami rooms as multifunctional bedrooms.[26] Many praised the flexible qualities of the tatami mats as during the day one can sit on them on square cushions around a low table while in the evening a futon can be rolled out over them to sleep on. Thus, the average tatami room is a rather small, lived-in space with an eclectic aesthetic (see Chapter 4) into which large chests and cupboards for storing clothing, bookshelves and other storage devices might encroach (see Chapter 5).[27]

Irrespective of this evidence, contemporary discourses surrounding tatami mats continue to associate them with tradition and Japaneseness. One common strategy used in advertisements to entice potential customers to create a Japanese-style room is to suggest that elderly relatives, who are nostalgic about the mats on which they grew up, will particularly appreciate this. Indeed, some elderly people in my sample seemed to comply with this stereotype. The Noguchis, the elderly couple living in Itami, for example, placed two tatami mats on the wooden floorboards in their Western-style bedroom while the Nishikis senior, who built a three-generation house in Gakuenmae, a commuter town in Nara prefecture, created a tatami corner to relax on in their Western-style dining-kitchen area.[28] This said, many elderly participants preferred to sit on chairs and sleep in beds. Mrs Kobayashi, who is eighty-five years old and occupies the ground floor of the Wada's family house in Osaka, possesses a Japanese-style room in which to receive guests. However, she likes to eat at a table while sitting on chairs in her modern dining-kitchen, and she prefers the convenience of a bed above 'aching legs and back from having to clean away the futon every day'. Mrs Kadonaga from Kobe, who is eighty-three years old, similarly, prefers to sleep in a bed placed on top of tatami mats on the ground floor of her house.

JAPANESE AND WESTERN STYLES

The examples given above demonstrate that sitting on chairs as well as sleeping in beds have been part of many people's lifestyles for decades. As Mr Nakae, born in 1947 (and whose family has lived in the centre of Kyoto since the 1940s in a house that is now over 100 years old), pointed out, 'My

83-year-old mother grew up eating Western-style breakfast (toast and coffee) at a dining table in a Western-style kitchen.' The fact that in many 2DK or 3DK apartments the flexible character of the mats is sacrificed in favour of sitting at a desk on a chair or sleeping in a bed further illustrates this. For example, both Mr Sawai and Mr Nasu, post-doctoral students who work from home, found it difficult to study sitting on the floor. Mr Sawai has turned a six-mat Japanese-style room in his 2DK apartment into his office by placing desks, bookshelves and storage on top of the tatami. As a result, the newly married Sawais' large double bed ended up in one corner in their living-dining area. Similarly, the Kagemoris, intellectuals in their early sixties, placed a desk for their computer, printer and scanner, bookshelves, a dresser, and storage furniture for clothing in a small Japanese-style room in their 3DK apartment in Osaka, which they share with their thirty-year-old daughter Shigeko. In the evening they roll out their futons in another carpeted room adjacent to

their dining-kitchen area. Under the carpet in this room, one can still see the evidence of a previous owner's urge to replace tatami mats with a concrete floor.

Those who live in rented accommodation are often driven by economic considerations to replace or cover the mats with another type of flooring such as carpet or vinyl. Because over time tatami mats discolour and get damaged, when moving house inhabitants may have to pay to replace them. The Iwaiis junior, a married couple in their early thirties with a one-year-old son, rent a 3LDK house in Kyoto.[29] When I enquired whether they had any tatami rooms, Mr Iwaii guided me to a room adjacent to their dining-kitchen area where he lifted a corner of a brown sheet of wood-patterned vinyl flooring that covered tatami mats. The vinyl was installed by the previous occupant of the house and, although the couple really like tatami mats, they decided to leave the mats covered because they hope that they might be able to save some money when they move house.

Mixing 'Western' and 'Japanese' stylistic elements is widespread and not considered problematic. All the participants in my study used terms like 'Japanese-style' (*wafû*), and 'Western-style' (*yôfû*), when discussing the various features of their home. However, 'Western' and 'Japanese' should not be interpreted as two mutually exclusive categories, but as consumer styles that are freely adapted and mixed (see also Goldstein-Gidoni 1997; Daniels 2001b). Indeed, in an article, entitled 'Was the Meiji Taste in Interiors Orientalist?', Sand offers historical evidence that supports this view. He strongly refutes that the Victorian styles adopted by the Meiji elite can actually be construed as 'Western'. In his words: 'Rooms were often appointed with furnishings both domestic and foreign in manufacture, along with Japanese, Chinese and other Asian antiques, arranged and designed in accordance with contemporary Japanese conceptions of Western taste' (Sand 2000: 637).

A HOME-LIKE ATMOSPHERE

For most, relaxing and feeling at ease in the home was not so much linked with tatami mats as with sitting, and for some sleeping, on the floor. Homes built since the mid-1990s have wooden flooring throughout. However, it is quite common to turn one corner of the central LDK area into a space where one can sit on the floor around a low table, which is placed on top of a rug in summer or on an electrically heated carpet (*hot carpet*) in winter. 'Hot carpets' are often used in combination with the *kotatsu,* a low table with a heating element attached underneath.[30] Both kinds of heating elements for warming the body while sitting on the floor remain common, although most contemporary homes contain powerful electric heaters/airconditioners (*aircon*) placed high up against walls, which can warm up a whole room.[31] *Kotatsu* are placed with the same frequency on tatami mats as on wooden floors or carpets. The Iwaiis junior, referred to above, placed a low table on top of a square carpet that covered the wooden floorboards in one corner of their dining-kitchen area. When I enquired about this space, Mrs Iwaii explained that at first they had used a Western-style table with chairs, but they decided to replace it with a carpet and a low table because, in her words, 'well, actually only this way can we really wind down (*ochitsukimasu*)'. Similarly, many others talked enthusiastically about the comfort and feeling of cosiness they experienced while sitting on the floor. *Ochitsuku* (settling down, make one's home) and *yutori suru* (being at home, at ease) were the two terms most frequently used to refer to this experience. A related term, but one with a strong connotation of individual wellbeing, was *bôtto suru* or 'being absent-minded, lost in thought', a state of bliss best achieved while sitting on the floor (tucked under the *kotatsu*) staring at the television while enjoying a snack or a drink.

The ideal LDK house with a central communal space may be configured as a shared, democratic space; in Japan, as elsewhere, inside the home the complex relationships between the individual and the family group are continuously contested, negotiated and created anew. Truly 'happy' homes are those that achieve a delicate balance between the need for intimacy among the family group and individual yearnings for relaxation and escape. One may relax during family-oriented activities such as sharing a delicious meal, but activities such as soaking in the bathtub or sitting or lying on the floor with a cold beer in front of the TV are equally important for the wellbeing of the family and the production and reproduction of a home-like atmosphere.

CONCLUSION: AFFECTIONATE TIES

In theory, in 2003 the conjugal 'happy family together', first proposed more than 100 years ago by the Meiji reformers, was the standard social unit. However, in practice, the disentanglement of marriage from vertical kinship relationships has only been moderately effective, and filial piety continues to play a significant role in the creation of smooth family relationships. The data presented in this chapter suggests that the happiness of the inhabitants of the Japanese home is not only based on the intimate relationship between the parents but also on the degree to which the whole family group (parents, children – increasingly, unmarried adult female children – and even grandparents) is able to create and recreate affectionate ties through everyday, embodied practices such as eating, sleeping and bathing. All three activities used to take place in the dark back areas of the house, but in the post-war, standard urban dwelling, the dining-kitchen, the bedroom and the bathroom are domestic spaces that are considered crucial for the successful (re)production of family life. Because of the strict division of labour, the hoped-for level of family sociality is rarely achieved as women tend to spend a lot of time alone at home while husbands are expected to spend long hours in the office, and school-going children are put through a highly competitive education system with many after school activities.

Through communal, bodily practices family members aim to achieve an intimate connectedness. Importantly, this notion of intimacy is disconnected from privacy, which suggests that strong affectionate ties may also be formed outside the romantic relationship between two individuals. The anthropologist David Lipset has recently argued that romance is not necessary linked with 'Western' modernity as elements of romantic love are experienced in a variety of configurations by different societies throughout history. However, he shows that outside Europe people seem to 'perceive romantic love as a distinctively modern relationship … they completely separate it from collective concerns of kinship and economy' (Lipset 2004: 208). As in other parts of the world, in contemporary Japan the notion of romantic love is generally associated with the 'West'. Romance has been eagerly embraced by the young, especially women in their twenties and thirties, and the recent drop in marriages, the rise in divorce, as well as the increase in intra-family generational conflict have all been linked with this phenomenon.

The commercial world successfully draws on this romantic ideal by linking it with consumer aspirations and promoting a range of romantic commodities ranging from intimate Christmas dinners for two (Moeran and Skov 1993) to exotic honeymoons packages (Goldstein-Gidoni 1997). During the 1990s the market also played a significant role in establishing the ideal of the intimate couple in China, associating it with 'leisure activities such as strolling together along the beach, visiting restaurants and singing karaoke, or taking trips to nearby cities' (Friedman 2005: 320). Likewise, in Japan romance between unmarried or recently married couples is primarily enacted through consumption practices in the public arena. Thus, commercialized leisure spaces, such as game arcades, karaoke parlours and parks, operate as pseudo-private spaces. Moreover, sexual encounters often occur in liminal spaces such as cars or short-stay love hotels. These examples illustrate the intertwined relationship between 'inside' and 'outside' in Japan, a topic I will explore in the next chapter.

SPREAD 2: THE CHOREOGRAPHY OF DOMESTIC SLIPPERS

After shoes have been removed in the entrance hall, one may step up the raised floor into the Japanese dwelling where an intricate choreography of slippers awaits. Rules concerning the 'proper' usage of slippers are directly linked with subtle distinctions made between degrees of cleanliness in various areas of the home. First, slippers are taboo in Japanese-style rooms. The necessary removal of slippers when stepping onto tatami mats is linked with them being used to sit or sleep on. This also explains why most automatically remove slippers when stepping onto rugs or carpets used to sit on. A second domestic space where slippers are off limits is the toilet. This space is considered impure and house slippers are abandoned for toilet slippers, clearly recognizable by their bright colours or by the letters 'WC' printed on them. In older houses a clear demarcation between the tiled toilet floor and the inside of the house acts as a physical prompt to switch back into house slippers. Unfortunately, this helpful reminder has ceased in contemporary houses with wooden floorboards (*flôringu*) throughout. Finally, when moving from inside to outside spaces such as backyards, gardens or terraces one changes into plastic outdoor sandals.

Kawasaki and Moteki (2002: 36) argue that slippers were introduced in the Japanese house during the Meiji period in order to keep people's feet warm in Western-style living spaces without central heating. Most participants kept a selection of slippers in the entrance hall, either in the shoe-closet (*geta-bako*) or arranged them on a rattan slipper rack (*sulippaa-tate*). Winter slippers are made of heavy, warm materials such as wool or felt, while in summer linen or cotton summer slippers with open toes or with tatami soles are common. In homes I visited, a pair of guest slippers

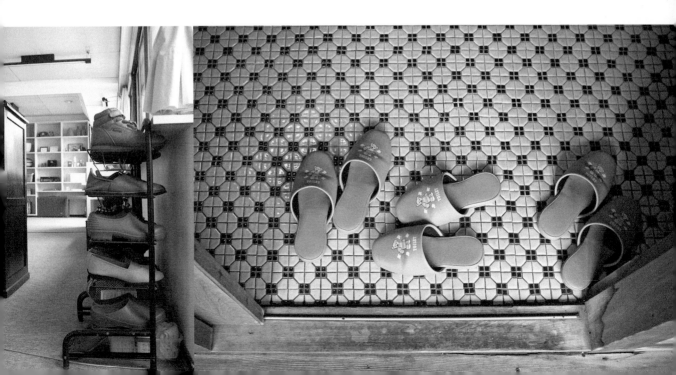

would generally be waiting for me on the raised step pointing towards the interior of the house. The Takahashi enjoyed selecting a different pair for each visit, while the Kuwaharas kept a special pair with my name embroidered. In some homes I was told slippers were optional as family members preferred to move around on their socks, but others never tired of fetching my neglected slippers from distant areas in the house.

Whenever I discussed the removal of shoes and the various uses of slippers the conversation would inevitably shift to queries about the European habit of wearing shoes inside the home. Questions ranged from 'how one could possibly have a baby crawl around on the 'dirty' floor' to 'how one could ever really keep one's house clean'. This concern about cleanliness does not only pertain to spaces used for sitting on the floor as slippers are also common in public spaces where people sit on chairs, such as doctor's surgeries or dentists, schools and community centres. The slippers supplied in these spaces are standard, plastic numbers that come in limited range of colours – dark green, blue or brown – and sizes – small for women and large for men. General hygiene might be behind changing from shoes into slippers at medical centres, but wearing slippers in schools or fully carpeted community centres is more surprising. On more than one occasion I have attended formal ceremonies such as weddings or graduation parties where everyone wore the same plastic slippers under formal dress. Other public spaces where slippers are common are Western-style hotel rooms where a pair of slippers – supplied with disinfected soles to put inside – might be arranged at the entrance to a fully carpeted room. This last example discloses that, as in other cultural contexts, wearing slippers in Japan is also associated with comfort and relaxation.

2

HOME AND THE COMMUNITY

GATES, FENCES AND WALLS

'We do not know any of these people [pointing at blocks enclosing their home]. Well, property developers knock on our door all the time. I have refused several very good offers but sadly most of our previous neighbours have sold.' These words were uttered by Mr Nakae, born in 1947, who is the president of a small wood distribution company, and whose family has lived for more than sixty years in a large house in the centre of Kyoto. He started his lament about the destruction of their once thriving neighbourhood while explaining to me why their two spacious Japanese-style guest rooms were hardly ever used. Like other participants in my ethnography, this family rarely received visitors, and mostly engaged in social activities outside the home, whether this meant having a drink or celebrating a birthday with friends, meeting colleagues after work, or gathering the extended family for a marriage or a funeral. Mr Nakae's answers to my queries about the absence of guests, like those of many others, highlighted the loss of local community. This rather pessimistic view is also echoed by Japanese social commentators (Funo 1997; Fujiwara 2003) who tend to link the phenomenon with progressive modernization and urbanization throughout the twentieth century.

The Nakaes' one-storey property, built at the end of the nineteenth century, is indeed dwarfed by large apartment blocks.[1] However, the physical outlook of their house also raises questions about an idyllic depiction of a past, close-knit community of neighbours. The fact that their plot is surrounded by a high mud wall with a robust wooden-roofed entrance gate, suggests that casual visitors were probably never that welcome. Indeed, the Nakaes' large house is modelled on the secluded dwellings of the

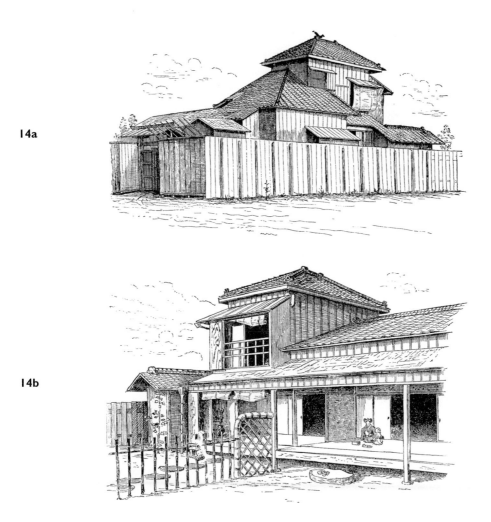

14a

14b

Tokugawa elite, who possessed a complex set of rules for receiving guests in their homes (Suzuki 2002b). South-facing guest rooms overlooking large ornamental gardens at the rear, and the ease with which access might otherwise be enabled towards the back of the dwelling meant that high walls and gates were necessary to secure the property (Sand 2003: 47).[2] William Morse's sketches of the front and back of an upper-class urban dwelling during the 1880s clearly illustrate how fences or walls were used to deal with this vulnerability (Morse 1886: 54–5) (figs 14a and 14b).

The exteriors of contemporary urban houses are also separated from the outside world by walls, fences and entrance gates.[3] Gates typically consist of the following four elements: (1) a rectangular sign with the inhabitants' family name, (2) a light that is automatically turned on in the evening (some houses have a hybrid light-cum-name sign), (3) a mailbox and (4) a buzzer with intercom through which visitors are expected to introduce themselves. Moreover, a number of stickers announce that the inhabitants have paid their TV license and that the gas system has been recently checked. Optional extras are a bag for newspapers and a small plastic box for the daily milk delivery. Some gates may also display signs with the Chinese character for dog to warn visitors and to scare

15a   15b

off intruders. These are the main elements of a generic entrance gate but, depending on when the dwelling was built, a number of variations in style exist. Houses dating back to the nineteenth century are commonly encircled by a high mud wall and possess either a large wooden roofed gate with reinforced doors or a smaller, lighter version with latticed sliding doors. This latter type of gate also became popular among the aspiring classes in the post-war period (fig. 15a). During the 1970s and 1980s, low concrete walls and iron gates were common but, since the mid-1990s, aluminium latticed fences and doors with automatic locks have prevailed (fig. 15b).

The entrance gates of the pre-modern elite not only secured the property, they also embodied social rank and status (Ueda 1998: 188–90). At the wealthier end of the contemporary housing market large entrance gates and high enclosures continue to be popular signifiers of social distinction (figs 16a and 16b). However, the reduction in the size of the average plot after 1945, bringing buildings closer to the edge of their property, has gradually led to a shift of focus from securing the perimeters of the plot to protecting the dwelling itself with devices such as steel doors and window shutters. Indeed, in 2003 a number of dwellings had removed enclosures altogether, while key elements of the entrance gate such as a mailbox, a buzzer and a nameplate with a light have been incorporated in a free-standing lantern pole.

16a   16b

'WE WOULD RATHER HAVE A NICE ENGLISH GARDEN'

Gardens, located on the side of the house furthest from the road, were considered a key component of the pre-modern, elite dwelling, and the inside of the home was thought to start at the enclosure (Ueda 1998: 180). The gardens were large and ornamental, consisting of shrubs, stones and sand (but no flowers) carefully arranged by professionals in order to represent somewhere else, such as the Buddhist paradise or iconic Japanese landscapes (Hendry 1997). Importantly, these miniature worlds were meant to be viewed from afar, preferably from a spacious Japanese-style room through large sliding doors/windows. Two families in my sample who possessed large Japanese-style guest rooms, the Iwaiis senior and the Nakaes, had these kinds of immaculately kept ornamental gardens. Five other participants also owned rear gardens. However, these plots were actively used, whether for relaxing on plastic garden chairs, drying washing, storing unused things or playing with a water hose on a sweltering summer afternoon. In other words, the Japanese garden has evolved from a 'viewing garden' to a 'doing garden'.

At the rear of the Nishiki's three-generation, two-storey detached house in Nara prefecture, for example, a large ornamental garden is beautifully arranged over a sloping mound. Mrs Nishiki junior, a 37-year-old housewife, told me that that her husband's father, Mr Nishiki senior, who is a widower and lives on the ground floor of their home, wanted this kind of garden. However, because 'it is very expensive to regularly have the trees trimmed by professionals' she and her husband 'would rather have a nice English garden'. Throughout the fieldwork, a cage occupied by the family cat and two large racks for airing futons obstructed the view towards the garden from Mr Nishiki senior's living room. The presence of a table with chairs in the back of the garden suggests some other uses, but the Nishikis junior's nine-year-old son, Hiro, and his friends seemed the only ones who truly appreciated the garden as an extra space to play in. Ms Nishimura, a single high school teacher who loves plants and regularly attends ikebana classes offers another example of the active use of gardens as extra outside spaces. In 1999 she moved from an apartment in Itami to a ground-floor flat with a large (10 metres by 5 metres) garden in a new apartment block in Takarazuka city. Ms Nishimura turned half the plot into a Japanese-style ornamental garden and laid out the other half, where she relaxes and holds barbeque parties in summer, in Western style, with an assortment of flowers. Like Ms Nishimura, three other families with gardens enjoyed tending to flowers and plants themselves and some, such as the Noguchis in Itami, even grew their own vegetables. All five gardens were further used to air futons or dry laundry, while part of the garden of the Kuwaharas in Itami and the Takahashis in Nara was taken up with storage sheds that compensated for insufficient storage space inside the house (see Chapter 5).

Gardens featured prominently in advertising for houses and apartments. In 2003 many pamphlets circulated in the Kansai region depicted a set of table and chairs placed in a large garden or a spacious decked patio decorated with potted plants. However, in practice most urban homes are built on tiny plots, and green exterior spaces like the ones described above remain beyond the reach of the majority of the population. The following description of her ideal house, given by Ms Kadonaga, a 55-year-old civil servant in Kobe, summarizes the mood: 'Even if I had lots of money I would prefer a small house. I would like a garden though. I would like to grow vegetables and flowers there. I would like to do some gardening (*gardeningu*)'. In reality, *gardeningu* boils down to growing some plants in pots. Large DIY stores, called home centres (*hômu sentâ*), which have sprung up in and around many urban cores, have profited from the widespread craving for private green space. In the spring of 2003, a home centre in the north of Kyoto regularly circulated pamphlets with gardening tips for tiny spaces, such as placing flowerpots on top of bricks next to the entrance gate, attaching special frames for pot plants to the balcony fence or hanging a shelf with miniature cacti in the bathroom.

Mrs Kubota and Mrs Matsui were the only two participants who kept plants inside their homes. The main reasons given for not growing plants indoors were that they would attract insects, gather dust and make it more difficult to keep the home clean. This was also why the Ebaras, the Sakais, the Noguchis and the Kuwaharas kept several bunches of flowers made out off silk in their home. On the whole, potted plants were kept outdoors. The Nakaos proudly showed me a melon they grew in a pot on their balcony. Mrs Ebara kept a few potted plants she received from her sister on the steps leading to their front door, while Mrs Sakai hung containers with flowers and placed several pots against parts of the wall surrounding their property (see Spread 3).

'EVERYONE NEEDS A GARAGE'

Very few people have the extra exterior space necessary to create a garden, because the average size of plots on which Japanese houses are built is comparatively small. In 2002, for example, the average house size in Osaka was 130 square metres and the plot size was 210 square metres.[4] By comparison, although houses in London and Paris are slightly smaller, they are built on plots that are on average 400 square metres (AS 2003: 190). In other words, in Japan the house fills up most of the plot. Of course, 70 or 80 square metres of outside space would still be enough to create a garden but, in practice, priority is given to the car.

In 2002, 84.4 per cent of Japanese owned at least one car (AS 2002: 183), and parking space is foremost in people's minds when they buy a house. In the UK, where many houses for sale are 'second-hand', properties tend to be promoted by showing colour photographs of the exterior and the interior. In Japan, on the other hand, most houses are newly built, and the main device used to advertise them are drawings of the prospective layout of the rooms and the private parking space (with parked car(s)) in front of the house.[5] Mr Togo, a 51-year-old architect and owner of a small

firm in Kyoto, discussed this focus on the availability of parking space with me and claimed that 'houses without a garage just wouldn't sell' because 'parking cars on public roads is prohibited and renting parking lots is very expensive'. Indeed, one month's rent for parking space costs between 50 and 150 pounds and, under Japanese law, one cannot register a car if one doesn't have proof of possessing a parking space, whether owned or rented.[6] Private parking spaces, called *gareiji*, are commonly indicated by a sloping plastic roof to protect the car from the elements and a low retractable fence to close the whole area off from the street (fig. 17a).

The need for private parking space has resulted not only in the disappearance of the garden but also, as the following two examples illustrate, in a decrease of living space. The Yanos are a couple in their mid-sixties who live with their 35-year-old unmarried daughter in the north of Kyoto. In 1963, Mr Yano, a retired public servant, built a small house on a plot of land owned by his father. In 2003 this house was torn down and a new dwelling was erected on the same spot. I visited the house several times before it was destroyed and was surprised at the plan to rebuild it as it seemed to be in a very good condition. Mr Yano explained that the main reasons for building a new house were, firstly, that the plumbing needed to be replaced, and, secondly, that they wanted to create a 'proper' parking space for the family car. In order to fit their vehicle in the space in front of their new house, the Yanos had to relinquish more than one metre of space in a tatami room located next to the hallway (Spread 8).[7]

The Ebaras offer another example of the importance attached to possessing a private parking space. After their marriage in 1978 they lived for two years in rented accommodation before they built a two-storey detached house in Nagaoka Tenjin in Kyoto prefecture. They borrowed a little money from Mr Ebara's family and the rest from the bank in order to buy a small plot of land. They did not want a ready-built house (tate-uri), and were actively involved in planning the layout of their home. Mrs Ebara disclosed the difficult choices they had to make, saying, 'We really wanted more rooms, especially one more room downstairs would have been nice. But then, you know, in the end we had to choose between en extra room or a space to park our car in front of the house.' Nevertheless, when their 24-year-old daughter, Yu, who lives at home, needed a car to drive to work, the Ebaras still ended up paying a high monthly fee to park on a nearby lot.

Multiple car ownership is on the increase in Japan, and some other participants with adult children possess two or even three cars. As a result of this trend, a variety of urban spaces, private and public, are progressively turned into parking lots. I have come across two striking examples of the destructive effects of this transformative practice in the north of Kyoto. The first was a wooden-roofed entrance gate and a fragment of a mud wall standing at the edge of a public parking lot that were the sole reminders of the traditional house that must have once stood there. The second, a miniature community shrine that had been placed in a corner of a public parking area to (re)present the full-size original that had previously occupied the whole space.

The number of cars one possesses and where they are parked are also markers of social status. The Kuwaharas in Itami, for example, place two of their cars behind a large metal gate in front of their home and rent additional parking space next to their property for a third. However, when I enquired about the size and layout of their house, parking space was never mentioned. Only when I prompted Mrs Kuwahara by asking, 'So having a garage was not a priority?' did their eldest daughter, Keiko, make it clear that, 'because renting parking space is expensive, for most people it makes a huge difference whether or not one owns a private parking space'. The younger daughter, Yoshiko, added, 'There are houses without a parking space and most have one in which only one car fits.' Whereas affluent families such as the Kuwaharas might not even consider the possibility of not having a parking space, the availability of private parking space is a pressing concern for those at the bottom of the housing market. In the case of cheap dwellings built on narrow strips of land the whole ground floor may be given over to garaging a car, and in order to increase the inhabitable space an additional floor might be added to the building. However, several architects I spoke with argued that these three-storey detached houses are often structurally unsafe and very dangerous, especially during earthquakes (fig. 17b).

Although, contemporary house exteriors are strikingly similar, the examples above demonstrate how the availability of exterior space, whether given over to gardens or parking, is used to create subtle distinctions among neighbours. Moreover, as room for cars has become a standard element of the contemporary dwelling, the focus of social competition seems to have shifted to the types of cars parked in front. In a recently developed street in the south of Kyoto, for example, all the houses

17a   17b

are the same size and the exteriors look alike, but the cars parked in front reveal the aspirations of their inhabitants. Examples range from tiny 'box-cars' to SUV vehicles and the latest Mercedes cars imported from Germany.

BETWEEN THE WINDOW AND THE HALLWAY

Like the Japanese dwelling, the Norwegian home is frequently referred to as being extremely private. Indeed, houses in both societies are closed off from the outside world by a series of physical barriers such as fences and gates. In her ethnography of Norwegian homes, Garvey argues that, although their houses are secluded, Norwegians still take great care in decorating their windows in order to reveal to passers-by that their homes are cosy. She, therefore, calls the window 'a visual field crossing domestic boundaries … a non-material interface where public and private boundaries appear indistinct' (Garvey 2005: 169). By contrast, in the homes I studied, windows do not function as interfaces. Window glass is often frosted, reinforced and/or covered with curtains. Moreover, windows facing the street tend to be small and barred. This is not a new development as, already more than 100 years ago, Morse repeatedly mentioned the 'close and prison-like aspect' of houses in Tokyo, their façade being 'perforated with one or two small windows lightly barred with bamboo, or heavily barred with square wood-gratings' (Morse 1886: 50).

Contemporary dwellings possess a number of large sliding windows/doors to the rear and on the first floor. However, the lower part of these windows is generally frosted, and fences and balconies obstruct the gaze from the street. Thus, these sliding windows are not comparable with their wooden predecessors covered with rice paper, which came in a great variety of shapes and sizes,[8] and which were opened up during the summer to allow the air to circulate through buildings. On the contrary, contemporary windows are placed in air-tight, aluminium frames that are kept shut in order to keep warmth in the house in winter and air-conditioned and cool in summer. This said, during the summer of 2003, some of those living in apartments build during the 1980s, such as the

Kagemoris, the Yamamotos and the Nakaos, created a pleasant breeze by leaving both their front doors and sliding windows at the rear ajar. Moreover, to deflect the strong summer sunlight, it is also common to put up exterior bamboo blinds (*sudare*), while many new houses have large steel shutters that are pulled over the windows for security during the night.[9]

In her PhD about consumption practices in Cuba, Anna Pertierra (2006) argues that, as in many other Caribbean societies, it is not the domestic window but the doorstep that functions as a liminal space. In her words, 'The doorstep is a space that is neither inside nor outside, that neither accepts nor rejects family and friends, where men and women can meet without lingering too long in an opposite gendered space, where disaffected youth and restless children can escape home without wrath, and that is not quite private whilst not totally public' (ibid.: 11). The description above is relevant for my study because it moves the discussion away from visibility issues by stressing the significance of everyday practices in creating notions of 'inside' and 'outside'. The doorstep also plays an important role in the Japanese home. However, at variance with its situation in the Caribbean, the Japanese step (between 10 and 25 centimetres high) is located inside the entrance hall (genkan), and acts as a social and physical demarcation between inside and outside worlds. Inhabitants remove their shoes in the entrance hall and then step up into the home, thus they 'physically leave society behind before entering a space in which they do not have to keep back' (Fujiwara 2003: 32–3).

Sand (2003) has pointed out that in-between spaces such as the hallway, but also the kitchen and the veranda, were common in farmhouses (*nôka*) and townhouses (*machiya*) belonging to affluent merchants and craftsmen in pre-modern Japan. They often function as spaces in which to entertain visitors. Moreover, more than three-quarters of the population in urban areas lived in cheap rented accommodation called *nagaya*. These were wooden tenement buildings consisting of a series narrow rooms, each one housing an entire family, separated by thin walls. There is only patchy information available about the daily life inside the *nagaya* and the relationships their inhabitants had with their surroundings. However, the urban planner/folklorist Nishiyama Uzo who discusses nineteenth-century 'tunnel *nagaya*' reveals that dirty alleys in the front and the back of these long, narrow buildings were simultaneously used as a play area for children, a spot to do the laundry and as communal toilets (Nishiyama 1989: 124–5).[10]

Contemporary urban homes do not have verandas or easy accessible kitchens, but all types of dwellings have retained an entrance hall.[11] This is a liminal space that enables informal exchanges between the inhabitants of the house and visitors. One item of material culture associated with the hallway that enables casual visits is the sliding door. In rural areas it remains common to leave the entrance gate and the sliding door unlocked during the daytime as it is acceptable for casual visitors and deliverymen to slide open the door, step into the entrance hall, and call out for the inhabitants of the house.[12] In urban areas, however, there has been a rapid replacement of sliding doors by more secure, outward pivoting, steel front doors. In my sample, in detached houses built since the mid-1990s such doors were generic, as in all the apartments.[13]

One could argue that this is but the latest type of physical barrier erected between the home and the street in a continuing process of emulation of the secluded houses of the pre-modern elite. However, another explanation for the popularity of the doors and the general decrease in liminal spaces might be sought in the growing concern – justified or not – with crime.[14] The Yanos in Kyoto exemplify this attitude. Before the demolition of their old house they carefully removed a pair of wooden latticed sliding doors engraved with a delicate, flower pattern, which they planned

to re-use. However, when I first visited their new house, a large steel, pivoting front door had been installed instead. According to their architect the old doors 'would take up too much space and did not provide security'.

Although pivoting doors have certainly reduced easy access to the entrance hall, the space has still retained some of its fluidity. For example, in homes with these kinds of front doors in which I stayed, neighbours, deliverymen and other visitors continued to be invited into the entrance hall. This explains why, in advertisements for new homes as well as home improvement literature, it is frequently suggested that one should place a bench in this space for visitors to sit on. Although, in practice, most hallways are too small to contain a bench. Instead, the shoe closet (*getabako*) is a virtually ubiquitous item of material culture inside the entrance hall that provides evidence of its liminal character. The closet is used to store a variety of things related to the outside world, such as shoes, umbrellas and walking sticks, but also golf bags, tennis rackets and footballs. More-over, the top of most closets functions as the main display area in the home (see Chapter 4). One particular style of shoe closet, found in some of the homes studied, perfectly embodies the dual

inside–outside character of the hallway. One part of this closet hovers over the tiled floor of the entrance hall, while the other half rests on the elevated, wooden floor. The outer part is generally used to store outside things, while the inner part contains domestic slippers as well as objects associated with postal deliveries such as scissors, pens and signature stamps.

RED BUCKETS AND NEIGHBOURHOOD COOPERATION

In contrast to Garvey's observations in Norway (Garvey 2005), none of those participating in my study made an effort to decorate the windows or any other part of the façade to show the outside world that their home is cosy. Most Japanese are also concerned with what neighbours – or passers-by – might think of their homes, but, as we will see next, this is expressed in different ways. One example is red plastic buckets filled with water with the word 'for fire fighting' (*shôkayô*) inscribed on them that are placed next to entrance gates and front doors throughout Kyoto. The power of

this innocent little bucket was brought home to me when the house of an elderly neighbour in Kyoto caught fire one cold winter night in February 2003. In no time the whole neighbourhood was awoken, a line was formed, red buckets with water were passed along, and the fire was put under control long before the professional fire brigade arrived. Efficiency apart, the presence of the red buckets indicates that the inhabitants of a particular home are concerned with the wellbeing of their family, neighbours and the community at large (fig. 18).

The Yanos were one family participating in my study who placed a red bucket outside their house in the north of Kyoto. They explained to me that the buckets formed part of their neighbourhood fire-fighting scheme, and that a red banner with the words 'fire watch',[15] passed around among neighbours and hung from the entrance gate of the particular house responsible for organizing the fire fighting, constitutes another important element of this fire-fighting technology. The Yanos, who have strong roots in the area, are members of the local neighbourhood association (*chônaikai*). This is a territorial unit that operates as a mutual support network organized around local institutions such as the shrine, the school and the fire brigade. The association consists of volunteers who work

together with the ward, prefectural and national government offices in tackling a range of local issues such as safety, security and schooling (Bestor 1989). Apart from the red bucket placed outside their own house, the Yanos' active involvement in their local community is also made visible in a number of other public spaces.[16] At their local shrine, for example, I spotted Mr Yano's name on one of a series of paper lanterns with names of benefactors written on them. One of the ways in which the shrine consolidates its relationship of exchange with donors and other members of the neighbourhood association is by sending them protection charms every year, a topic I will return to in Chapter 3. The community also shares responsibility for taking care of small street-side shrines dedicated to neighbourhood protection deities (*jizô-san*) (figs 19a and 19b). Mrs Yano, who performs these duties for her family, explained that they include making small offerings of water and rice, burning candles and refreshing flowers.

The red buckets embody the positive qualities of social cohesion and mutual cooperation of the neighbourhood association. However, as Mr Takahashi junior, a 58-year-old university lecturer in geography, rightly observed, the peril of reciprocal scrutiny and surveillance is never far away

18a   18b

(Spread 4). At the start of the 1960s Mr Takahashi's father bought their current three-generation house in Gakuenmae, a commuter town between the cities of Nara and Osaka, 'a place where there is not much sociability (*tsukiai*) between neighbours'. Mr Takahashi junior thus grew up in a *machiya* in Nara city and, although he remembers that the 'house itself was very dark', he speaks fondly of 'the spirit of mutual cooperation' inside the neighbourhood. However, as the following abstract reveals, throughout our conversation Mr Takahashi junior remained in two minds about the benefits of living in a typical neighbourhood community:

> Well, there were many nuisances as well. There is, for example, not much privacy (*puraibashii*) in these old towns. But then, I also think that there is something good about that, in particular, when something bad happens. One really feels like one is part of a big family. Yes, these benefits exist, but then, after all, the way we live now is probably better.

The neighbourhood associations might continue to be a powerful force in the everyday lives of people living in historical towns such as Kyoto and Nara, where 'natives' with strong roots in the locality continue to make up a large percentage of the population. However, the majority of those participating in my study who live in or close by large urban centres were not much involved in their neighbourhood associations. As a matter of fact, more than half admitted that they did not know their neighbours at all, while others uttered phrases such as 'we seldom meet' (*mettani awanai*) or 'I don't know them very well' (*amari shiranai*). Still, façades in large urban centres such as Osaka, Itami and Kobe also reveal the existence of a form of local community. One common example is a sign displayed at the gate or front door to announce that inhabitants participate in a neighbourhood crime-watch schemes. Nakano (2005) mentions a similar scheme organized by the local junior high school in a Tokyo neighbourhood where one evening a week a patrol consisting of educational staff, mothers involved in the PTA and other local volunteers walk around the neighbourhood for eighty minutes to prevent juvenile crime and to create a sense of community. Similarly, most women with school-going children in my sample, such as Mrs Matsui, Mrs Nishiki junior and Mrs Kubota, created local ties through their active engagement in their children's schools. Moreover, in several neighbourhoods in Nara, Kyoto and Osaka, people hung small flags or stickers outside their homes in order to show their support for local schemes that aimed to protect children walking to school.

19a

19b

All these examples confirm Bestor's (1989) observation that in urban areas community activities are frequently organized around schools.

Those living in large apartment blocks seem to have the least contact with their neighbours. Most have resident groups that have taken over some of the functions of the neighbourhood associations, maintenance of the building, for example, but also the monitoring of bicycle parking spaces, children's play areas, noise, the drying of clothes or garbage collection. However, only two of the nine participants living in this kind of accommodation frequently attended meetings. A number of physical boundaries also separate inhabitants of apartment blocks both from their fellow residents and from the surrounding areas. During the daytime, apartments are guarded by a porter, while, in the evening, keys or security codes are necessary to enter most premises. A buzzer/intercom is either installed downstairs close to the mailboxes or next to the front door of each individual apartment. Moreover, newly built apartment blocks such as that of Ms Nishimura (the 45-year-old single high schoolteacher) in the centre of Takarazuka city are equipped with CCTV and an intercom system with video. Post is collected from a row of boxes located in the entrance hall. Pointedly, the red buckets have been replaced by fire extinguishers on each floor.

One reason for the dearth of neighbourly contact is the fact that the main residents of apartments, such as families of salaried white-collar workers and professionals, but also single people and students, are generally more mobile than homeowners. Regular work transfers are among the causes of a more transient lifestyle. Mr Kubota, a fifty-year-old banker with a large international bank, is transferred to another branch about every five years. Each time his family accompanies him to his new destination and the Kubotas currently rent a mansion belonging to Mr Kubota's employer in the centre of Osaka. Moving house is also driven by a strong desire to change to another type of accommodation as one's career progresses and/or as children grow up and leave home (Suzuki 2002a). Mrs Terayama, a 45-year-old 'part-time' nurse, who has lived in the same 3DK apartment in Itami since 1985, repeatedly complained that she did not know any of her current neighbours. By contrast, when they moved into the building there was a real sense of community because everyone had children of the same age who went to school together. In her words, 'Everyone moved in at the same time, and our children were all around the same age. There were forty-five children from the same block in my son's class. It was a bit like living inside a *nagaya*

(pre-modern accommodation for commoners), where people visit each other freely. But then, you know, most have long since moved on.'

LOCAL COMMUNITIES OF LIMITED LIABILITY

The examples above provide evidence for the weakening of community ties and the increasing significance of school and work relations in contemporary Japan. However, I disagree with some researchers who argue that these changes suggest that neighbourhood networks based on long-term reciprocal dependency have been completely replaced by occupational and educational solidarity (Fujiwara 2003: 25–34; Suzuki 2002b: 217). Through a comparative study of two types of urban

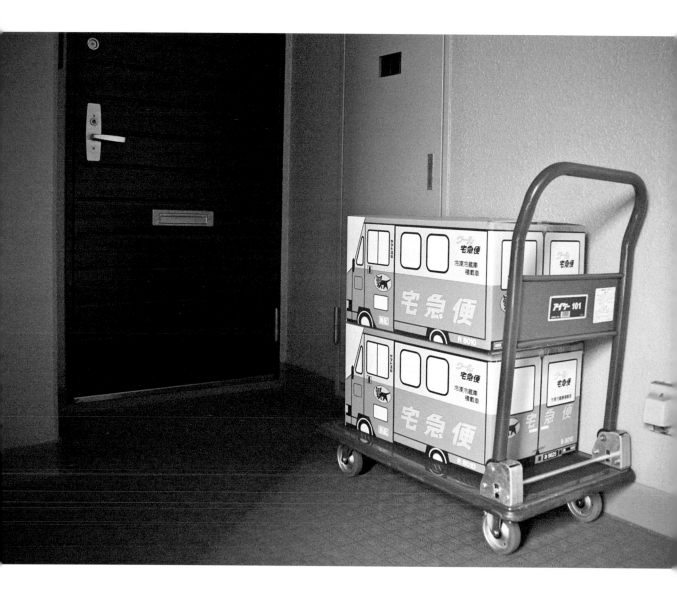

Japanese communities, a commuter village and a housing estate in Otsu east of Kyoto, the Israeli anthropologist Eyal Ben-Ari (1991) reaches a more attractive conclusion. He holds that although ties between neighbours have weakened, locality remains important in the creation of what he calls a 'community of limited liability which is more specialised, dependent and volitional' (Ben-Ari 1991: 11). In other words, contemporary neighbourhood communities might consist of only a limited number of the local population, and people may have multiple alliances with different groups at the same time (ibid.: 272–3). My data confirms that in contemporary Japan local community is just one option among many as most participants looked for personal fulfilment and created feelings of identity through belonging to multiple groups. These alliances, which often centred around consumption practices, may or may not have a strong spatial, local element. Clammer has similarly argued that Japanese urban neighbourhoods are held together 'through networks

or patterns of relationships (friendship, work or common interests) often based on consumption activities (shopping, eating, producing, selling) ... which in many cases transcend the boundaries of any particular locality' (Clammer 1997: 34–5).

The Kagemoris, intellectuals in their early sixties who live in a 3DK apartment in Osaka, offer a good example of how local communities of limited liability are created. Although they have no close relationships with their immediate neighbours they are part of a lively local community of people who share an interest in food and drink. This community strongly identifies with the rich food culture in Osaka, and the group, among them a number of local cooks, wine sellers and restaurant owners, frequently gathers in local restaurants to sample unusual foodstuffs and explore new wines. Moreover, this community of food buffs regularly organizes trips to other regions of Japan to taste regional produce. The Kagemoris have formed a particularly strong friendship with Mrs Fujii, a married 55-year-old cook/teacher with two children. On many occasions I have witnessed her casually dropping by their home, always bringing along one of her original dishes.

A second example of a local voluntary community is exemplified by two participants, Mrs Matsui and Mrs Nishiki junior, both housewives in their mid-thirties who live in Nara prefecture.

They first met at the end of the 1980s while studying at Nara's University of Education. During their student days they belonged to a small group of students, mainly women, who organized flea markets to sell their own crafts and homemade food and sweets. The group continued these activities after graduation because many settled down in the Nara region. Ties were only strengthened with marriage and the arrival of children, and in 2003 the women regularly met in each other's homes, sharing food they brought along while their children played together. They also continue to enjoy selling things at flea markets. However, these days their main focus is on ridding themselves of the surplus of gifts stored inside their homes (see Chapter 5 and Spread 10).

A final, perhaps more surprising, example of a how locality continues to play a central role in creating community is offered by the Takahashis of Nara prefecture. This is a very closely tied, three-generation family consisting of Mr Takahashi junior and his wife, both in their late fifties, their two adult daughters and his elderly parents. Because the Takahashis repeatedly travel to Okinawa, the most southern island of Japan, over the years they have created lasting friendships with several Okinawans. These connections are manifested in their home through elaborate displays of Okinawan crafts. Moreover, Mrs Takahashi grows plants and vegetables that originate in the

いよいよ、夏ですね。ゴーヤを食べて夏バテ知らず!!

ちゃ工房 通信

第四四号

2006. 7.17

発行所 奈良市登美ヶ丘三丁目六-一七 ちゃ工房

インターナショナル交流記

ちゃ工房通信でおなじみのインゲさんが、ロンドンより京都にやってこられました。今回の来日の目的は、来年出版されるインゲさんの研究書につかわれる写真撮影です。

まず、5月の20日すぎに京都に到着されました。24日に大きな荷物を持って、わが家に来てくださいました。久しぶりの再会に、家族みんなで大喜びしました。うれしかったのが、家族それぞれにおみやげを、もってきてくださったのですが、イギリスという国は、日本のような進物包装はないそうです。ロンドン出発前に、夫のショーンさんとショッピングに行き、おみやげを選んで帰り、ショーンさんが全部ラッピングしてくださったそうです。一緒に夕食をして、撮影の日の打ち合わせをしては、3年前の思い出話に花が咲いたり楽しいひとときでした。

真剣に撮影中 →

勢介は女なんです

いよいよ6月4日、インゲさんがスーさんを伴ってわが家に来られました。前にも増してすごい荷物。スーさんの撮影に使われる機材がその大半です。りっぱな研究者のインゲさんもこの日ばかりは、スーさんの撮影助手。わが家に到着されてすぐに、スーさんの写真家としての作品をいくつか紹介してもらいました。そしていよいよ撮影開始です。それまでになかった緊張感が家の中をみなぎります。どんなに薄暗くても、フラッシュは使わず直径1メートル程もあるかと思われる白い反射板を使って、撮影は続けられます。身長2メートル近い女性2人、会話は英語。大迫力です。あたりまえのことですが、すごいカメラ、それにレンズ。仏壇、神棚、床の間・・・玄関の飾り物や市松人形。わたしたちがふだん、なにげなく接している空間が、彼女たちには新鮮に写るんでしょうね。スーさんに写してもらった玄関ポーチの写真なんてどこのごりっぱなお宅かしら?と見間違えるほどすてきに写ってます。インゲさんのための撮影が一段落すると、スーさんがご自分のテーマとして集めておられる家族の写真を写させてほしいと言われ、大家族6人せいぞろいでスーさんのカメラにおさまりました。半日だけの間でしたが、とても貴重な経験をさせてもらいました。あとはおきまりのビールでかんぱぁーい!

ちゃ工房(高橋家)はインゲさんとスーさんによって、どのような紹介がされるのでしょう。楽しみです。　　(ち)

7月16日現在の気温

	最高	最低
奈良	33.9℃	23.6℃
那覇	30.5℃	27.3℃

ついに、今年奈良の方が暑くなってしまったよ。

第七回 世界遺産をめぐる旅 ～玉陵(たまうどぅん)～

首里城から西に三百メートルの地点にある玉陵(たまうどぅん)が、今月の世界遺産です。その名前は推測できますが、一五〇一年に築かれた、琉球王家(第二尚氏王統)の陵墓です。

首里城にほぼ隣接しているにもかかわらず(しかも世界遺産登録されているにもかかわらず)、観光で訪れる人のほとんどが立ち寄らないスポットですが、りっぱな石造建造物に、墓域に踏み入れられたん、そのおごそかな雰囲気に圧倒されてしまいます。

歴代国王のほか、国王の家族な ども埋葬されていて、約七十人もの人々を祀る玉陵を訪れたあと、この玉陵を訪れると、王朝の栄華と繁栄を改めて感じずにはいられません。

第二次世界大戦で大きな被害を受けましたが、3年余りの歳月をかけ、修復工事が行われ、現在では往時の姿を取り戻しました。一九七二年には重要文化財の指定も受けています。

建造物の上、東西の屋根の端にそれぞれ雌雄の獅子が乗ってい

朱色に輝く首里城とは、とで、この玉陵を訪れると、

で訪れる人のほとんどが立ち寄るかのように、広い空を背に私たちを見下ろしている姿がとても印象的でした。私たちが訪れた七月中旬、陵墓全体には降りしきるような蝉の声に包まれて、静かにそして蝉々と、そこに玉陵はありました。　(や)

歴史の重みと、琉球王朝の大きさを感じる玉陵。

お菓子紀行～大和編③

とってもおいしい。→

今回は奈良の生駒にあるバームクーヘン屋さんの紹介です。奈良といえば和菓子のイメージが強いかもしれませんが・・・。

地元では知る人ぞ知る、根強い人気店だった「リンダーホフ」は、2～3年前からテレビで何度か紹介され、今や幻のバームクーヘン屋さんになりました。予約販売のみで、月の初めに来月分の受付が開始されます。予約が多いので、さらに抽選で当選した人のみが購入できるシステムなんです。しかし先日、たまたまお店の近くを通ると、いつもは閉まっているはずのシャッターが開いているではありませんか!!!お店に余裕があるとき(ごく稀)は、店頭販売もするみたいです。しかも開店してまだ5分、ラッキー!それでもプレーン味はすでに売り切れ、月替わりのバームクーヘン(このときは黒ゴマ)が少し残っていたので迷わず購入しました。

「リンダーホフ」は、ドイツの南の端の森の中にあるお城「リンダーホフ城」からきているそうです。森の中にひっそりとたたずむ質素なお城ですが、一歩中に入るとそこは別世界のような豪華絢爛なお城なのです。このお店のバウムクーヘンも見た目はとてもシンプル。バームクーヘンによくある白い砂糖のコーティングはなく、お店の焼印のみ。ひとつひとつが手焼きで、甘さもひかえめで、でも一口食べると、名前の由来どおり、口の中で別世界が広がるような、味わい深い味でした。

また「リンダーホフ」とは「リンダー(菩提樹)」「ホフ(館)」と「菩提樹の館」という意味で、「木のお菓子(バウムクーヘン)」と、ぴったりの名前ですよね。地方発送もしているみたいですので、ぜひみなさんも予約挑戦してみてください＊＊＊(ゆ)

TEL 0743-75-5246　　URL http://www.Linderhof.jp/

ちゃ工房5周年記念 植樹祭 いたしました。

7月8日

早いもので、ちゃ工房を立ちあげてから、この7月で5年目に突入いたしました。これもひとえに皆さまの応援のおかげです。いつもいつもありがとう。そこで勝手に記念樹を植えてみました。何の木にしようか、さんざんスタッフ会議の結果、風にそよぐユーカリの木にしました。大きくなるかな?これからもよろしく!!

region to cook typical Okinawan dishes. Yasuko, one of the daughters, has taken up playing the Okinawan guitar (*shamisen*) and has mastered the complicated, local singing technique. Finally, Mr Takahashi junior has managed to combine his family's passion with his work, and has recently written an award winning academic book about one of the islands.

The 'voluntary community' the Takahashis have created with their Okinawan friends might not be 'local' in the strict sense, but the way in which they have drawn on their strong interest in this particular locale to strengthen local ties is interesting. The artefact that most clearly embodies this process is the monthly 'family newspaper' called *chiyakôbo tsûshin* (Studio Chiyorko News), a contraction of the names of the three editors: Mrs Takahashi junior and her two daughters, called, respectively, Chiyuki, Yasuko and Yuko (fig. 20). This one-page, illustrated circular offers comparative information about Nara, where the family lives, and Naha, the capital of Okinawa. Key topics discussed are local dishes, sites to visit and annual festivals, while the latest antics of the three family cats is an endearing, reoccurring feature. There are also special reports on unexpected events such as their participation in my study or the photographer Susan Andrews taking pictures in their home. The newspaper, circulated to local and Okinawan friends, also offers both daughters a platform to sell their original postcards and personal crafts. A more unusual spin-off, however, is that twice a year the Takahashis organize an open house during which their friends are informally entertained with Okinawan music and food.

The three examples discussed above illustrate that some of those participating in my study created strong personal relationships with people outside their immediate locale and their extended kinship group. Although it is important to stress that, as with all social relationships, these ties are based on both sentiment and obligation. However, they may be called friendships as they 'show none of the formality and reserve that so often characterize relations among neighbours. Friends are much more likely to entertain each other informally in their homes' (Bestor 1989: 215). This said, during my fieldwork only two other families (the Sakais and the Kuwaharas) informally invited friends inside their homes. Although some of my participants aspired to possess a formal guest room (see Chapter 4), regardless of their ability to formally receive guests, the majority preferred to entertain non-family members in public spaces.

CONCLUSION: HOMES INSIDE OUT

In this chapter I have shown how the 'mainstream' urban home is encircled by a large number of physical barriers. Historically, this seclusion can be traced back to the houses of the pre-modern elite with large rear gardens secured with walls, fences and entrance gates. However, these previous dwelling forms were not merely imitated. Because contemporary urban dwellings are built on small plots, rear gardens are replaced with garages at the front of the house. Instead of having enclosures erected around the whole plot the dwelling tends to be sheltered from the outside world with enforced doors, barred windows, shutters and balconies. Although most urban home exteriors consist of a number of generic elements, the size and height of the entrance gate, the security system and the number and brand of cars parked in front are all markers of social status.

In studies about the Euro-American home, the creation of domestic boundaries is commonly associated with a need for privacy. However, 'privacy' is an ill-defined concept, historically linked with the supposed alienating consequences of Western modernity (Giddens 1991: 151). It generally pertains to the need to protect the individual self from others and from outside, harmful influences in a personal space. Although the idea of the private individual and privacy has become well established in post-war Japan, what it means to be private in the Japanese context needs to be investigated within the light of native notions of the self.

In the extended literature about the Japanese self, reference is made time and again to the opposed social and spatial categories of inside and outside, *uchi* and *soto*. As recently as 2006, Ozaki and Rees Lewis state,

> The distinction between the inside and the outside is particular salient to Japanese people as it relates not only to physical spaces, but also to psychosocial values. That is, the inside is associated with purity, cleanliness, safety, and intimacy (inside the group as well as inside a physical space), and the outside is associated with impurity, dirt, danger, and strangeness. (Ozaki and Rees Lewis 2006: 93)[17]

It cannot be denied that the inside–outside categorization plays a key role in creating a sense of self in Japan. *Uchi* and *soto* are ubiquitous terms that people use in their everyday lives to associate with a particular group and distance themselves from others. The stress is on us versus others instead of the individual versus society. *Uchi* is always relative to the point of view of the speaker, and the family group is considered to be the key 'inside' group. Japanese individuals are socialized into the construct of the group as they move through a number of formal and informal groups throughout their lives, and they 'acquire the capacity to move from one frame to another' (Ben-Ari 1991: 19). Inter-connectedness and cooperation also plays an important role in European or North American notions of personhood. However, I should like to argue for a difference in emphasis. In other words, Japanese subjects, as well as others living in the larger Asian region (Helliwell 1996; Yan 1996), seem more aware of the limits of individual, rational decision-making and most view autonomy as one among many other culturally acceptable choices.

In Chapter 1 I discussed the range of domestic, bodily practices whereby families produce and reproduce themselves as a social and spatial unit (Daniels 2005a). In this chapter I have focused on the changing relationship between the domestic inside group and the immediate local community. The presence of large numbers of spatial divisions between the house and the outside world suggests a clear-cut, inside–outside distinction. However, my research provides evidence for the argument that these categories are fluid and continuously recreated. The entrance hall, for example, is a liminal space where inside and outside merge into each other. The red buckets, which embody both mutual cooperation and control among neighbours, further demonstrate that although the inside is considered to be distinct from, it is always connected with, the outside world of the community. In contemporary urban Japan, local communities endure, but they tend to be more specialized, informal and voluntary. For many urban Japanese, work and school relations and networks formed around consumption practices have become more significant than ties between neighbours. Although these new networks continue to be understood as collectives of close 'inside' relationships, the fact that they are spatially distant from the home has also resulted in a decreased fluidity between inside and outside domestic spaces.

SPREAD 3: STREET GARDENS

Clusters of potted plants occupy the space between the house and the street in urban areas throughout Japan. These street gardens differ greatly in the quantity of plants used and the way in which they are displayed. Some people carefully select colour coordinated, terracotta pots, but most opt for more of a DIY feel, using a mixture of recycled containers. White rectangular boxes, previously used to transport fish, seem particularly popular. Some decorate barred, frosted windows with flowers baskets, others position small groups of plants at either side of their front door, while still others place a series of plants on top of concrete bricks arranged around their property. In the most extreme cases, potted plants are stacked high on tiered display platforms against the façade of the house. All these intricate creations function as a 'green' barrier between the house and outside world. However, other street gardens expand horizontally and colonize every available space between the house and the street, spilling out onto the pavement or even continuing across the street.

The Yanos living in the north of Kyoto created such a horizontally expanding street garden. The family loves gardening, and every time I visited their home they displayed several vases with fresh flowers. Moreover, when I did not call around for a period of time during spring 2003, I was given

a CD with pictures of flowers that had bloomed during my absence. I was, therefore, not surprised to find that when they built a new house they dedicated a patch of land at either side of their home to growing plants. When these spaces were filled with their favourite flowers, they began to line potted plants against the wall of their neighbours' house on the opposite site of the alley leading to their home. When I inquired about this practice, I was told that their neighbours did not care as 'before there had only been an ugly strip of gravel'.

The consensus among Japanese urban planners and architects is that 'illegal' street gardens are untidy eyesores. According to the Japanese architect Watanabe, the chaotic mix of flower pots in front of Japanese homes proves that 'most Japanese are not concerned about how their private actions might affect the overall aesthetic outlook of their street or city' (Watanabe 2002: 69). By contrast, the majority of those participating in my study considered street gardens to be expressions of creativity that could significantly enhanced the rather dull and monotonous appearance of their neighbourhood. Blomley has demonstrated that a similar view was expressed by those living in a area in Vancouver where locals began growing plants in public spaces that were left uncultivated by the authority. Although in theory this practice was an encroachment of public space, unlike other 'illegal' border crossing activities it was tolerated by the local government as well as local citizens because the plants were thought to enhance the quality of life for all (Blomley 2005).

SPREAD 4: WIFELY DUTIES AND NEIGHBOURHOOD SURVEILLANCE

Laundry and garbage disposal are two everyday domestic practices primarily conducted by women that question a simple dichotomy between the private-inside and public-outside. Both activities are associated with cleanliness and domestic order, in turn associated with morality. Kawano rightly argues that 'a clean house embodies a morally positive state' and when 'the order is violated, morally relevant questions arise concerning a person's reputation and upbringing' (Kawano 2005: 48). Japanese women are considered to represent their families to the outside world, and it has been argued that through public activities such as hanging out washing and disposing of garbage women not only judge each others' reputation, but also control the neighbourhood (Kondo 1990; Buckley 1996; Broadbent 2003). This connection between female labour and neighbourhood surveillance is by no means particular to Japan. In a recent study about interactions between elderly widows in a village in the Republic of Macedonia, Lozanovska calls this type of reciprocal female control 'surveillance through exposure' because 'women are never out of each others' sight … and are also *seen* to be working' (2002: 146). Clarke's account of interactions between female neighbours on a council estate in North London offers an interesting urban comparison (2001). In this case, women living in the same block constantly negotiate the tension between the need to protect their privacy and to create sociality with neighbours. The dangers of gossip and rumours, and the threat of being ostracized resulted in other women acting as 'a sort of super-ego' through which the estate is controlled (Clarke 2001: 30).

In most of the homes studied the laundry was done daily, while futons were aired a few times a week. Buckley has argued that time-saving devices such as a dryers are not common in Japan because if a woman is not seen hanging out the washing regularly her neighbours 'condemn her for not performing her wifely duties' (Buckley 1996: 451). Large drying racks placed at the front of the house, drying platforms raised on rooftops, and the cacophony of colourful futons slung over the balconies of intercity apartments seems to confirm the important role laundry plays in neighbourhood surveillance. However, most women participating in my study avoided dryers

because they did not like the feel and smell of artificially dried clothes and preferred to dry their washing and air their futons in places hidden from view.

Garbage disposal, on the other hand, is a boundary crossing public performance that continues to play an important role in creating good neighbourly relations. 'Improperly disposing of garbage' was listed as the number one activity 'that may lead to disputes with neighbours' by 34.7 per cent of the participants in a 1996 survey conducted by the Ministry of Buildings (Kawasaki 1996a: 59). Every town has its own set of rules concerning the time the garbage should be placed outside, what kind of bag should be used, what each particular category of garbage consists of and how items need to be prepared for collection. Garbage is not collected in front of individual homes but at dedicated communal pick-up spots. Moreover, because many towns produce official garbage bags made of see-through plastic and people are advised to write their name on each bag, garbage is easy traceable to its owner. This system allows for a woman's domestic credentials, and by extension her family's reputation, to be scrutinized by her neighbours. All married women in my sample made sure to separate specific items according to the rules and dispose of bags at the designated times. However, the time and energy each individual invested varied.

In Japan everyday practices that mediate between the inside and the outside, such as garbage collection – and perhaps to a lesser degree drying washing – are used to create notions of sameness and difference. This also explains why garbage disposal is often at the centre of tensions between Japanese and non-Japanese neighbours. The landlady of the guesthouse in Kyoto where I stayed during my 2003 fieldwork repeatedly stressed the importance of garbage disposal because neighbours were very sensitive to the fact that the 'foreigners do not dispose of garbage properly'. The two main points of contention were that garbage bags were placed outside the night before, which resulted in crows and dogs spreading the contents throughout the neighbourhood, and that the time consuming garbage preparation guidelines were not followed to the letter. A number of recent studies have, similarly, shown that the Norwegians (Garvey 2005) and the Dutch (Van de Horst and Messing 2006) use native ideals of domesticity such as decorative windows to highlight difference between native inhabitants and their multi-ethnic neighbours.

3
DOMESTIC SPIRITUALITY

BONDS WITH THE ANCESTORS

Eight of the thirty homes participating in my study possessed a Buddhist altar. This number corresponds with recent statistics that reveal that forty per cent of urbanites have an altar (Kawano 2005: 240). The *butsudan* is a standing cabinet with double doors that usually contains a representation of the Buddha, mortuary tablets of the family's dead (*ihai*)[1] and a range of ritual utensils such as offering containers and vases.[2] When a person dies, family members start a long sequence of memorial rituals in order to remove his or her spirit *(shirei)* from the world of the living. As the memory of the dead person fades, after at least thirty-three years, the spirit will ultimately become a guardian or ancestral diety *(senzo)* who takes up a regular place in the family altar (Smith 1974: 40–1).

At the altar, offerings of rice, green tea and water are made to the ancestors on a daily basis and flowers are habitually renewed so that they remain fresh. Moreover, it is common to present a particular deceased person with his or her favourite food or drink. Mr Nishimura senior, for example, was frequently given cans of beer or cigarettes, while Mrs Nishiki senior enjoyed mandarins and chocolates. By allowing the deceased to partake in everyday meals and by giving them treats, bonds between the dead and the living family members are constantly affirmed and maintained. Moreover, by placing all gifts they may receive in front of the altar, a family further acknowledges the continuity between current and past networks of relationships.

Offerings are generally the responsibility of the matron of the house, but in those homes where three generations co-resided, the senior generation would take care of the altar.[3] This said, every family member may express wishes for the wellbeing of the family as well as personal greetings and petitions in front of the altar. This activity, called *omairi*, generally comprises of opening the altar's doors, lighting candles, burning incense, ringing a chime and putting one's hands together to say a short prayer or briefly contemplate the deceased. The attention a particular person pays to the Buddhist altar varies according to their feeling of duty and respect for the deceased as well as their emotional attachment to them. Mr Takahashi junior, for example, greets his grandparents at the start as well as the end of each day, while every night Mr Nishiki senior and his grandson pray together at their ancestors' altar for the happiness of their family.

The domestic altar is firmly connected with the family grave, where the cremated remains of the deceased are interned, which in turn links each home with a particular temple. Graves should be visited and cleaned regularly and offerings made of flowers and incense. Neglecting the family grave may have dire consequences as ancestors can become wandering spirits (*mu-en botoke*, literally *buddhas* without attachments or bonds), who are thought to intervene directly in the world of the living and cause misfortune (Smith 1974: 41–2). This said, a visit to any cemetery reveals that 'graves without ties', so-called *mu-en bôchi*, are a common sight. This is not a new phenomenon,[4] but the weakening of territorial ties (*chi-en*) as well as changing relationships between extended family members since the early 1960s have affected attitudes towards the dead. Among those participating in my study, some – such as 55-year-old Mr Kuwahara, who now lives in his wife's home town of Itami – regularly travel to their place of origin in the countryside to fulfill obligations to their family grave. However, others have resolved the problem by donating money to local

temples which, in exchange, look after their ancestors' graves. Still others disclosed that they were unsure about how to maintain the upkeep of the family grave once the elderly relatives who cared for it had passed away.

THE DUTY OF CARE OF THE ELDEST SON

The Buddhist home altar and the grave are central to a more than three-century-old Buddhist funerary system based on ancestor worship and family obligation. In the patrilineal extended family, the eldest son becomes the successor who inherits the house and the land while other sons move away and create branch families. Daughters take the names of their husbands and become part of their families. Together with the privileges bestowed on the eldest son, when he returns to live in the family home as a married man, it is also his responsibility to care for the elderly parents who continue to live there with him and his wife. Moreover, male descendants need to fulfil their obligations towards ancestors by maintaining both the *butsudan* and the family grave. The duty of care is particularly important on occasions when the dead are honoured, such as during the *Obon* celebration when the spirits of the ancestors are thought to return home,[5] and members of the extended family are expected to travel to their family homes to pay their respect to the ancestors.

In 2003 approximately half of those that participated in my study did not celebrate *Obon*. These were three single students, two recently married couples without children and nine nuclear families who did not feel the need to venerate ancestors of stem families to which they had once belonged. Still, apart from one family, who were Christian, all anticipated that once a close family member had passed away, they would probably built their own family grave, buy a Buddhist altar and start actively participating in the *Obon* celebrations (fig. 21). Two families in my sample bought an altar during the 1990s. These were the Kubotas in Osaka, who had lost their infant daughter after a short illness in 1995, and Ms Nishimura in Itami, whose aging father passed away in 1991, and who made the purchase with her mother and married elder sister.

The eight families who possessed an altar celebrated *Obon* in their own home, while six families and two single students returned to their family home to honour their ancestors. This data is surprising as it is generally claimed that after the Second World War progressive urbanization and industrialization led to the demise of the patriarchal family unit. However, as the sociologist Ochiai has demonstrated, demographic conditions between 1945 and 1975 (large families with many siblings) meant that the stem family system continued to exist alongside nuclear families created by spare children who were not successors (Ochiai 1996: 149–50). It is only since 1975 that there has been a steady decline in the number of co-residing three-generation families: from 54.4 per cent in 1975 to 33.3 per cent in 1995 (Wu 2004: 9) and 19 per cent in 2000 (AS 2005: 85).[6] The fact that, at the start of the twenty-first century, approximately one-fifth of Japanese households continue to be modelled on the stem family shows the resilience of this kinship model. Indeed, my 2003 sample contained four homes where three generations lived together.

DOMESTIC CYCLES OF 'ANNUAL EVENTS'

Sectarian Buddhism, introduced from China during the sixth century CE, has a long history of amalgamation with Shinto, the indigenous religious tradition.[7] Architectural styles and material

21

culture related to both constituencies as well as the deities worshipped and ritual practices enacted are highly syncretic.[8] Overall, those participating in my study did not make clear-cut distinctions between Shinto and Buddhism,[9] but, generally, Buddhism was linked with death, funerals and, by extension, the *Obon* festival when the spirits of the ancestors return home, while Shinto was associated with auspicious occasions such as New Year and life-cycle events such as birth and weddings (Reader 1991a).

Both the *Obon* and the New Year celebrations form part of a cycle of prescribed rituals performed to attract good fortune, generally referred to as 'annual events' (*nenjû gyôji*).[10] Auspiciousness or luck is considered to be an important quality in the world that affects people's everyday lives (Daniels 2003).[11] Japanese notions of luck can, firstly, be traced back to Taoist cosmic principles of change and transformation (Kiba 1997). One example of the continuous importance of Taoist thought is the popularity of astrological calendars that provide practical guidelines for individual practices to avert misfortune during life-cycle events (Hayashi 1996). A second, is the widespread concern with unlucky numbers as well as unlucky years during which individuals might attract bad fortune. Japanese notions of luck also draw on popular Buddhist ideas about karmic causality, whereby an individual is thought to be able to influence his or her destiny by accumulating merits for proper actions (Keyes 1983: 19).

Ishikawa (2000) distinguishes between five different types of celebrations that constitute the ritual year. These are: (1) events linked with the cycle of rice cultivation; (2) festivals to celebrate spirits and ancestors (New Year and *Obon*); (3) the five auspicious days (*sekku*) concerned with the celebration of life and reproduction (9 January, 3 March, 5 May, 7 July and 9 September); (4) specific days to celebrate Shinto and Buddhist deities (*ennichi*); and (5) rites of passage. However, progressive industrialization and urbanization throughout the twentieth century have greatly influenced people's everyday perceptions of 'annual events' and their involvement in them,[12] and during my ethnography it became clear that Ishikawa's classification needs to be updated for the twenty-first century.

Before the Second World War more than seventy per cent of the population lived in rural farming communities (AS 2003) that depended on mutual collaboration between extended families for their survival. The whole community participated in 'annual events' that were organized around spatial units such as local shrines and temples. Knowledge about these events and the domestic ritual observances associated with them was passed on through the generations (Ogino 2000: 65). By contrast, the majority of Japanese born after 1945 grew up in (sub)urban families, commonly organized along strict gender roles (Ishikawa 2000: 5). Although neighbourhood networks continue to exist (see Chapter 2), for most urban Japanese, school and work associations have become equally – if not more – important. Ritual knowledge, no longer transferred through the extended family or the local community, became the preserve of commercial companies such as those offering professional wedding (Goldstein-Gidoni 1997) and funeral services (Suzuki 2000; Murakami 2000), or others providing advice literature (Daniels 2009b).

Local festivals linked with agriculture continue to be organized at religious institutions throughout Japan. However, for most urbanites this particular category of 'annual events' has very little resonance, and most celebrations are but widely advertised tourist attractions. Days devoted to special deities, celebrated at community shrines or temples, still attract local audiences, rural and urban, but the majority of those involved are elderly. By comparison, in the case of auspicious days that remain popular, such as the Girls' Festival (3 March), Boys' Day (5 May) and *Tanabata* (7 July), young people are central. From mid-February until 3 March families will celebrate female children with temporary displays of dolls depicting a royal wedding. In contrast, on 5 May, boys are honoured with indoor displays of warrior paraphernalia, such as a samurai helmet or arrows, and virile animals such as tigers, while wind socks in the shape of carp, which are associated with strength and potency, are flown outside. Finally, *Tanabata*, literally 'seventh night', celebrates the meeting of two stars (the herdsman star and the weaver maiden star) imagined as lovers. On this occasion, schoolchildren are encouraged to make ornaments and write wishes that are then hung in bamboo branches. Again, among the celebrations linked with rites of passage, those that focus on children are the best attended. Examples are the Seven–Five–Three (*sichi–go–san*) festival, when boys of five and girls of seven and three visit religious institutions or school graduation ceremonies. Most children learn and actively engage in activities surrounding life-cycle events in schools. This provides further evidence for my earlier claim that social relationships surrounding children and schools carry more weight than local community ties, although both kind of social networks are territorial and often overlap. All these celebrations are also rare opportunities for the young to wear traditional dress (see Chapter 5 and Spread 7).

Although children form the prime focus of most annual events, celebrations for spirits and commemorations of ancestors are equally important. They are particularly pertinent for my discussion because many of these festivities focus on two domestic altar: the *butsudan*, associated with ancestors and the spirits of the recently dead, as discussed above, and also the Shinto shelf

(*kamidana*) for protective household deities associated with themes of wealth, plenty and good fortune.[13]

GOD SHELVES AND AUSPICIOUSNESS

The standard god shelf consists of a flat wooden shelf hung high against a wall. A miniature Shinto shrine and a variety of white ceramic containers for offerings of rice, water or sake, and sasaki leaves are placed on top. One or more spirits (*kami*) who assist in influencing the fortune of the inhabitants are enshrined inside. They are generally embodied in rectangular-shaped paper or wooden charms (*ofuda*) with the name of the deity and the shrine of its origin written on it, but statues or prints of deities are also common. *Kami* are territorial spirits that protect homes or larger residential units such as neighbourhood communities, but their powers also extend to public spaces such as shops (fig. 22a), trains or sport stadiums.

While there is a typical look to a *kamidana*, during my ethnography I have come across shelves that differ greatly in size and content. Only five of the urban homes studied possessed a *kamidana*.[14] All were hung high against a wall in the dining-kitchen area.[15] In the Wada household the shelf contained two miniature shrines with two *ofuda* charms placed on each side and three ceramic containers for offerings (fig. 22b). The Kubotas and the Yanos, on the other hand, simply had the façade of a shrine hanging against the wall without any space for offerings. The two remaining shelves did not contain a shrine at all. The Iwaiis junior placed three paper and two wooden *ofuda* on an otherwise bare wooden shelf (fig. 22c), while the shelf of the Takahashis was a box-like construction containing one paper charm, centrally placed, two vases filled with evergreen leaves, and some containers with water and rice offerings. An additional item standing on this shelf was a small statue of the good luck diety Ebisu. Statues, lucky strips (*ofuda*) and other auspicious objects, which are distributed through religious centres, enable people to create and consolidate connections with various deities in their homes.[16] Because of their sheer variety in size and price these lucky objects transgress the boundaries of status and class. Moreover, the power of these devices is not

coercive as they are intended to motivate people in their efforts to influence their fate by seeking divine help (Daniels 2003).

Ideally, the material culture of luck should be placed on god shelves. However, because *kamidana* are a rarity in contemporary, urban Japan,[17] people tend to keep lucky objects in various loci in their homes. My data suggests that the kitchen is the prime location for placing objects such as *ofuda* that embody connections with religious centres. The Ebaras, for example, pinned two paper *ofuda* on one wall in their dining-kitchen, while a lucky arrow rested on a doorframe. When I inquired about these items, the daughter, Yu, answered, 'Well, these are all things to protect against evil (*yakuyoke*)', and, pointing at one of the protective strips on which Mr Ebara's name and the age forty-one were written, 'that one is actually father's.' Mrs Ebara explains that her husband brought this charm home when he went to pray for protection during his unlucky year (1994) at their local shrine.[18] The other charm on display was an entrance ticket for the Silver Pavilion, a major tourist attraction in Kyoto, which may double as a protection charm.

Mrs Matsui claimed, like many other people in my sample, that she did not purchase luck objects for the home. However, during successive conversations it became clear that, because the family is affiliated with the Kasuga Taisha Shrine (located close to their home in Nara) that they regularly donate money to, the Matsuis are each year sent *ofuda* and lucky arrows to protect their house against bad influences. One *ofuda* lies hidden from view on top of a closet in their spacious dining-kitchen area. Mrs Matsui thinks that 'this kind of thing does not suit [the aesthetics of] the room, as it would start to resemble a storehouse'. In contrast, her husband 'has an interest in lucky charms' and displays a collection of them in his office. Other families, such as the Yanos and the Takahashis, also received charms through the mail from their local shrine or temple. Thus, auspicious objects are used in the continuous production and reproduction of connections between households, deities and the religious centres where they are enshrined. These examples also show that some temples and shrines have successfully adapted to the busy lifestyles of contemporary

22b   22c

Japanese by providing mail delivery services as well as by advertising and selling their wares through the internet (Reader and Tanabe 1998).

The lucky objects discussed above are placed inside the home to protect its inhabitants. However, religious institutions also distribute a range of charms that assist in fulfilling particular individual needs such as finding love, passing exams or driving safely. Although these lucky objects might also be placed in the home, they are often miniatures that may be carried close to the body, whether they are kept in wallets, hung in cars or attached to key chains, mobile phones or bags. Thirty-year-old Kagemori Shigeko, for example, carried two lucky charms in her wallet: a magic five-yen coin to help her find a boyfriend and a miniature rake to rake up money. Takahashi Yasuko and Ebara Yu, both in their twenties, had a protective charm to keep them safe when driving. These examples draw attention to the fact that interactions with the divine may be driven by individual motivation. However, as we will see next, in the Japanese context individual interest and collective morality are not considered exclusive (Kawano 2005: 26).

What it means to be a good Japanese person is strongly influenced by Confucianist ideas of self-cultivation (shûshin). Whereas in China self-cultivation was primarily a scholarly pursuit, in Japan the concept became coupled with notions of filial piety, social harmony and reciprocity, and changed into an everyday virtue that might lead to improvement for all (Ornatowski 1998: 349).[19] This blurring between individual and group goals means that drawing on the spiritual world as much in order to find a love match or do well in school as to win at sports or in elections, or make profit in business is not seen as problematic. Indeed, as we will see below, it is the careful articulation between individual desires and group ideals that is also at the base of the successful operation of the domestic, spiritual defence system. Still, this is a delicate balance, and throughout Japanese history elites have exploited the notion of self-cultivation for their own ends. During the first half of the twentieth century, for example, the promotion of self-cultivation in order to boost national goals led to devastating military consequences. A more recent example is the

strong pressure placed on employees in large companies to cultivate themselves by working long hours, thereby sacrificing family life in order to increase company profits. Similarly, promoters of traditional arts have repeatedly drawn on the notion of self-cultivation in order to turn everyone into 'mainstream' Japanese citizens (Ackermann 1997).

ZODIAC ANIMALS AND THE TEMPORALITY OF LUCK

Apart from the kitchen, two other key areas where the material culture of luck might be found are decorative alcoves and hallways. Japanese-style rooms with alcoves, usually also the designated space for placing the Buddhist altar, continue to be strongly associated with ritual in contemporary Japan.[20] Of the eight people in my sample who possessed a contemporary alcove (see Chapter 4), five chose to place one or more lucky arrows inside.[21] However, centrally placed in all alcoves are figurines in the shape of zodiac animals (*etomono*). Twelve zodiac animals correspond to a prescribed sequence of twelve years embedded within a larger sixty-year cycle of growth and decay. Zodiac animals are considered to invite luck during the year with which they are associated. Ideally, representations of a particular zodiac animal should be replaced with the next one in the series at the start of each new year.[22] Some zodiac animals are ornaments, but many are utilitarian goods. For example, 2003 was the year of the sheep, and sake bottles, soaps or candles in the shape of sheep, as well as plates, cushions and slippers covered in sheep motifs, were ubiquitous. Most of the zodiac shapes, like the majority of lucky objects, are gifts that entered the home en masse during the New Year period,[23] whether or not the recipients actually want them (see Chapter 6).[24] Like *ofuda* and lucky arrows, discussed above, zodiac animals assist in the creation and recreation of relationships between people, and between people and religious institutions. However, zodiac shapes, as well as a number of other lucky objects, are distributed by both religious centres and commercial companies.

Some lucky charms were placed in decorative alcoves, but most were on display on the top of the shoe closet in the hallway. The space is generally built to face east, where danger is considered to be located, so that auspicious objects can be placed there to watch and protect the house and its inhabitants against bad influences. Some of the objects displayed aimed to drive away evil. Common examples are representations of devils, whether printed on a paper protection charm (Iwaiis junior), or in the shape of a roof tile (Nasu) or a clay bell (Takahashis). In Okinawa, pairs of jishi lions, protective guardians of the house, serve the same purpose. However, charms that invite good luck are more common. A big bamboo rake to rake up good fortune is one such example, but the most popular items within this group are lucky animals, such as cats with their paws raised, frogs and owls.

As with zodiac animals, the power of these lucky animals does not emanate from religious centres. Instead, their efficacy is grounded in homophonic association. Owl miniatures were ubiquitous in the homes studied. The Yamamotos and the Noguchis displayed owl statues on top of their hallway shoe closets while Mrs Sakai's owl collection occupied any possible surface in the entrance hall (see Chapter 6). The Japanese word for owl is *fukurô*, a homonym for (1) *fu-kurô*: 'without trouble' and (2) *fuku ga kuru*: 'to invite luck'. In the case of frogs, *kaeru* is a homonym for the verb 'to return', and frog shapes are thought to assist people to return safely home from travel or to return to a normal state, after an illness, for example. I found an interesting adaptation of the frog theme in

the Takahashis home in Nara. Mrs Takahashi senior has created a display with six miniature frogs in the hope that the six members of her family 'would return home safely'. Frogs are not only common in domestic entrance halls but are also placed in buildings such as temples and businesses to pray that people will return safely home.[25] Finally, the beckoning cat (*maneki neko*), which appears with the same frequency in both domestic and commercial settings, is worth mentioning here as it has achieved a global presence, inviting luck with its raised paw.[26]

One of the main characteristics of all lucky charms is that they have a temporal character. In theory, because their efficacy only lasts until they have served their purpose or, even if they have not achieved this, for at most one year, they must be frequently replaced; old charms have to be regularly exchanged for new ones. During the New Year, a key period in the yearly ritual cycle of regeneration,[27] a large percentage of the population visits temples and shrines (*hatsumôde*) to pray for good fortune, and many make it a habit to exchange charms on this occasion. Still, because of blockages in the circulation of luck between religious institutions and local community, many 'old charms' are never returned. Some examples from my fieldwork in 2003 are an ink painting of a

horse dating from 2002 hanging in a hallway and a lucky arrow with an image of dragon dating from 2000 kept on top of a kitchen closet, god shelves with *ofuda* from as far back as 1995 and ravelled brocade protection charms forgotten inside handbags and brief cases.

Faced with this evidence, some claimed that old charms were not replaced because of time constraints, others, however, admitted that had simply forgotten about these items that got lost in the back areas of the home (Chapter 5). Still others explained that their mothers or grandmothers used to take care of these matters. For example, Mr Iwaii junior from Kyoto, born in 1969, told me that at the beginning of each year his mother, Mrs. Iwaii senior, who lives in Nara, sends *ofuda* from a local shrine for him, his wife, and since 2003, for his son, with their names and ages imprinted on them. Each year, on receiving a new batch, the old ones are returned to Mrs Iwaii senior, who disposes of them at the shrine. Likewise, the Takahashi seniors and Mrs Wada's 85-year-old mother, Mrs Kobayashi, regularly returned used-up charms to religious centres (figs 23a and 23b).

My observations at temples and shrines confirm that the majority of those who return charms for ritual disposal are middle-aged or elderly women. It is common for one person to take responsibility for performing religious activities as a representative of a larger group, and in my sample married women were the ones held accountable for the happiness and spiritual wellbeing of all members of their family. They were in charge of preparations for annual events, visited religious centres when needed, and managed the domestic material culture of luck. Moreover, women are also the ones who are held responsible for caring for the ancestors both at the *butsudan* and at the family grave.

TENSIONS BETWEEN THE GENERATIONS

We have seen that central to the patrilineal family model, influenced by Confucian ethics of filial piety, is the idea that a male successor lives with his parents and takes care of them into old age. Mr Takahashi junior of Nara is a typical example of an eldest son who has fulfilled his obligation of care towards his parents and his ancestors. He spent the first year of his marriage in a rented house in Takatsuki, north of Osaka. However, after the birth of his first daughter in 1975 a second floor was added to his parents' house in Nara and both families started to live together. In 2003, the elderly couple (both in their mid-eighties) occupied two rooms on the ground floor: a Western-style living room and a large Japanese-style room that contained the family's Buddhist altar cared for by Mrs Takahashi senior. The entrance, the kitchen, toilet and bathroom were shared spaces, while Mr Takahashi, his wife and their two adult daughters would relax and sleep on the first floor. Mr Takahashi dutifully moved in with his parents after the birth of his first child, but these days it is also common for eldest sons to pursue a career elsewhere and only return to the family home later in life, often after retirement. Mr Sakai's older brother, for example, worked as a sarariiman in Hokkaido for more than thirty years before he eventually returned home to Osaka to become head of the family and take care of his parents.

Although his brother received the family house and the status that comes with it, Mr Sakai does not envy him as 'it is a really tough life with not much freedom, and it is especially difficult for his wife'. In the literature, the relationship between the wife of the eldest son and her mother-in-law

23a

23b

(*shûtome*) is generally described as tense and problematic (see Daniels 1996) and, as the following example illustrates, some women in my sample who were married to eldest sons refused to live with their husbands' aging parents. About twelve years ago, Mr Nishiki's father built a large two-storey house in Gakuenmae, a commuter town between Nara and Osaka. His eldest son was planning to get married soon, and Mr Nishiki senior had assumed that he would live together with his new bride on the first floor in their new house. However, because his daughter-in-law did not get along with his wife, the elderly couple continued to live alone in their three-generation house for another seven years. It was only when Mr Nishiki senior's wife passed away that his son's family (which by then included a four-year-old son) moved in. In theory, the generations agreed to live separate lives, but this proved impractical because the young Mrs Nishiki cooked meals for everyone, and the extended family ended up spending most of their time together in the ground-floor dining-kitchen (see Chapter 4). Interestingly, in this case, Mr Nishiki senior, an eldest son himself, cares for his deceased parents and wife, tending their shrine in a large Buddhist altar in the Japanese-style room on the ground floor. As she has never warmed to her husband's parents and their ancestors, 37-year-old Mrs Nishiki is not particularly interested in the altar, but occasionally she may offer some rice or place gifts in front of the altar (Daniels 2009c) (fig. 24a).

Children might feel reluctant to cohabit with elderly parents or parents-in-law. However, my data suggests that these negative feelings might be mutual. Mr Togo, an architect in his early fifties who lives in Kyoto with his wife and two teenage sons, raised this point as follows:

> Probably parents do not want to live with their children either because their lifestyle is too different. Therefore, if it was the case that there were places where one could live alone as an elderly person I would honestly prefer that. It would be easy if my children would want to live close-by, but not if it was in the same house, and one had to be careful all the time.

A number of other parents over sixty in my sample also valued their independence. An extreme example are the Kagemoris, who used to live with their unmarried adult daughter Shigeko in a 3DK apartment in the centre of Osaka. However, in 2004, when Mr Kagemori retired after a long career as a high schoolteacher, the couple, who were by then in their mid-sixties, set up home in Borneo, a place where they had dreamed of living since they had conducted fieldwork there as graduate students. Shigeko continued to live on her own in the family flat and her parents visit her once every three months. Still, living independently into old age becomes much less feasible when one spouse falls ill or dies. As Mr Togo hinted above, elderly people living alone (only five per cent of the over sixty-fives in 2000) have a hard time because they are often discriminated against. It is, for example, common in urban areas to refuse them the opportunity to buy a flat. In December 2002, a programme on NHK television revealed that the main reasons for this kind of prejudice are that other tenants feel: (1) uneasy because there would be no responsible person around if something happened, for example, sickness; (2) unsafe, because, for instance, they may cause fires; and (3) that they might not be able to take proper care of the property.

NEW FAMILY MODELS AND FEMALE REBELS

The elderly in Japan, unlike their contemporaries in other developed countries, continue primarily to be cared for at home (Wu 2004). This said, both parents and children have developed strategies

to adapt to changing social and demographic circumstances. One option, briefly introduced earlier, is to build a house large enough to allow two generations to live separate lives under the same roof. However, the fact that these so-called three-generation houses need to be build on relatively large, expensive plots of land make them unachievable for many. Most people negotiate the pressures associated with patrilineal kinship in other, innovative ways.[28] The Matsuis in Nara are both only children. In theory, after their marriage in 1996, Mrs Matsui's loyalty should only have been to her husband's parents in Osaka. She would, therefore, have not been able to care for her own aging parents. The Matsuis could probably afford to place them in a home or a special apartment block for the elderly,[29] but, like most children I talked with, both preferred to fulfil their duty of care personally. Because Mr Matsui's parents were younger and in better health, the couple decided that they would first care for Mrs Matsui's parents.[30] Soon after their first child was born in 1999, the couple assumed they could moved into her parental home in Nara, but to their great surprise, Mrs Matsui's mother opposed this plan.

A : I did not think she would say no!
Q : Why do you think she refused?
A : Well, when my mother came here as a bride there were still five people in the house and my father's mother was ill. She had to make food and wash for all of them. She doesn't like to work for other people again. She finally is free!

Mrs Matsui's parents did not refuse their daughter's generous offer outright. Instead, they funded the construction of a new house for their daughter's family on a plot next to theirs. This strategy enabled them to remain independent, while at the same time having their daughter, their future caretaker, and their granddaughter close by. For the time being at least, the *butsudan* belonging to each family remained in the care of the senior generation. However, as we will see below, some households with two sets of altars (and graves) already exist, and this dual burden of care might become more common in the future (Ochiai 1996: 152–3).

Another increasingly popular solution to the parental care problem is for an unmarried daughter to reside with one or both elderly parents. Japanese women in their late twenties and early thirties are under considerable pressure to marry, but once they have passed the age of thirty-five many give up hope of ever finding a partner.[31] One reason for this trend might be the disparity between the romantic ideal held by many young Japanese women (see Chapter 1) and the practicalities and problems involved in securing a marriage contract between families competing for successors.[32] Another factor is that growing numbers of women continue working after they marry (see Chapter 4). Ms Kadonaga is a 55-year-old civil servant with a law degree from a highly regarded university. She has never married and lives together with her 83-year-old mother in Kobe in a two-storey detached house build on the family plot after Mr Kadonaga died seven years ago. Mrs Kadonaga occupies a Japanese-style room with a bed adjacent to the dining-kitchen on the ground floor while Ms Kadonaga has her own living space and bedroom upstairs. This is a so-called 'barrier-free' home that accommodates Mrs Kadonaga's current and future special needs. The kitchen, for example, has a low stove and working space at which one can cook while sitting on a chair while the bathroom is easy accessible with a wheelchair.[33]

Because the Kadonagas are Christians they do not possess a domestic altar, but the following example serves to illustrate how the obligation of care towards the ancestors may be fulfilled in this kind of family model. When Mr Nishimura died in 1991, Ms Nishimura, who had lived with both her parents in their family home in the city of Itami, moved with her mother into an apartment close to the local temple graveyard, and with the support of the family of her older, married sister she purchased a Buddhist altar and family grave, which was regularly visited and tended by Mrs Nishimura. Following Mrs Nishimura's death, Ms Nishimura cared for the altar on a day-to-day basis, and her older sister's family shares her duty of care towards their ancestors. In 2003 the altar was placed in a custom-made recess (*butsuma*) in Ms Nishimura's ground-floor apartment in Takarazuka city (fig. 24b).

CONCLUSION: THREATS TO THE SPIRITUAL DEFENCE SYSTEM?

The *butsudan*, the grave and the material culture of luck form part of a domestic, spiritual defence system activated through a series of ritual performances at specific times throughout the annual cycle. The anthropologist John Traphagan calls this a 'total life care system', whereby 'the Kami, the ancestors, and the living are linked together through social interactions enacted in the context of ritual performance' (2004: 79). This system builds on traditional conceptions of the family that stress patrilineal blood ties and strong relationships between homes and religious institutions within a particular locale. In practice, both types of connection are sustained through the relentless effort of (married) women. We will see in the next chapter that some women use humour to negate tensions between their individual desires and the collective ideal of domesticity that places enormous pressures and obligations on them. However, few directly question the legitimacy of their domestic burden. Furthermore, for many of the elderly women, engaging in ritual actions as representatives of their extended families gave them a purpose in live. But then it comes as no surprise that those who are nearer to death and thus closer to becoming ancestors themselves are probably eager to sustain these funerary practices.

Still, changing family relations as well as new work and lifestyle patterns threaten the continuation of the 'total life care system'. This danger is clearly illustrated by the slowing down or even the complete blockage of the circulation of luck between religious centres and homes. Moreover, a number of recent ethnographies about new Japanese burial practices offer compelling evidence for an increased tension between notions of interdependence and individual self-determination (as opposed to the Confucian notion of self-cultivation). Whether discussing new graveyards set up by burial societies that do not require the care of descendants or more progressive practices such as the scattering of ashes in natural surroundings that cuts bonds with the living altogether (Rowe 2003: 109–10), this research highlights the conflict between the right of the family to do what is socially acceptable and the right of the individual to determine their own burial (Murakami 2000: 345–50).[34]

The Buddhist funerary system, based on ancestor worship and family obligation, seems difficult to sustain in a society where households without children or single-person households are on the

24a   **24b**

increase, gender and generational relationships are contested and people generally lead more mobile lives. One family in my sample illustrates what the future might have in store. The Wadas in Osaka live in a 'three-generation house'. Because Mr Wada's parents had already passed away, the Wadas decided to construct a new home for their own family as well as Mrs Wada's 85-year-old mother, Mrs Kobayashi. The house was built on the same plot on which the Kobayashi's family house had stood for more than forty years. It has two separate entrances, and Mrs Kobayashi occupies the ground floor while the Wadas live with their adult, single son on the first floor. Moreover, this family possesses two Buddhist altars. Mrs Kobayashi cares for her deceased husband and his ancestors at the Kobayashi's altar, while Mr Wada, who is an eldest son, venerates his mother at a small portable altar on the first floor. Mr Wada's mother was one of a growing number of women of her generation who have decided to 'divorce' their husbands after death either by purchasing their own grave or by opting for a range of new burial practices. By choosing to be buried separately Mrs Wada placed an extra burden on her son and his family, who will not only have to buy an altar but will also need to fund regular memorial services for two sets of graves.

I will not be able to discuss this example in more detail here, but the fact that it concerns an elderly person rebelling against the system raises interesting questions about uncritically associating change and rebellion with youth. Still, although some people may say 'no' and opt out of the system, this is currently only a very small minority. I therefore think it wise to refrain from jumping to any conclusions about the collapse of Japanese religious structures and practices grounded in a particular value system that stresses collectivity, as this has been predicted since the 1970s, whether the blame is placed at the door of Westernization, urbanization or individualization. My research

does, however, demonstrate that anxieties about separation and alienation remain strong among contemporary Japanese, and many continue to engage in those ritual practices that are relevant to the specific circumstances of their lives at the start of the twenty-first century.

> The continuous focus on belief as the primary dimension of religious life has led to mistranslations and misunderstandings of other religious traditions, and … to the failure to explore the faith of others in their historical and communal contexts.
>
> Good (1994: 17)

Since the early 1970s, growing numbers of anthropologists have raised epistemological questions about the usability of the concept of belief, defined as an inward, psychological state, as a universal, comparative category in the study of religion (Needham 1972; Ruel 1982; Asad 1993). As a result, the idea that 'religion as action' is equally important as 'religion as faith' has steadily gained weight (Tambiah 1985). A number of ethnographies carried out by anthropologists working in Japan have provided strong evidence in support of this view. In *Practically Religious*, a seminal study about economic activities at Japanese religious sites, for example, Reader and Tanabe astutely argue that 'human understanding is not a prerequisite for ritual to have power or effect … practical and rational technologies supplement each other in the production of good results' (1998: 127). John Traphagen (2004) is another anthropologist who uses Japan as a case study to launch a powerful critique of the Western conceptualization of religion as faith, arguing that 'rather than being organised around doctrine or institutional affiliation [Japanese] religious activity is centred on the idea of concern about personal and collective well-being' (2005: 81).

This book focuses on how concern is expressed in the domestic arena by creating connections among people, dead and alive, with deities and with the inanimate world. However, the home is

closely connected with religious institutions, and in times of need people will visit temples and shrines to express concern about their personal or collective wellbeing. The Japanese religious world is orientated towards this worldliness and there are no parameters for areas of concern. The power of religious practice may, thus, be employed to reach material, social and political goals ranging from recovering from illness and passing exams to improving business and finding a love match.

Buddhist, Shinto, Taoist and Confucianist thought have a long history of amalgamation, and deities that fall out of fashion are easily replaced with new ones that deal better with the existing circumstances. Moreover, institutional affiliation is not linked with commitment to faith and people generally mention multiple affiliations when asked about their religion. Because they operate in a highly competitive, changing climate, those religious centres that efficiently market the deities worshipped and the wares sold are most successful.

When a particular concern arises, people (generally women as representatives of the family group) visit temples and shrines to pray to multiple deities for assistance. Religious professionals, who are concerned with doctrine and larger transcendental problems, may act as mediators between people and the deities by reciting sacred texts and conducting purification rites. However, a huge variety of material culture allows people from all walks of life to express concern by enacting a series of embodied actions while moving through the sacred space. These ritual performances include washing hands and mouths with water on entering the sacred site, dressing and putting make-up on statues, ringing the bell, offering coins and clapping hands, writing wishes on votive boards (*ema*) that are left behind, and, finally, purchasing lucky charms to take home.

4
TATAMI TASTES

FROM MALE TO FEMALE DOMESTIC TASTE

> The assertion of an aesthetic judgment is not simply that of the autonomous agent but most commonly part of a social context in which the expression of aesthetics is intended to be part of relationships.
>
> Clarke, 'Taste Wars and Design Dilemmas'

Of the thirty homes studied, two – those of the Nakaes and Iwaiis senior – stood out because they possessed spacious, sparsely furnished tatami rooms with a decorative alcove or *tokonoma*. These kinds of minimalist rooms are modelled after the *sukiya*-style guest rooms of the Tokugawa elite, with an alcove dedicated to showing the taste and status of the inhabitants. The display inside these elite rooms consisted of one or more scrolls hanging on the wall and 'three objects used in Buddhist ceremonies' (*mitsugusoku*), namely an incense burner, a flower vase and a candleholder, set out in front. In the homes of the most affluent, a large wooden post (*toko-bashira*), often a tree trunk in its natural state, separated the *tokonoma* from another large recess called *chigai-dana*. This second alcove contains a top shelf closed off by sliding doors and one or more shelves for displaying a selection of art treasures or antiques (figs 25a and 25b).

The content of the *tokonoma* in the homes of the Nakaes and Iwaiis senior emulates this ideal: a scroll appropriate to the season was hung in the middle of the wall, while a subtle arrangement of fresh seasonal flowers was placed in a vase before it. For their *chigai-dana*, the Nakaes selected a quirky display of large antique clocks that Mr Nakae's father used to collect, while the Iwaiis chose a more 'traditional' display of *objets d'art*, such as an antique penholder and ink container. The fact that both families displayed objects expressive of masculine taste, whether tools associated with scholarship or a

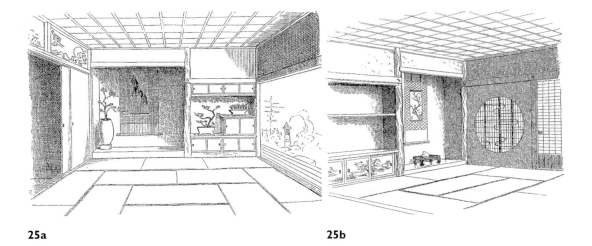

25a   25b

male collection of antiques, is of interest here as the selection and the placement of objects in the alcove used to be an exclusively male pursuit. The stress was not on demonstrating personal taste but on possessing 'not only a capacity to discern objects of generally regarded worth but also the means to own a stock of such objects sufficient to select and match in accordance with the aesthetic principles prescribed' (Sand 2003: 104–5).

As we have seen in Chapter 1, since the end of the nineteenth century the Japanese state has endorsed the ideal of the nuclear family. Within this family model, the male domestic role changed from that of a host proficient in the appreciation of art and antiques to a father engaged in family activities. Female achievements, on the other hand, were measured against the ideal of 'good wife, wise mother' (*ryôsai kenbo*), which meant that 'a woman's role was essentially home-based. Women were expected to carry the burden of domestic work and care for the wellbeing of all family members alone' (Bishop 2005: 88). However, in reality a large female workforce employed in factories, mines and agriculture was essential to the successful industrialization of the country. It was only after the Second World War, with the introduction of a new constitution, that the extended patriarchic family unit slowly ceased to be the economic and legal foundation of the nation and the gendered division of labour became a reality.

During the 1950s the number of female workers in full-time jobs declined sharply (Broadbent 2003; Bishop 2005).[1] An immediate reason for this decrease was that large number of returning service men needed jobs. However, socio-economic factors had a more lasting impact. Because of the steady wage rises it was economically no longer necessary for middle-class women to contribute financially to the household. Their early retirement helped to secure the much-discussed Japanese system of life-long employment and payment by seniority.[2] By the mid-1960s the state-driven gendered ideology had become firmly established and spawned two powerful stereotypes; the professional housewife, or *shufu*, who is completely devoted to domestic life and her male antipode the *sarariiman*, the hardworking white-collar breadwinner.

FULL-TIME AND PART-TIME HOUSEWIVES

All twenty-three married women in my sample were responsible for daily domestic routines such as cleaning, food provisioning, cooking and childcare.[3] If unmarried adult daughters were living at home they would assist with housework. Still, the majority of the married women were in sole charge of interior decoration. When examining their attitudes towards home and work a clear distinction could be made between women over and under forty-five years of age. Of the fifteen women over forty-five years of age, twelve became full-time housewives when they married (between 1960 and 1985), while only three continued to work throughout their married lives. These were Mrs Kagemori, who was sixty-three years old and had a long and successful career as a academic, 55-year-old Mrs Nakao, who was an independent book designer, and fifty-year-old Mrs Kuwahara, who was working as a high school teacher.

Until the mid-1980s Japanese mature womanhood continued to be primarily defined by a strong commitment to the domestic domain. However, the Japanese-American anthropologist Doreen Kondo (1990) has rightly critiqued the widespread assumption, often propagated by Western literature about Japan, that all Japanese women are professional housewives. Her ethnography of working-class women employed in a small factory in Tokyo in the late 1970s and early 1980s demonstrates that depending on economic and social differences women express their devotion to the domestic in different ways. The working-class women Kondo worked with showed their commitment to their families by participating in the world of wage labour (Kondo 1990: 285).[4]

The prolonged economic recession that began at the end of the 1990s has resulted in an increased participation of women, from all backgrounds, in the labour market. A survey carried out among unmarried women in 1997 showed that only 20.6 per cent wished to become full-time housewives, 34.3 per cent would like to stop work temporarily and 27.2 per cent wanted to work throughout their married life (National Institute of Population and Social Security Research, 1999). The eight married women in their thirties and early forties in my sample continued to work after they had married, but they all left employment once they became pregnant. The main reason for this trend is that mothers are considered to have sole responsibility for the upbringing as well as the educational credentials of their children, regardless of whether they are active in the workforce. As Bishop puts it, they are 'expected to attend regular parent–teacher meetings, provide highly elaborate lunchboxes according to school recommendations and arrange for children to follow specific timetables, even during vacations' (Bishop 2005: 93). Moreover, as we have seen in the previous chapter, there is an expectation that children will care for elderly parents at home, which means that many women are also domestic caretakers of the elderly.

Still, half of the women under forty-five had returned to work or were planning to return once their children went to junior high school.[5] They had decided to re-enter the job market in order to supplement the family income – either to save for their children's further education or to contribute to mortgage payments. It is important to stress here that Japanese women are on average paid 60 per cent less than men (Ishii-Kuntz 2003: 211). The main reason for this income gap is that most are either employed in low-skilled jobs or in positions without much prospect of advancement.[6] Many female workers are *paato*, or part-time employees. However, while in Europe and North America this term is associated with fewer working hours, in Japan part-timers work as long as their full-time colleagues but without being entitled to job security, bonuses or regular pay rises (Matsunaga 2000). It is often the only kind of work available for middle-aged women who want to

return to work after their children are going to school, which they do in order to contribute (even if very little) to the family income in general, but also, for many, in order to start saving money to allow their children to embark on a university education in the future. The situation has only grown worse with the continued recession in Japan and many people, often university graduates, work part-time through their twenties and into their thirties. Some younger people claim they prefer this kind of work to having to endure the stress of working in a large company.

A NATIONAL DOMESTIC TASTE?

Japanese married women are in charge of the domestic arena, and the aesthetic outlook of the home is one among their many responsibilities. In the two homes with large empty Japanese-style

guest rooms, Mrs Iwaii senior and Mrs Nakae, full-time housewives in their early sixties, created a 'Japanese' aesthetic. They carefully selected decorations and produced fresh flower arrangements in accordance with the season that were displayed in designated areas in the home, such as decorative alcoves and hallways. Both told me that, through studying the Japanese tea ceremony, they have gained special knowledge of colours and shapes about decorative objects, food and plants associated with the specific seasons (Moeran and Skov 1997: 199). An important part of this formal ceremony, held in a Japanese-style tea room, revolves around the aesthetic appreciation of a few unpretentious objects such as a hanging scroll and a flower arrangement in the alcove.[7,8]

The historian Jordan Sand has elucidated how, during the 1920s and 1930s the state supported the creation of an unified national taste based on decorative practices drawn from the tea ceremony but also on aesthetic ideas imported from elsewhere, particularly the 'West' and China (Sand

2000).[9] The 'art of tea' was appropriated in two distinctive ways. Firstly, architects integrated key elements of the *sukiya* style, used in the traditional tea room, to produce a new aesthetic for the home characterized by 'closed exteriors and a mix of tatami and chairs indoors, featuring a number of native aesthetic markers such as exposed wooden posts, round windows and unglazed roof tiles' (Sand 2003: 370). Secondly, tea schools, which were once male-centred spaces linked with connoisseurship and elite taste, began training women in etiquette that could also be put to use outside the tea room. Moreover, the incorporation of the tea ceremony into the girl's high school curriculum during the 1930s resulted in the widespread association between tea and female self-cultivation (ibid.) that continues to this day. Within this context it is interesting to refer to Ackermann's argument that throughout Japanese history the ruling elite has linked expertise in seasonal representations with correct social behaviour in order to establish their authority. He calls this phenomenon 'authoritarianism behind the veil of aesthetics' and singles out master's of the tea ceremony as well as presidents of large companies as those who continue to successfully exploit this ideology (Ackermann 1997: 40–2).

Seasonal expertise is linked with socio-economic status and Mrs Iwaii and Mrs Nakae, discussed above, are privileged women whose level of expertise and commitment in creating a 'Japanese' aesthetic in their homes was exceptional among my female participants. Indeed, the creation of elaborate displays based on prescribed sequences of motives and patterns requires an intricate knowledge of the complex 'native' aesthetic iconography of the seasons. Moreover, only those who possess large numbers of seasonal goods, as well as ample space in which to store them, are able to keep up with the cycle of change (Daniels 2009b). Nonetheless, most married women over 45 years of age aspired to assimilate at least some of these aesthetic elements into the decoration of their homes. A good example is Mrs Terayama, the 45-year-old part-time nurse from Itami, who, although she occupied a tiny urban flat with insufficient storage, still kept a small selection of vases and display plates to create seasonal displays on a shelf above the towels in the bathroom/utility room.

Interestingly, all the women in the over forty-five age group had at some point in their lives studied traditional arts and crafts, such as the tea ceremony, flower arrangement, calligraphy or playing the *koto* (Japanese zither). Many told me they took up one or more of these 'traditional' pursuits (*okeiko*) while at school or university to enhance their chances of making a good marriage. Mrs Kubota, a 50-year-old part-time secretary living in an apartment in the centre of Osaka, told me that she studied the tea ceremony and calligraphy while at university, which she jokingly referred to as 'the place where they turn women into 'good wives'. She regularly practiced these skills after she got married, but about ten years before we spoke she had discontinued them because she became too busy assisting her two teenage sons with their education. Other women told me that they had started classes in traditional arts during the 1980s nationwide revival of Japanese arts and crafts. However, like Mrs Kubota, many stopped practicing soon after they had children, while others developed new interests such as oil painting, karaoke singing lessons or volunteering (Nakano 2005).[10]

Whether or not they were still active, most women in this age group displayed objects they associated with the traditional arts. For instance, Mrs Takahashi junior had a wooden box with tea ceremony utensils that she brought with her as a bride and Mrs Noguchi had a wooden circular box containing teacups. Those who possessed a *tokonoma* chose to display these paraphernalia in there, but Mrs Kubota, for example, proudly showed me a portable tea ceremony set she received from her teacher when she got married that she kept in a glass display case in the LDK area. Moreover, in several homes there were wooden plaques to commemorate that the woman of the house received a teaching qualification for traditional Japanese arts. Mrs Yano, for example, qualified to teach flower arrangement, while Mrs Kuwahara could teach the tea ceremony. As the examples given above suggest, utensils for preparing tea, kimonos and a range of other objects used to enter the house as part of a women's dowry, and I will discuss these domestic female objects in more detail in Chapter 5.

ECLECTIC ALCOVES

Aspirations to create a 'Japanese aesthetic' were the strongest among those women who possessed a Japanese-style room with a *tokonoma*. As we have seen in Chapter 1, most contemporary tatami rooms are everyday, multifunctional living spaces without decorative alcoves. Apart from the Iwaiis senior and the Nakaes, who live in houses that are more than 100 years old, only eight of the contemporary dwellings studied contained a *tokonoma*.[11] In the immediate post-war period, the popularity of alcoves suffered from their strong association with the nationalistic agenda (Ueda 1998). However, by the mid-1970s, with more than seventy per cent of the Japanese living in cities, there was a growing nostalgia for a more 'traditional' Japan, and Japanese-style rooms with alcoves became desirable again. Still, it was not until the 1980s that the *tokonoma* became mainstream. The revival of the traditional Japanese arts might have played a role, but the general increase in affluence and the rise in home ownership enabled a large proportion of the population to built alcoves in their homes.

The displays in the eight contemporary alcoves studied retained two traditional aesthetic elements: a hanging scroll and a flower arrangement. However, the rules of seasonality were not strictly adhered to in these alcoves. Only some, such as Mrs Yano and Mrs Takahashi junior, displayed fresh flowers, and silk or dried flowers or paintings of flowers were far more popular. The Sakais, for example, placed a large antique vase in the middle of their alcove, while several large bouquets of silk flowers, some wrapped in plastic to protect them against dust, were placed on the side. Moreover, hanging scrolls were rarely changed, and in some homes the same framed painting was on display throughout the year. Most alcoves also contained a large quantity of other decorative objects, such as gifts, souvenirs and handmade things. Overall, in contemporary displays the stress was not so much on taste and connoisseurship but more on variety and volume. One could argue that this is because most families do not possess the collection of precious objects such as scrolls and antiques necessary to create the typical aesthetic of the Japanese-style room.[12] However, the primary use of tatami rooms as multifunctional spaces meant that the alcove's main function changed from a space to exhibit the status of the inhabitants to guests to a more dynamic area where the extended networks of relationships that are important to the creation and recreation of the family group are on display. (see Spread 6)

Importantly, from the onset the 'native' aesthetic, based on complicated sets of rules, was only discussed in relation to formal, performance spaces such as guest rooms and tea rooms with decorative alcoves. By contrast, 'official' guidelines for decorating rooms for everyday use were non-existent (Sand 2003: 100–2), and the aesthetic in these spaces generally consists of an eclectic mixture of gifts, souvenirs and homemade things. It is important to mention in this context that in all family homes, whether or not there was a *tokonoma*, a 'formal' display area was created in the hallway – often the only space in contemporary homes where outsiders are received – on top of the shoe closet (see Chapter 2). Although most hallway arrangements attempt to adhere to some degree to 'native' aesthetic rules, as in the case of the contemporary *tokonoma*, the focus is more on volume than on minimalism.[13]

'NEW IS JUST BETTER': TRADITIONAL AND MODERN AESTHETICS

Some of the married women under forty-five distanced themselves from what they considered to be an aesthetic associated with a more 'traditional' way of life. The 37-year-old housewife Mrs Nishiki junior, for example, showed me a ten-mat Japanese-style room on the ground floor of their two-storey detached house in Nara prefecture. She apologized for not being able to answer my queries about a rather unusual disarray of decorative objects – fans, monkeys, decorative plates and dolls – placed in one corner of the room. In her words, 'I don't have any knowledge about these objects on display. The room and all the things in it belongs to my husband's father who lives on [this] floor of the house. Neither me nor my husband particularly like this kind of taste.' When the Nishikis' three-generation house was built in 1990, Mr Nishiki junior's mother, who has since passed away, had insisted on a ten-mat Japanese-style room for organizing formal tea ceremony parties for her female friends. Arranged on several shelves hidden behind a screen in a corner of this room were cups, teapots and other utensils used in the tea ceremony. However, these once treasured objects were now gathering dust and Mrs Nishiki junior had turned the space into a storage area for unwanted gifts (see Chapter 6). Moreover, the large Japanese-style room, devoid of furniture, made for an ideal play area for their eighteen-month-old daughter. A yellow, plastic slide placed on top of a rug in the middle of the room attested to its new function.

Many of the younger women dreamt of owning a house with wooden flooring throughout, and 37-year-old Mrs Matsui possesses just such a home in Nara. When their house was built in 2001 she insisted on wooden flooring because in her view 'tatami rooms are a waste of money'. However, because her husband refused to sleep in a bed, they decided to build an eight-mat Japanese-style bedroom on the first floor (see Chapter 1). Like Mr Matsui, other men under forty-five years old had a more positive attitude towards tatami than their female counterparts. The Sawais, a recently married couple in their late twenties, illustrate this contrast. The couple were living in a small rented apartment in Kyoto, but both saw this as temporary solution. Mrs Sawai dreamt of owning a 'modern western-style (*yôfû*) home with wooden flooring throughout'. Because she grew up in the countryside in an old house that only had Japanese-style rooms she associated tatami mats with an unsophisticated, traditional way of life. By contrast, her husband, who had always lived in urban apartments wanted to live 'in a "real" Japanese house with Japanese-style rooms (*washitsu*), the kind that can only be found in the countryside'.

Mr Sawai's comments disclose widely held stereotypical views about the Japanese countryside as a more 'traditional' place. As anyone familiar with rural Japan will concur, newly built homes, identical to their urban cousins, are on the increase, but a large percentage of the rural housing stock continues to be constructed in a more distinctive style. Because these houses are commonly erected by smaller, local contractors they might have kept certain regional characteristics such as heavy tiled roofs or large wooden entrance gates. Still, efficient transportation and communication

networks have made the same services and goods available anywhere in Japan, and rural citizens are very much part of a national Japanese consumer society. Hence, however 'traditional' the façade, behind it generally awaits a standard LDK home with the latest domestic appliances and modern furnishings.

MALE MINIMALIST DESIGN

Apart from Mr Iwaii junior, an academic who studies the tea ceremony and admires the beauty and simplicity of the mats, the men in my sample primarily appreciated tatami for relaxing and sleeping on (see Chapter 1). Moreover, many saw no ill in placing desks and tables on top of the mats to create a workspace in their home. This said, some younger men expressed a keen interest in the aesthetics of their home. Mr Nishiki junior in Nara prefecture offers a particularly interesting example. He originally worked for a design company in Osaka, but a few years ago he returned to Nara to work in his father's construction company. Interestingly, another participant in my study, Mrs Matsui, introduced me to the Nishikis because 'everyone thinks their home is very "unusual"'. Indeed, the aesthetics of their LDK area was unlike any of the other spaces studied as it contained a number of well-chosen modern design classics such as an Eames table and chair set, a Yanagi coffee table and a Ron Arad bookworm. Moreover, on a large, white display rack 'design' objects such as an old Olivetti typewriter, Nael toys and a Michelin doll were tastefully mixed with colourful

ethnic goods such as African baskets and Mexican pottery. Mrs Nishiki stressed her husband's interest, telling me that he was 'really into these kind of things', while pointing at several large stacks of interior design magazines arranged on the floor. A similar rack was used to display Mr Nishiki junior's large collection of CDs, while two large African drums occupy one-third of their living area.

The fact that Mr Nishiki junior trained as a designer offers an explanation for his unusual interest in domestic aesthetics.[14] However, since the late 1990s the minimalist, designer look has become very popular among men and women in their twenties and early thirties. The increase in designer furniture shops in urban areas throughout Japan is a direct consequence of this phenomenon. Nasu, a 27-year-old post-doctroral researcher in Kyoto, explained the attraction of a 'smart' space with wooden flooring filled with designed furniture and objects as follows: 'Well, yes, you know, it has a cool (*kakkoii*) image. And when going to university one would of course like to live smart (*oshare*). Well, tatami, how should I say it, euhhhh, well, you know they have a rather trashy image among young people.' The fact that Nasu as well as Kageyama Naoko, a single 26-year-old secretary who also expressed her admiration for these types of interiors, each rented a tiny, multifunctional tatami room reveals that this kind of home, and the lifestyle with which it is associated, is expensive and difficult to achieve.

Returning to Mr Nishiki junior, the reason why he, as a married man with a family, was able to put his mark on the domestic interior was revealed on a subsequent visit when his wife showed me the rest of their large house. When Mr Nishiki junior moved into the house with his wife and

son in 1998, they planned to live on the first floor, while his now widowed father would live on his own on the ground floor. However, because Mrs Nishiki junior cooks for the whole family in the kitchen downstairs, the couple and their son ended up spending a lot of time there too. As the family only retreats upstairs in the evening to sleep, their minimalist living-dining-kitchen area primarily functions as a space in which to entertain friends and guests. Thus, this space is not that dissimilar from the minimalist Japanese-style guest rooms of old, rarely used on a day-to-day basis. By contrast, the mixture of Japanese and Western styles, functional and aesthetic, gifts and chosen things, toys and decorative trinkets in the spaces on the ground floor of the Nishiki's home is typical of the 'eclectic aesthetic' found in everyday use spaces in the majority of the homes studied.

A number of anthropologists have discussed how the placing of decorative objects in the home is influenced by whether or not one adheres to an overall interior aesthetic scheme. Chevalier distinguishes between two schemes of decoration prevalent in French homes: the interior is either expressive of a certain decorative style, and objects must comply with specific aesthetic criteria, or it consists of an accumulation of things, which allows for a range of different objects, liked and disliked, to be easily integrated (Chevalier 1999: 510). Clarke (2002) subsequently argues that both schemes are more intertwined and most people participating in her London ethnography mixed individually chosen items with goods they received as gifts. My study, similarly, reveals that in Japanese homes two (or even more) types of aesthetic schemes tend to coexist.

Most women over forty-five attempted to produce a 'Japanese aesthetic' in designated spaces, preferably decorative alcoves, but more commonly hallways. Although these formal displays may express a family's taste to outsiders, they mainly function as a focal point for the inhabitants of the home and objects displayed embody a range of social relationships that constitute the family group. Importantly, this space-specific 'native aesthetic' contrasts sharply with the aesthetics in everyday used domestic spaces, which tends to consist of a blend of liked and disliked objects: souvenirs, handmade items and gifts (see Chapter 6).

By contrast, the younger generation – like their counterparts all over the world (see, for example, Reimer and Leslie 2004) – aspired to create an overall aesthetic scheme expressive of a certain style. The minimalist designer look preferred by Mr Nishiki junior (discussed above) is a popular example of such an aesthetic scheme. However, even if one is able to produce such an overall scheme it is difficult to maintain. The sociologist McCracken (1990), for example, has famously discussed the 'Diderot Effect', a phenomenon whereby when new goods are introduced into the home other objects must be removed or updated in order to maintain an overall symbolic unity of space. Because of limited available space and the surplus of goods an average family possesses, everyday, lived-in spaces tend not to adhere to any particular, aesthetic scheme. This said, Japanese families also update their homes, but instead of regularly overhauling the decor in accordance with fashion cycles, they might install the latest system kitchen or a high-tech bath or, as we will see in the next chapter, they might carry out structural reforms to improve storage facilities.

AN OVERALL AESTHETIC SCHEME

Mrs Matsui, aged 37, who lives with her husband, a 38-year-old professional photographer, and their four-year-old daughter, Nao, in a newly built house in Nara, was the only married woman in my sample who expressed a strong interest in interior decoration and was knowledgeable about current fashions and styles. She has a university degree in German linguistics, but after graduation she worked as a salesclerk in a small company selling Japanese crafts. When her daughter was born she became a full-time housewife. She seemed to have taken to this new role with real gusto and, like the majority of my female participants, she was firmly in charge of all things related to the home. However, unlike the women in the older age bracket who tended to decorate specific areas according to 'Japanese aesthetic' rules, Mrs Matsui aimed to create a 'modern', overall aesthetic scheme.

She was an eager consumer of home interior magazines that supply her with the necessary inspiration for decorating her home. While flipping through issues of *Interia*, her favourite monthly magazine, she enthusiastically pointed at examples of interiors she liked. She was particularly fond of the 'white-paint-look', in which every piece of furniture is painted white, which she tried to emulate in her own home. Two shelves more than twenty years old, which she had used as a child in her bedroom in her parent's house, received the 'white-paint-treatment'. An old chest of drawers

that she had received from a friend who was planning to throw it away and a low table, a gift from her mother, were all painted white too. By covering a range of disparate pieces of furniture that had entered the home through various second-hand channels with white paint Mrs Matsui had also been able to successfully neutralize the Diderot-effect discussed above.

Gregson and Crew have argued that discourses about good housekeeping in the UK feed assumptions that men should not be interested in the domestic (Gregson and Crewe 2003: 120–1). Similarly, in Japan men are not supposed to show much interest in domestic work.[15] Mr Kagemori, the high school teacher in Osaka, was the only man in my sample who actively engaged in domestic labour. He enjoyed cooking and frequently prepared meals for his family and for dinner guests. I never witnessed any of the other men cooking, doing the dishes, putting up decorations or tidying the house, although some would occasionally go grocery shopping or pour drinks at the table.[16]

On closer inspection I discovered that some husbands had not completely conformed with their anticipated domestic roles. Mr Matsui offers a good example. As the fieldwork progressed

he became bolder and disclosed, for example, that his wife's 'taste (*shumi*) is quite different' and even dared to question her cherished white-paint-look, asking, 'Don't you think it really looks like a hospital?' This rebellious attitude prompted Mrs Matsui to say, 'When we just got married he would often complain about things I put on display that he didn't like, but these days he does not bother anymore. At the end of the day, I spend most of my time inside, so I can decorate any way I like. Yes, I decide! High-handedly!' Mrs Matsui repeatedly joked about her dictatorial style of managing the house, thereby typecasting herself as the full-time housewife and her husband as the passive breadwinner. The fact that she has firmly taken control of the look of the domestic interior is epitomized by a small shelf hanging on the wall in their dining-kitchen area. Mr Matsui made this piece of furniture when he was in high school, but it was painted white and integrated in Mrs Matsui's domestic scheme. Unlike most other women, Mrs Matsui seems to have succeeded in keeping the eclectic aesthetic at bay. We will see in the next two chapters that her success is based not only on decisive aesthetic choices she made, but also on her ability to store or dispose of unwanted goods.

'WE HAVE "A SON IN A BOX"'

Like Mrs Matsui, many of the other women, but especially those in their fifties and sixties, used humour to remark on the reluctance of their husbands (and children) to share any housework. Mrs Takahashi junior from Nara, for example, called her husband 'a son in a box'. This is a parody on the term 'a daughter in a box' (*hako-iri musume*) used to refer to daughters of the elite who were brought up sheltered from the outside world (and resembled dolls in their glass boxes). Many men happily joined in the banter. When Mrs Sakai proudly showed me the large collection of souvenirs displayed in their living room, Mr Sakai, a retired manager of a prefab housing company, sighed, 'In this house there is not one thing that belongs to me. These are all mother's things.'

Mr Sakai enjoyed taunting his wife but, during my fieldwork, he also showed that he was very aware of the sacrifices made by women of his generation saying,

> My wife trained as a schoolteacher but after we married she followed me around. I don't know whether it is good or bad but in Japan this is common; I didn't want her to work after we got married and well we also had a child right away. Therefore, from the age of twenty-six, she only took care of the children and managed the house.

This said, 56-year-old Mrs Sakai has skilfully turned the gendered division of labour to her advantage by creating strong local support networks of female friends. During the mid-1970s, the family bought a house in a suburban housing settlement south of Osaka. Because many people bought their homes during the early 1970s, they have been neighbours for a long time. Most women in the neighbourhood had children around the same time and they socialized together while their husbands commuted to their offices in Osaka. Mrs Sakai is a particularly well-known person locally because after her own children grew up she opened a prep school for local children in a room on the first floor of their house. She loves cooking and regularly invites her female friends and neighbours for meals. Moreover, the women have embarked on various hobbies together and the result of her own and her friends' handicrafts are on display throughout the house.

Mrs Sakai's informal female network, which was initially arranged around children but over time came to focus more on hobbies and leisure activities, is yet another example of a 'local community of limited liability', discussed in Chapter 2. Mrs Sakai's busy social life, contrasted sharply with that of her husband who had recently retired. Mr Sakai pointed out that he 'only worked and [had] no friends locally'. However, in contrast to the widespread negative stereotype of retired men as unable to cope, Mr Sakai seems not too bothered about his lack of friends, and he is eager to enjoy his retirement to the full.[17] He told me he would really like to start a hobby, 'perhaps something creative such as photography'. When I visited their home in 2006 he had happily joined his wife as a volunteer teaching Japanese to migrant workers from South East Asia in their local community centre.

The typical marital mockery described above was generally good-natured, but, as the following example illustrates, humour may also conceal darker feelings of gloom and loneliness. The part-time nurse Mrs Terayama has lived in the same small apartment in Itami city that she and her husband share with their sixteen-year-old daughter; their son moved out when he started university in 2001. They first moved into their current home in 1985 because it was close to the workplace of her husband, now in his fifties, who at the start of his career was expected to work particularly long hours. Although he was able to limit his commuting time, Mr Terayama still ended up spending

a lot of time away from home. First he was separated from his family for several years because he was transferred to a branch office in Hokkaido, the most northern prefecture.[18] Moreover, when he finally returned to work in the Kansai region, he was expected to go regularly on business trips, which often took him abroad.[19] Like many other women, Mrs Terayama made relentless jokes about her husband's passive behaviour in the home. When we discussed the aesthetics of their home she told me, for example, that she would really like to purchase a particular type of Swedish chair to read books in, laughing, 'but if I buy any new furniture that I need to throw something else out, perhaps my husband'. However, as the following exchange illustrates, Mrs Terayama's humour also conceals her distress about her lonely existence.

> *Q*: who is in charge of the interior decoration?
> *A*: I don't have a good sense (*sensu*) at all but … yes, it is all me. My husband only lies down and sleeps there (pointing at Japanese-style room adjacent to dining-kitchen), he does nothing. My daughter is only interested in volleyball. No one is interested in anything.

Like Mrs Terayama, other women in this age bracket also expressed resentment towards their children. Unmarried daughters in their twenties and thirties who continued to live at home were a common target. Mrs Ebara in Kyoto prefecture, who is forty-nine, complained, for example, that her unmarried, 24-year-old daughter Yu did not appreciate the sacrifices they had made for her. For example, she and her husband paid for a two-year graduate course at an American university for their daughter, and the fact that she was 'still unable to find a proper job' seemed to be a matter of particularly contention. Marriage is another common source of inter-generational conflict. A frequently recurring topic was the strain placed on parents because adult daughters who struggle to find husbands continue to live at home well into their twenties and thirties, while some have even giving up hope of marrying all together (see Chapters 3 and 5). As in the case of gender conflicts, these tensions were often alleviated through humour.[20]

MALE DOMESTIC STEREOTYPES: 'JAPANESE FATHERS HAVE NO HOLIDAYS'

Since the mid-1990s the gendered division of labour has come under fire from various sides.[21] I have already pointed to the steady increase in the participation of middle-class women in the labour force in order to retain their lifestyle. This development, which poses a real threat to the seniority system, is amplified by the growing numbers of younger men who are discontent with their job prospects (Ishii-Kuntz 2003: 200).[22] Moreover, the state has finally begun to change its long-held conservative view of the family by introducing policies that facilitate men's participation in the home. However, no legislation has been implemented yet and the continuing hostility in the workplace towards the small minority of fathers who are trying to increase their involvement in childcare and housework illustrates that much still needs to be done to make this possible.

The domestic behaviour of those married men in my sample who were in demanding white-collar jobs matched the widespread male stereotype of the *sarariiman* (Allison 1994). They showed no interest in domestic things and saw their homes primarily as a place to sleep and recover from a gruelling work schedule. However, this male role model is not – and has probably never been – as ubiquitous as was once thought. Ten married men in my sample questioned the proscribed domestic gender roles because they were in jobs that allowed them to work from home. They were owners of small local businesses (Mr Nakae, Mr Iwaii senior, Mr Nishiki senior and Mr Nishiki junior), independent professionals (Mr Matsui, Mr Nakao and Mr Kuwahara), or academics (Mr Takahashi junior, Mr Sawai and Mr Iwaii junior). Moreover, three men (Mr Wada, Mr Noguchi and Mr Sakai) were retired.[23] Although I have no evidence that these men were more prone than others to engage in any domestic labour, they were able to spend more quality time with their families.

In the homes of *sarariimen* no space was specifically devoted to them. If any private rooms were available they were commonly given to teenage children. By contrast, most of the men in other professions had laid claim to a private room in their home. This space was mainly used to work in, but some had private hobby rooms (Mr Nakao) or bedrooms (Mr Kuwahara). Mr Takahashi junior, the university lecturer, had turned the only private room in their three-generation house in Nara prefecture into his study, while his two adult daughters, Yasuko and Yuko, did not possess their own space and had to sleep together in a Japanese-style guest room. This room, which, according to Mr Takahashi junior, was just filled with piles of books and papers, was clearly an eyesore for his wife who declared that this space in the house was off-limits for my research.

The presence of a male room in the home enabled some couples to successfully mediate tensions about taste. The newly-wed academic researcher Mr Sawai had his own study room in the couple's

rented 2DK flat in Kyoto. In this space he displayed 'the things I really like'. Mr Sawai is a scientist, and the walls were covered with sketches of wildlife and nature scenes along with some photographs of his parents' dogs pinned on a cork board. He is fond of small ornaments and soft toys, and he has chosen to surround himself with a number of collections. His stuffed bear collection is prominently displayed on computer equipment on his desk. Nearby, in front of some books on a shelf, he has placed his collection of miniature animals and favourite *manga* characters (see Chapter 6). As we have seen earlier, Mr Matsui's taste also differs from his wife's and the fact that he possesses a home office/darkroom offers him an aesthetic outlet. In his room, for example, he displays an impressive collection of protective charms from local shrines, objects his wife dislikes. Similarly, adult children with private rooms can customize these spaces with objects of their choice. In my study, examples of such objects ranged from posters of television celebrities to collections of hello-kitty charms and photographs of school friends.

In all the homes studied, even those from which men were largely absent, the women of the house displayed objects associated with their husbands. Among the male objects on display business gifts such as ashtrays and clocks were common. Those with an alcove exhibited such items in there, but others placed them in areas of the home in everyday use. On a windowsill in the Wadas' kitchen, for example, stood a clock Mr Wada received when he retired as a chemist. A second group of 'male things', ubiquitous in the homes of *sarariimen*, are objects associated with sports. Trophies won at golf, the 'manager sport' par excellence, were everywhere. Moreover, bulky golf bags or tennis rackets would frequently occupy precious space in entrance halls. Some husbands, all non-*sarariimen*, were represented in the domestic interior through the fruits of their creative endeavours. Here, examples are pictures painted by Mr Takahashi junior, wooden models of famous religious buildings produced by Mr Kuwahara and photographs taken by Mr Matsui. However creatively inclined these men might be, only two husbands engaged in DIY.

DO-IT-YOURSELF

The Noguchis live together with their 39-year-old unmarried daughter Tomoko in a large twelve-year-old house in Itami city. Mr Noguchi, a seventy-year-old retired manager of a carpet producing company, is a real DIY devotee. His main accomplishments are the garage and large annex that he built at the rear of their house. This latter space is primarily used by Mrs Noguchi to wash and dry clothes, but it also houses a number of aquariums with Mr Noguchi's collection of exotic fish. Smaller DIY jobs include erecting walk-in closets in all bedrooms and replastering cracks that appeared in the walls after the 1995 Kobe earthquake. Finally, Mr Noguchi also liked to design gadgets to make housework not only more convenient but also more environmentally friendly; he had, for instance, recently made a device to recycle their bath water for use in the washing machine.

Mr Nakao, the only other DIY enthusiast in my sample, is a 56-year-old graphic designer. He has his office in the fifth-floor apartment in central Osaka that he shares with his book-designer wife and their 27-year-old daughter who is studying to become a professional singer. Over the years Mr Nakao has carried out numerous small DIY jobs.[24] He removed the wall that had once stood between two individual children's rooms to create the six-mat Western-style room that the couple use as their bedroom, while another six-mat Japanese-style room he painted white 'because the walls were so dark and dirty'. Mr Nakao also produced some furniture, such as a large black chest of drawers standing in the reception area and a bedroom dresser made from old wine crates. Finally, like Mr Noguchi, he invented a number of contractions to make home life more efficient: rails to dry towels and laundry in the bathroom, for example, and shelves for large pots and pans hidden above doors.

The increase in DIY-type stores or home centres across Japan (see Chapter 2) – particularly in the suburbs – since the beginning of the millenium initially led me to conclude that Japan must be encountering a DIY boom similar to the one that occurred in the UK during the 1990s (Shove, Watson, Ingram and Hand 2008). However, the fact that only two of the men who participated in my study showed any interest in DIY made me reconsider this assumption. Furthermore, staff at two DIY stores in Kyoto made it clear that their main customers are professional builders, carpenters or plasterers. The general public primarily purchased everyday commodities sold at very competitive prices, such as bicycles, fans and heaters or cleaning products, although a small minority might buy materials to embark on 'very small domestic projects such as gardening or replacing paper on sliding doors.' Indeed, gardening is a very popular hobby (see Chapter 2) and replacing the paper on sliding doors is about the only aspect of general maintenance that the majority of those participating in my study actively engaged in.

This said, over time many had made some changes to their homes whether small-scale projects such as building closets and replastering walls (Terayama), or more substantial work such as turning Japanese-style rooms in Western-style ones (Matsunaga), changing the interior layout (Sakai and

Kagemori) or adding an additional floor (Takahashis). Apart from Mr Noguchi, all had hired professionals to carry out this kind of work. I was given a variety of explanations for this strong reliance on specialists. Mr Sakai in Osaka, for example, thought that the majority of men were just too busy with work to do things around the house, saying, 'Japanese fathers have no holidays'. The time squeeze might indeed be a factor to take into consideration as the stereotypical Japanese male breadwinner tends to spend his time at home either relaxing or sleeping. However, as we have seen above, only one-third of my male participants fitted the *sarariiman* stereotype. The others were either professionals working from home, academics with flexible working hours or retired men with time on their hands.

Others such as Mr Takahashi junior, in Nara, claimed that it was 'just impossible for amateurs to make these kind of changes'. This statement points at the widespread appreciation of the expertise of specialists. However, Mr Noguchi, the only one among those participating in this study who actually owns a toolbox and enjoys repairing and building things in his home, drew attention to another reason for depending on specialist labour. He argued that most Japanese do not do things around the house themselves because they want to show that they can afford the very expensive services of professionals. Mr Togo, the Kyoto-based architect, also raised the issue of cost when he discussed the popularity of television programmes about reforming the home: 'In reality it is all very expensive, even something small … will cost about ¥20,000 or ¥30,000 [about £100–150]. The majority of people will not be able to afford this.'

CONCLUSION: HUMOUR AND GENDER STEREOTYPES

Contemporary anthropological literature about gender highlights the fact that notions of maleness and femaleness are fluid and that both categories are continuously reiterated in relation to each other (Strathern 1990; MacKenzie 1992; Moore 1994). Drawing on these ideas, several ethnographies focusing on material culture inside the home have further demonstrated that domestic gender relationships are produced within the exchange of labour between husbands and wives. Miller, for example, has famously discussed the exchange of male DIY labour and female aesthetic advice in working-class UK homes (Miller 1988), while, more recently, Marcoux has discussed the exchange of male physical labour and female cleaning skills when moving house in Canada (Marcoux 2004). By contrast, my data suggests that this kind of gendered exchange of domestic labour is virtually non-existent in contemporary Japanese homes. Still, one could argue that the Japanese roles of husband and wife are also complementary as men are expected to earn money while women are responsible for managing the domestic finances (and the rest of the home). In Smith's words, 'marriage is seen as a mutual commitment made by two people of complementary competence. The man commits himself to providing for his family, the women to maintaining a comfortable home for all' (Smith 1987: 19).

This widespread view regarding Japanese gender relations does not necessarily mean that Japanese men and women are trapped in their anticipated gender roles. As Marcoux has rightly demonstrated, relations of domination are not naturalized in the female body, and women frequently accept their role without necessarily feeling dominated (Marcoux 2004: 57). In his words, 'people invest themselves in stereotypical relationships … they "make" stereotypes … [and] they are "made by" stereotypes' (ibid.: 55). Both men and women in my sample were aware of, and many happily complied with, the domestic performances associated with their gender. This said, women generally have fewer choices outside their expected gender roles.[25] A number of female participants in my study challenged the domestic status quo by drawing on the power of irony, which allowed them 'to entertain the idea that even though apparently nothing changes, there is room for free action, joy, resistance, or at least fugitive behaviour' (Torres 1997: 20).

In a seminal sociological study about couples and their laundry practices in France, Kaufmann demonstrates that 'many descriptions of conflict were peppered with laughter, [and] many criticisms made of the partner were highly ironic' (Kaufmann 1998: 177). In his view, humour used by both male and female participants performs a dual function: it is a means to channel emotions and annoyance while allowing the couple to distance themselves from conflict and protect their relationship. The anthropologist Tanuma rightly argues that one cannot ignore the context in which jokes are uttered, and in her study of the usage of irony in Cuba, she distinguishes between the perspectives of insiders and outsiders. The latter consists of 'sarcastic or skeptical accusations of incongruities between what is expected and what actually occurs … scrutinizing others from an alleged distance' (Tanuma 2007: 48). Insiders' irony, on the other hand, is sympathetic 'because the two sides are thought to have shared beliefs and practices of which the insider became sceptical' (ibid.: 48).

The banter between married couples as discussed is an example of insider's irony that combines criticism and sympathy. This kind of humour should, therefore, not be seen as an act of resistance against gender stereotypes and the larger power structures in which they are embedded. As Mary Douglas points out, joking is not an act against the value system but 'a temporary suspension of the social structure' (Douglas 1975: 106). One might add that it is during this suspension of the dominant value system that the need of the individual is momentarily foregrounded. The use of humour in the home, thus, plays a vital role in balancing the needs of the individual and the expectations of the collective, in this case the family unit.

SPREAD 6: CONTEMPORARY ALCOVES

The presence of a *tokonoma*, especially in a room located close to the entrance hall, might imply a certain eagerness to demonstrate to outsiders that one has the means and expertise – however patchy – to (re)produce a 'Japanese' aesthetics. However, my data questions any simple association between decorative alcoves and guests as very few participants actually entertained formal visitors inside their homes. Most contemporary alcoves are a focal point for the inhabitants of the home, and unlike their minimal predecessors, these contain a relatively large quantity of goods that celebrate the accomplishments and skills of family members. All eight examples in my sample fit into a continuum ranging from being relatively empty (Takahashis) to rather full (Kuwaharas).

The Takahashi junior's *tokonoma* is located in a six-mat Japanese-style room on the first floor that is used as a living-room-cum-informal-guest room as well as a bedroom for their two adult daughters. The display consists of three seasonal items: a vase with flowers, a calligraphy and a statue in the shape of a zodiac animal, while a wooden box containing a sake set that Mr Takahashi junior received from a famous writer is placed in one corner. Two large glass cases with Ichimatsu dolls clad in kimonos (gifts received from Mrs Takahashi junior's parents at the birth of each of their daughters) are prominently displayed. On the shelves above stood, firstly, a clock, a return-gift from a wedding they attended, secondly, a beckoning cat, a lucky charm presented to them by their go-between for their own wedding, and finally, a small silver display plate Mr Takahashi brought home from a trip to China.

The Takahashi juniors, like the majority of other people in my sample, displayed three types of gifts in their alcove. These are: (1) gifts received for life-cycle events, (2) gifts received from people of high status and, finally, (3) souvenirs (see Chapter 6). The presence of large numbers of gifts demonstrates that this family has been flourishing in creating and consolidating a variety of formal and informal social relationships over time. Contemporary alcoves, thus, bears witness to

the successful (re)production of the family unit, which is further stressed by putting things made by family members on display. An extreme example of this practice are the Kuwaharas who, apart from gifts such as dolls in glass cases and lucky arrows, also display several pieces of calligraphy by their eldest daughter Keiko, glass boxes with architectural models of temples made by Mr Kuwahara, a small swan statue made by Yoshiko, the youngest daughter, and an ikebana flower arrangement made by Mrs Kuwahara's unmarried sister, who is considered to be part of the family. Finally, in many homes official certificates were given a prime spot in the displays. Some women, for example, displayed plaques that certified their accomplishments as teachers of traditional arts, while men tended to display official documents they received for services to the country. Mr Yano, for example, received a certificate from Kyoto Town Hall for assisting with the local youth baseball team, while Mr Noguchi obtained an official document from the emperor for assisting in rebuilding a local shrine after the 1995 Kobe Earthquake.

Another display feature similar in aesthetics and function of the contemporary *tokonoma* is the 'memory wall'. These displays, created by hanging two-dimensional objects on the walls in the main living area, were common among the students in my sample. For example, Nasu-san, a 27-year-old post-graduate student, displayed a number of posters depicting his favourite films, a chart with different types of moss in Sweden (where he had lived for a while) and an illustrated list of Japanese regional plants and liquors. Some of the other young men in my sample appropriated their working spaces in a similar way. However, memory walls were popular among all those who were well-travelled. One example is Ms Kadonaga, who covered one wall on the landing of the first floor of her house with an eclectic mix of two-dimensional objects such as photographs and letters that embody her international travel experiences. In McCracken's view the abundance of pictures and other two-dimensional items commonly grouped together on walls in American homes embodies the family's past and present, internal and external relations as well as accomplishments (1989: 172). In contrast, Japanese memory walls tend to be created by individuals to reference personal experiences that underscore self-cultivation and taste associated with specific people, places and events.

5
STUFF AND STORAGE

THE IDEOLOGY OF TIDINESS

> What housewives desire most when they buy a house is 'a lot of storage': I Iike a storage room (*nando*), and a built-in closet (*oshi-ire*) in every room, and in the kitchen one wall should be covered with shelves and there should be storage under the floor, and walk-in closets in the bedrooms and can we also have a loft?
>
> Miyawaki (1998: 51)

The architect/essayist Mayumi Miyawaki unveils a strong longing for storage among Japanese housewives. Indeed, any discussions with married women about interior decoration and domestic aesthetics inevitably turned to the limited availability of storage space and personal battles against the deluge of goods that enter the home. Mrs Takahashi junior of Nara prefecture, who is fifty-five years old, exemplified this attitude, saying, 'It is a bit all over the place. I place things wherever there is space, I am really not able to put away much stuff (*shûnô*).' Storing things, like other domestic tasks linked with ideas of cleanliness, such as doing the laundry or disposing of garbage (see Spread 4), is associated with the respectability of the family (Kawano 2005: 73). In other words, it is a major domestic concern that forms part of the post-war ideology of what it means to be a good housewife.

The advice literature industry has successfully exploited female anxieties about keeping the home tidy by producing a dazzling range of storage manuals with detailed advice on how to use domestic spaces more efficiently. Moreover, women's magazines run large sections about storage and special storage issues are regular features. The April 2003 issue of *Interia* (*Interior*), for example, carried a section with twelve hints and thirty examples for 'improving storage and increasing the efficiency of the home'.

26a 26b

Popular television programmes in the before/after makeover format also draw on the urge to improve the practical use of the dwelling by advocating 're-form' (*rifōmu*), a term that refers to structural changes carried out by professionals. Finally, the attention paid to storage in promotional materials for new houses and apartments suggests that this is a topic of the utmost importance to homebuyers. Major areas of concern are efficient kitchen storage, large built-in closets in bedrooms and storage units for shoes, coats and other items in the hallway. Moreover, those promoting accommodation at the top end of the market offer walk-in closets, interior storage rooms and lofts.

My fieldwork confirms that storage is considered to be a highly desirable commodity in contemporary Japan. All ten participants in my study who had bought a home within the previous ten years had made storage a priority. They had installed the latest system kitchens as well as built-in bedroom closets and a range of other storage options had also been explored. The Yanos, for example, had created several storage units under the floor in their dining-kitchen of their newly built house in Kyoto (fig. 26a). The Wadas built a storage room (*nando*) on each floor of their detached three-generation house in the north of Osaka. Finally, both the Kuwaharas and the Kadonagas, who built on very narrow plots, were the proud owners of lofts.

The ideology of tidiness might be prominent but in practice homes vary enormously in degrees of orderliness. Only a small minority of participants actually had the time and energy to keep to a strict tidying and storing routine. One example is 85-year-old Mrs Kobayashi in Osaka who occupied the ground floor of the two-storey house that she shared with her daughter's family, the Wadas. Mrs Kobayashi repeatedly told me she loves housework, and not only does she clean and dust all her rooms daily, she also rearranged things inside her closets and cupboards on a monthly basis. Moreover, in a covered recess (*oshi-ire*) in her main tatami room she keeps stacks of neatly folded futons and sheets, blankets and pillow cases that she washed at least once a month (fig. 26b).

Her effort is even more admirable considering that the textile items stored away are supposed to be used primarily for accommodating guests, something she admitted rarely happens.

Mrs Nakao, the 55-year-old book designer, offers another good example of someone who displayed an exceptionally pragmatic attitude to keeping her home tidy. Everything in the Nakaos' fifth-floor apartment in central Osaka had its proper place because of their desire to 'live a convenient life'. During my visits, Mrs Nakao would nonchalantly open drawers and slide open doors to reveal the neatly arranged contents inside. Like most of my respondents, the Nakaos possess a large collection of clothes, and one whole tatami room had been turned into a 'walk-in' wardrobe. Clothes and accessories are neatly ordered according to type and colour in a large built-in closet and several large wooden closets that line the other walls.

By contrast, most women expressed anxiety about not being able to keep up with things that accumulated in their homes. Indeed, many storage facilities were off limits for my research because people felt embarrassed about the disorder inside. Mrs Kubota in Osaka, for example, had converted a tatami room into storage space, but she only opened the door briefly to let me peep at the chaos inside. The Kuwaharas invited me into their orderly loft, but the stuff in their garden shed was not considered to be appropriate for my investigating eyes. Similarly, the Takahashis conveniently forgot about showing me the storage sheds in their garden. Domestic cleaning, tidying and storing routines are especially daunting for those women who work outside the home and who, as we have seen, are still expected to do all the housework by themselves. However, it is important to stress that some women did not subscribe to the housewife ideology. Mrs Kagemori, a 63-year-old retired academic, for example, told me that she only bought a washing machine after her retirement. While she worked she would only wash underwear; all other clothing was taken to the dry cleaner.

STOREHOUSE LIVING: CIRCULATION VERSUS ACCUMULATION

Among the avalanche of literature marketing domestic storage solutions I have come across a number of ingenious innovations. One example worth mentioning is the 'kura-house', the most popular house in the Misawa Homes range for over a decade.[1] Misawa is one of the four main providers of ready-made homes (see Introduction), and in its catalogue the 'kura-house' is promoted by highlighting its unique storage facilities as follows:

> Storage space normally takes up almost 9.2 per cent of the total surface of the home. Misawa Home has come up with the original idea of making storage and relaxed living spaces more compatible. Because we place a large storage space called "*kura*" between the ground and first floor one can ensure almost 25 per cent of the surface for storage. Of course you can put your everyday goods, but also seasonal items and so forth in there. (Misawa Homes 2003: 78)[2]

The kura-house allows inhabitants to reduce the number of goods placed in spaces in everyday use by circulating things in and out of storage (ibid.: 81).[3] Misawa has thus cleverly reinvented the pre-modern, fire-resistant free-standing storehouse called *kura* (figs 27a and 27b). Starting in the sixteenth-century, *kura* were built by the elite to protect family treasures against fire and theft (Sand 1996: 155).[4] The building also played a pivotal role in a complex spatial mechanism whereby domestic objects were moved around in accordance with the ebbs and flows of everyday life, the seasons and life-cycle events (Koizumi 1995; Sand 1996; Hanley 1997).[5]

27a   **27b**

The Iwaiis senior and the Nakaes are the only two families participating in my research who possess a *kura*. Mr Iwaii senior and Mr Nakae are both first-born sons who inherited a large plot of family land with a spacious house and a *kura* on top. As we have seen in the previous chapter both families were also able to create a minimalist aesthetic in their large Japanese-style guest rooms. One would assume that this extra outside storage space enabled them to achieve this. However, a closer look at the storage practices of the Iwaiis senior and the Nakaes brings into question the function of the *kura* as a contrivance for the regular circulation of domestic goods. Both families possessed antiques and other valuable objects that were regularly taken out of storage. However, these items were actually stored inside the house. In the Iwaiis' home, for example, scrolls, pottery or vases that were regularly displayed in the guest rooms were kept in a small storage room. Objects stored inside the *kura* were moved less frequently. Some functional seasonal goods were exchanged half-yearly: as spring approached, for example, blankets, winter futons and heaters were swapped for electrical fans, bamboo blinds and summer futons. Still, most of the material culture inside the *kura* had come to a standstill. Heirlooms such as hanging scrolls or kimonos, but also items once used in everyday practices, such as individual eating tables and ceramic charcoal heaters, had morphed into a large heap of miscellaneous stuff 'that has just accumulated over time'. In other words, the contemporary *kura* is used as a container for the long-term, or even indefinite, storage of large quantities of unused and unwanted goods. Indeed, we will see below that the majority of domestic storage space assists in the accumulation rather than the circulation of things.

STORAGE STRATEGIES

> Because inside Japanese houses there are so many goods and because storage space is insufficient, the home is inundated with things.
>
> CDI & CORE (1993: 232)

Participants in my study expressed a strong desire for storage in order to accommodate the surplus goods in their homes. Most expected that as one progressed though life one would be able to move into a larger space with more storage. However, in practice, this upward progression is not necessarily achieved, and next I will explore a range of storage strategies common among those who can expand the home and those who have to stay put.

EXPANDING THE HOME

I was surprised to find that affluent families in my sample who had build their dream homes with excellent storage facilities still expressed a need for extra space. Indeed, over time most would continue to expand their homes by adding floors, building garden sheds or even renting storage boxes in specialized premises. The Kuwaharas, the family of four living in Itami, offer a good example of this process. In 1986, when their second daughter Yoshiko was about one year old, they moved into a two-storey house built by Mrs Kuwahara's father, a carpenter. During the 1995 Kobe earthquake this house was severely damaged and a new dwelling was built on the same plot. Mr Kuwahara, who is a pharmacist but who also trained as an architect, carefully explored the most efficient storage solutions for their new home. Large built-in closets were installed in every room on the first floor, and a spacious loft was created to store valuable things such as Mr Kuwahara's large collection of surreal poster art or their daughter Keiko's calligraphy paintings. Moreover, in their small rear garden they placed a shed for storing seasonal goods.

The Kuwaharas thus possessed a luxurious quantity of storage spaces inside and outside their house. However, by 2003, six years after they had moved, their storage needs had increased considerably. Mrs Kuwahara repeatedly complained about the uncontrollable mass of, what she called, 'unnecessary (*muda*)' goods. Built-in bedroom closets were stuffed with clothes, bedding and towels, seasonal goods and unopened gifts spilled out of large recesses and their garden shed was filled with documents from Mr Kuwahara's work. The Kuwaharas therefore decided to create two external storage spaces. First, the first floor of Mrs Kuwahara's former family home was turned into additional storage space.[6] Here, domestic appliances and functional goods such as tableware, often in perfect condition but no longer used, found a resting place. Second, because of temperature fluctuations their loft could not be used for storing fragile goods such as Mr Kuwahara's art collection and so they decided to rent a special temperature controlled storage box instead.

Since the early 2000s renting external storage has become popular. A search of the Internet in March 2005 discovered a large number of sites that offer storage for rent such as trunk-room. com, nissokyo.or.jp or sumitomo-soko.co.jp. The Sumitomo Warehouse offers the most specialized service, with earthquake proof, temperature-regulated spaces for storing specific items such as seasonal dolls, art collections or filing cabinets for documents. In October 2003, a pamphlet distributed with the *Kyoto Shinbun* newspaper advertised storage boxes for rent with twenty-four hour access that cost on average ¥20,000 (about £100) a month for four *tsubo* (about 13.2 square metres) and ¥30,000 (about £150) for eight *tsubo* (about 25.6 square metres). Suggestions for goods one might want to store in these boxes were 'off-season things, leisure goods (ski, golf, outdoor goods), books or memory albums, and display items'.

Rented external storage spaces, similar to the elite storehouse of the past, enable people to circulate goods in and out of storage in order to keep the house tidy. Although the Kuwaharas stored-away art collection clearly resembles the *objets d'art* kept by the pre-modern elite, most of the artworks concerned were considered too valuable to be displayed. However, as the following

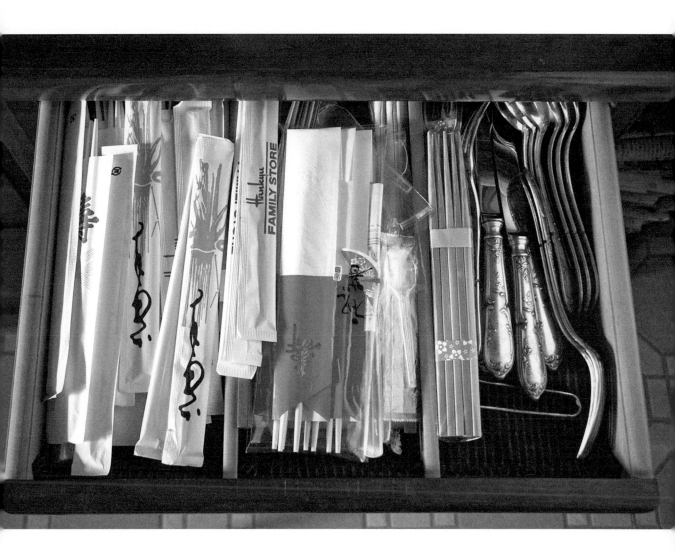

example illustrates, the types of goods stored away matters as more everyday used, functional items such as clothes, for example, are regularly circulated. The Kagemoris were the only other participants in my study who rented extra storage. They repeatedly told me that they chose to live in their 3DK apartment in the centre of Osaka rather than in a big expensive house because they preferred to spend their money on food and clothing. Indeed, as I have shown in Chapter 2, this family's social life evolves around food. Moreover, each family member possesses an expanding collection of clothes, among them many designer brands. Shigeko, the Kagemoris' daughter, stores her clothes in a large wardrobe in her bedroom, while the couple's clothing fills a built-in closet in a corridor and a number of free-standing racks placed in a Japanese-style room turned into an office/storeroom. The Kagemoris only managed to stop their clothes from spilling out into their everyday living spaces by circulating winter and summer clothes between the home and two storage boxes they rent close by.

'LIVING AMONG ONE'S FURNITURE'

The hunger for more storage might lead some to move into larger properties or build a bigger home on the same plot. Others expanded the domestic space outwards into sheds and rented storage units. However, those at the other end of the spectrum, who are living in small apartments with insufficient storage but do not have the means to move, have no other option than to store their possessions in their existing homes. Over time, as goods accumulate, more closets, chests and drawers are added and, in many of the smaller homes studied, these storage devices encroached upon limited living space. Thus, the use of more storage devices, which are supposed to help in tidying up the home, paradoxically leads to a decrease in available space. I discussed the general lack of storage with Mr Oka, an architect in his fifties working at Misawa Homes, and he formulated this paradox as follows: 'In most Japanese houses storage space is limited and therefore people place many closets and so on in their house and the space available for living decreases. Well, it is as if they are living among their furniture.'

The Terayamas are a good example of a family who 'live among their furniture'. The size of their eighth-floor 3DK apartment in central Itami was a constant source of regret to Mrs Terayama, who repeatedly expressed her disappointment that her family was unable to move into a bigger house of flat that would better suit their changing lifestyle and family set up. The Terayamas 60-square-metre home contains only one built-in closet (*oshi-ire*) located in a Japanese-style room once occupied by their son, who is currently at university. This space is used to store the family's futons and bedding, while towels are kept on some shelves raised above the washing machine. Their teenage daughter, who occupies the only private room in their home, stores her clothes in a free-standing Western-style wardrobe, while Mrs and Mr Terayama's clothes, as well as a range of other possessions, are stored away in several large pieces of heavy wooden furniture arranged against the walls of a second Japanese-style room adjacent to the dining-kitchen. These closets and chests of drawers protrude deep into the living space and Mrs Terayama can just about roll out the futon she sleeps on.

FURNITURE WALLS: STORAGE AND DISPLAY

The Terayamas' domestic set-up resembles those of participants in an architectural study of sixty-three apartments in a municipal housing block built in the 1980s in Tokyo (Yasuda 2002). The apartments concerned have an identical 2DK (dining-kitchen and two rooms) layout with a toilet and a bath. Over time, all the inhabitants had actively personalized their environment by creating a 'second wall' with their furniture and possessions (Yasuda 2002: 93–5). Through a detailed examination of this wall Yasuda identifies two different storage practices that corresponded with the age of the woman of the house. The older the women concerned, the more likely it was that things would be stored out of view in large pieces of furniture such as chests of drawers and closets. Younger participants, in contrast, tended to store their belongings in/on smaller pieces of furniture that could not be closed off, such as wooden shelves or steel-pipe racks. They also seemed to place things closer to the ground and covered a larger percentage of the surface of their walls with things such as posters and calendars. Yasuda links each storage practice with a different attitude towards creating domestic space. In her view, the former group prefer to place things out of view in order to create a functional, tidy place, while the latter arrange things in view as an expression of their personal taste (ibid.: 94).

Yasuda's study raises important questions about the association between storage and display that also surfaced during my fieldwork. My data supports her suggestion that approaches to storage differ among female participants belonging to two different age cohorts. Overall, women over forty-five possessed large free-standing storage units, while younger women seemed to be less inclined to use these kinds of storage devices. However, Yasuda's argument needs some fine-tuning. To begin with, as I have already hinted at above, it is important to distinguish between four different kinds of goods that are stored away in Japanese homes. First, there are seasonal things that may be taken out of storage at regular intervals, such as heaters and fans, but also seasonal display dolls or decorations for festive occasions that are more easily forgotten and may become lost in the back areas of the home. Second, people store books and paper documents and, third, gifts and memory items. However, by far the largest number of goods placed in storage is textiles, particularly clothes but also bedding and towels.[7] Futons, sheets, blankets and other items of bedding as well as towels were generally stored in large enclosed recesses located in Japanese-style rooms. Clothes, on the other hand, were hung in free-standing wardrobes and folded in chests of drawers by those over

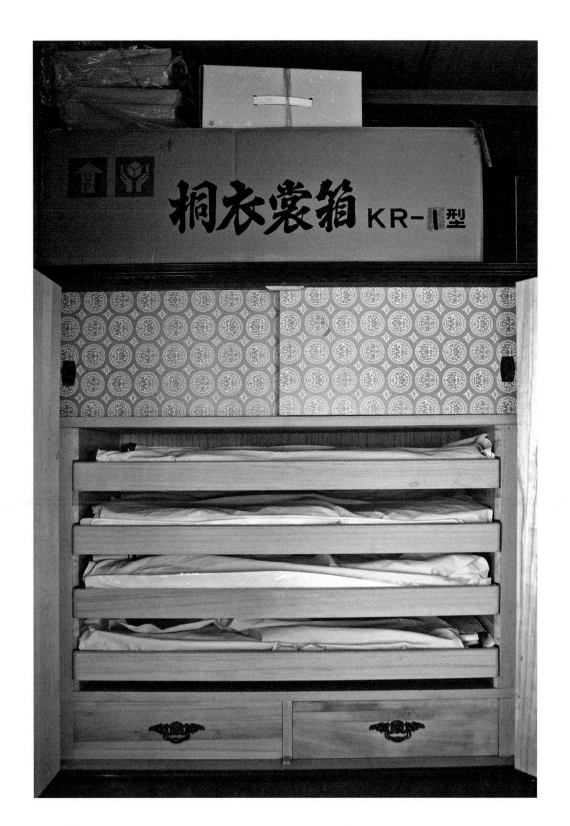

forty-five, while the younger generation primarily used built-in wardrobes. However, as this latter type of storage device has become standard in contemporary dwellings, they were used by those of all ages living in relatively new homes.

Everyone stored textile objects and seasonal goods out of view. Only the storage of paper and decorative items, whether gifts or commemorative objects, corresponded to some degree with Yasuda's age-related distinction between 'hidden' versus 'on view'. In the majority of cases, placing and ordering practices, whether based on practical or aesthetic concerns, were only partially driven by individual preference. The processes through which storage furniture ended up in the home were equally important. Those in my sample who got married before 1985 stored goods away from view in large closets and chest of drawers that were part of their dowry. Mrs Terayama, for example, slept surrounded by her 1982 dowry furniture consisting of two Western-style closets, two chests of drawers and a Japanese-style closet for kimonos.

Importantly, all participants in my study preferred to place their dowry closets and chests of drawers outside their daily living spaces. However, only those who live in large homes with sufficient storage space are able to do so. In two-storey detached houses large pieces of storage furniture were placed out of view in first-floor bedrooms. Moreover, a minority of those studied were fortunate enough to possess storage rooms (*nandos*) to cram their storage furniture in. The *nandos* built on either floor of their house by the Wadas in Osaka were used separately by Mrs Wada and her mother. Each storage room contained the particular woman's dowry closets for Western clothing as well as a Japanese-style chest of drawers for kimono. Both rooms were chock-full, and the heavy dowry closets blocked access to an additional storage unit created under the floor.

DOWRIES AND FURNITURE PROVISIONING

The Japanese historian Koizumi has shown that from the time of the seventeenth century elite women were expected to bring goods as a contribution to their new homes. The samurai military class, which governed Japan until the end of the nineteenth century, operated a system of landownership based on male inheritance whereby eldest sons inherited the family property and daughters received a dowry (Koizumi 1995: 258–64). Possessions kept in these elite homes were, thus, divided into two distinct categories: first, decorative items for guest rooms that were acquired through inheritance or ordered from craftsmen and antique dealers (see Chapter 4); and second, objects for daily use and chests for storage that were part of a woman's dowry (Sand 1996: 176–8). The elite were quickly emulated in their family system of male inheritance and female dowries by wealthy peasants and merchants, but the practice only became law at the end of the nineteenth century (see also Chapter 3).

Department stores played an important role in spreading the use of dowries among the larger population. At the beginning of the twentieth century they began to sell ready-made, Western-style furniture, but initially sales were poor as most Japanese were not familiar with purchasing 'domestic goods' (*kagu*)[8] in this way (ibid.: 175). Department stores were only able to turn this situation around through the sale of dowry sets, thus drawing on existing distribution channels for the acquisition of goods for the home. During the 1910s and 1920s dowry sets were frequently advertised in department stores' own magazines-cum-mail-order catalogues and in women's magazines. In 1918 *Fujin no tomo* (A Housewife's Friend), for example, published a list of goods that should be part of a woman's trousseau (Koizumi 1995: 342–3), such as futons, kimonos, *zabuton* (sitting cushions), a set of tea ceremony utensils, mirrors, coal heaters, but also a variety of closets and chests of drawers for storing clothes in (fig. 28a). The depiction of expensive novelty items such as sewing machines and organs highlights that *Fujin no tomo*'s readership consisted of upper-class and intellectual women (ibid.: 350). Before the Second World War most of these luxury goods were out of reach for the majority of the population, and a standard dowry consisted of a more modest assemblage of chests for clothing and bedding, a toilet table and mirror, a sewing box and kimono (Sand 1996: 177).

Four types of storage devices formed part of the pre-war dowry. First, there were Western-style closets (*yôfukudansu*, literally 'closets for Western clothing'), which are large chests with pivoting doors in which to hang clothes. Second, there were chests of drawers (*seiri dansu*), which were a common piece of storage furniture. Third, there were Japanese-style closets (*wadansu*), which consist of two parts, an upper part with a number of large wooden drawers on which folded kimonos, sometimes wrapped in special rice paper protection covers, can be stored,[9] and a lower part for obi and other kimono accessories (see Spread 7). These three types of closet continue to be common pieces of storage furniture in the homes of women who are over forty-five years old. However, the final type of dowry closet, i.e. the Japanese-style tea closet (*chadansu*), mainly used for storing tea utensils (Koizumi 1995: 345), is unusual and I only came across a handful of examples placed in empty Japanese-style rooms. One could argue that this piece of furniture has been replaced by the so-called 'glass case', a display closet with a lower section consisting of drawers and an upper section of shelves arranged behind a glass door; I will return to this in Chapter 6.

From the 1960s onwards, dowries also began to include home electronics such as televisions, radios, stereos and appliances such as washing machines and rice cookers. After a decade of hardship, the 1960s brought high economic growth and better wages. Moreover, the introduction of a democratic education system and the increased accessibility of information through the mass media resulted in the consolidation of a 'mainstream' consumer culture. By 1965, the once utopian ideal of the nuclear family that lived in a two-storey detached house surrounded by the three Cs – colour TV, cooler (air conditioning) and car – had become attainable for most (Sôgô josei rekishi no kenkyûkai 1993: 244).[10] During the 1970s and 1980s, the consumption of domestic appliances and home electronics increased steadily in cities and in the countryside (Koizumi 1995: 351–2) and 'their presence and placement within Japanese dwellings … homogenised Japanese domestic space' (Ivy 1995: 249).

In 1993 the Communication and Design Institute in Kyoto found that, over three decades, people had not only gathered more goods but the size of kitchen appliances such as fridges, freezers and televisions had also increased (CDI & CORE 1993: 23). In 2003 more than 98 per cent of the Japanese possessed at least one colour television (53.1 per cent of which were larger than 28 inches), a washing machine, a vacuum cleaner and a refrigerator (75.4 per cent of which had a capacity in excess of 300 litres) (AS 2004: 181).[11] All those participating in my study possessed similar appliances, and large fridges and washing machines occupied valuable living space. Few possessed flat-screen televisions, but it was common to have a large colour television in every room. Moreover, computers were common in half the homes; desktop models were placed in studies, and about one-third were laptops.

STARTER HOMES

The women in my sample who married between 1960 and 1985 possessed large pieces of storage furniture that formed part of their dowry. Electronics and kitchen appliances had either been bought by the husband or purchased using money the couple collected at their wedding. When Mr and Mrs Ebara married in 1978, Mrs Ebara's parents bought them futons and major pieces of furniture such as closets, while Mr Ebara's family supplied kitchen appliances and other electrical devices for the kitchen. These latter goods have been replaced several times since, while the majority of her dowry furniture, placed in the master bedroom on the first floor, has remained. Similarly, most other women in this age group continued to use their dowry furniture to store their possessions, even if this meant, in the case of those living in small homes without built-in closets or storage rooms, that the bulky furniture compromised their already limited space available.

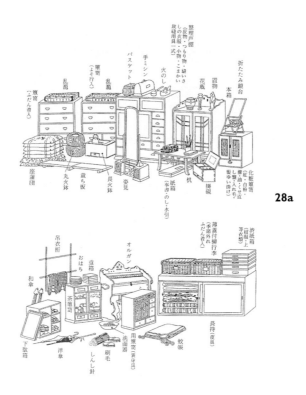

28a

In many European countries, furniture acquired during particular moments in the lifecycle, such as birth, marriage or death, is considered to be imbued with family lineage and will therefore be maintained across generations.[12] Traditionally, the Japanese dowry also embodied genealogical connections and expressed the status of a women's family. However, the goods that a Japanese bride brought with her were only supposed to last for one generation, and it has been usual for the majority of dowry possessions to be disposed off upon the death of the owner. Mrs Kema, a single researcher in her mid-forties, who lost both her parents in 2003, kept some of their personal items, especially jewellery, while formal clothing such as suits and kimonos were distributed among relatives. However, because 'they had too much wear and tear', most other possessions, including her mother's dowry furniture, were thrown away.[13]

By contrast, during their lifetime most women treasure their dowry furniture (as well as other dowry items such as kimonos) as these items are often the only remaining connection between themselves and the families they had to leave behind as brides. This attitude was particularly strong among several elderly widows who lived happily among their dowry furniture. For example, Mrs Nakae senior, who is in her mid-eighties and lives with the family of her eldest son in the family home in Kyoto, has surrounded herself with her 1930s dowry furniture in her six-mat tatami bedroom. Similarly, 85-year-old Mrs Kobayashi proudly showed me a large standing mirror, a common dowry item from before the Second World War, that was centrally placed in her Western-style bedroom while her dowry chests were stored in a storage room nearby. Mrs Yamada, a 91-year-old friend of the Kuwaharas, offers an interesting final example. During the mid-1930s, when she was of marriageable age, her family commissioned Mrs Kuwahara's father, a carpenter, to produce her dowry furniture. Aware that after her death her own family would dispose of these possessions,

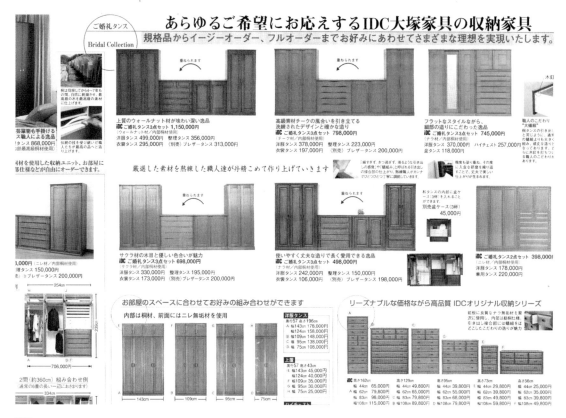

28b

which she cherished, Mrs Yamada repeatedly enquired whether Mrs Kuwahara would like the furniture as an example of her late father's craftsmanship.

My fieldwork data suggests that, since the 1990s, brides (and their families) are no longer considered solely responsible for buying furniture and other households goods for the starter home.[14] The main reason for this change is a shift in marriage patterns. The average age at which people marry rose from 27.6 years for men and 24.6 years for women in 1970 to 30.4 and 28.2, respectively, in 2000. It remains unacceptable for unmarried couples to live together, but most young people experience an extended period of time living on their own, whether as students or as company employees before they marry.[15] Upon marriage they will bring possessions, particularly furniture, that have accumulated during this period to the shared home.

The Sawais, who are both in their late twenties, married approximately eighteen months before my study began. They live in a rented apartment in Kyoto. With some of the money they received during their wedding party they purchased a double bed, but most pieces of furniture in their home, such as two chests of drawers, they had used while at university. Some bookshelves in Mr Sawai's study even dated back to his high school days. When the Iwaiis junior, another married couple in their early thirties with a one-year-old baby, moved in together they used some of the money received at their wedding to buy a number of appliances, such as a stove and a fridge. The other furniture in their home consists of pieces that each of them purchased when they lived on their own in Tokyo. Two large display shelves in their dining-kitchen are actually bookcases that Mr Iwaii bought when he moved to Kyoto to start his PhD. Another bookshelf is used to store tableware in their dining-kitchen. Their television is more than 17 years old and once belonged to Mr Iwaii's grandmother, a VCR was a wedding gift from a friend, and they received a small desk and plastic storage units from foreign students who had since returned home.

Finally, when the Matsuis married in 1996 they used money received at their wedding to buy much of the furniture that was in the two-storey house in Nara where they were living with their four-year-old daughter when I met them in 2003 (fig. 28b). For example, there are the two steel racks they had bought at a local home centre. They used the top shelves to display decorative items on and the lower shelves for storing documents. When they moved from rented accommodation into their current home in 2001 they only bought a wooden sideboard for storing tableware that matches their other furniture. A second, new purchase was their large kitchen table, imported from Italy, which they bought in a local design shop. The other pieces of furniture in their LDK area were either gifts, handmade items or things from their childhood. A number of display shelves in their living room had belonged to Mrs Matsui when she was a child and there was the small shelf that was made by Mr Matsui when he was at high school. A chest of drawers belonged to a friend who had planned to throw them away, while a low table was a gift from her mother. As we have seen in the previous chapter, Mrs Matsui had painted most of this furniture white so that it blended into the overall aesthetic scheme of their home.

Like most other people of their generation, the three couples discussed above did not possess the range of bulky, free-standing closets that constituted inalienable wealth for their mothers. Instead, most used the built-in wardrobes that are standard in recently built accommodation. Other pieces of furniture and appliances were individually purchased before marriage, jointly bought for the starter home or passed on by family and friends. These latter objects make manifest a variety of social, formal and informal, relationships that constitute the couple but also the individuals within that relationship. These changes across the generations thus point at a more general shift from the extended paternal family unit based on primogeniture to a family structure that also values the bond between a couple, and does not necessarily disadvantages women (see Chapter 3).

LIFE CYCLE RUPTURE POINTS: 'IF I HAD A HOUSE LIKE A CASTLE, I WOULD TAKE EVERYTHING'

> A house with many shelves, storage rooms and wardrobes is considered to be a good house but is this really so? It happens that when storage space increases the number of hoarded goods also increases.
>
> Fujiwara, *Tatakau maihomu*

The Japanese sociologist Fujiwara frames the paradox at the base of the Japanese storage problem by making an important link with hoarding. My research, similarly, suggests that we need to rethink storage within the context of the amassing of goods and disposal practices. Since the 1960s there has been a steady increase of the number of possessions in the Japanese home. The relatively small size of the contemporary dwelling,[16] but more importantly the scarcity of pragmatic disposal strategies means that a large number of possessions 'hang around, get in the way and seem to fill all

available spaces' (Cwerner and Metcalfe 2003: 237). As Gregson, Metcalfe and Crew (2007) have pointed out in the UK context, social processes such as couple formation or separation, increased geographical mobility and house purchase may lead to things being cast off.

The last three examples discussed above shed light on couple formation in contemporary Japan. It is common for the recently married to live temporarily in rented accommodation. However, because the ideal of home ownership remains strong among Japanese of all classes and ages, soon after the birth of their first child most would like to move into their own house.[17] This said, because most newlyweds move into relatively small residences, children leaving the nest does not necessary mean that parents will be able to release space. Kuwahara Keiko, who is twenty-three years old, directly linked her ability to take her things with her with the size of her future marital home, saying, 'if it was a house like a castle, I would take everything'. Moreover, Ueda narrates the example of an elderly couple whose home was turned into an extra storeroom for their married children (Ueda 1998: 142–4). This last case might be extreme, but my data confirms that children's possessions tend to linger in the parental home for much longer than anticipated. When the Sakais' 28-year-old son married in 2002, for example, he left many of his things behind, and as a result his room eventually became used as an extra storage space.

Two related issues that add to the Japanese domestic storage problems, and which I have already discussed briefly in Chapter 3, are, first, that increasing numbers of women in their mid-thirties, who have missed the window of opportunity to marry, continue to live at home. Second, if the husband is an eldest son, it remains common for his family to move back in with his parents. The merging of two families into one home leads to new, pressing storage needs, as the following example illustrates. After his first child was born in 1975, Mr Takahashi junior moved back into his parents' house, built during the 1960s in a commuter town close to the city of Nara. In order to accommodate the young family a second storey was added to the house, and as the family expanded with the arrival of another daughter, and as they accumulated more possessions, a number of storage spaces were added, including, for instance, a closet above the staircase, a loft under the roof and two sheds in the garden.

In Chapter 2 I have discussed the tensions between natives and newcomers in urban areas, and have identified the geographical mobility of the latter as an important contributing factor to these disputes. Indeed, it is common for young couples such as the Sawais, who are renting, to move house frequently in accordance with job opportunities, while ambitious employees and professionals have to consider frequent work transfers. Still, geographical mobility in Japan is relatively low as once people have bought a house they are unlikely to move.[18] The main occasion on which Japanese people may sort through and possibly dispose of some of their accumulated surplus is when they rebuild their house. Because the average life expectancy of Japanese houses built during the 1960s and 1970s is only about forty years, it is common for couples in their sixties to destroy and rebuild their homes on the same plot (as the Yanos did) (see Spread 8). Other reasons cited for rebuilding a house were the death of elderly relatives and the return of a son or daughter to the family home (as with the Nishikis and the Wadas), but also the occurrence of disasters such as fires (the Noguchis) and earthquakes (the Kuwaharas).

CONCLUSION: CONDUITS AND CONTAINERS, CIRCULATION AND ACCUMULATION

> Objects are also discarded much more rapidly in Japan than probably anywhere else. Perfectly functional but simply out-of-date equipment, fashions or furnishings will be replaced rapidly by those who can afford to do so; possession of the latest enhances cultural capital like almost nothing else. Variety or originality is not the point: newness is. (Clammer 1997: 24)

This statement, made by one of the foremost specialists on Japanese consumption, could not contrast more sharply with the findings of my research. It brings to the fore problems inherent in the early research about consumption that tended to focus on the beginning of the consumption process, for example by exploring shopping practices, and primarily highlighted issues such as fashion, taste and style (Hetherington 2004). More recent research about mundane consumption practices in the home, by contrast, reveals that consumption is a much more complex social and material process, and that taste and aesthetics are just one among many ideological concepts with which people may or may not engage. Within this context a number of recent pioneering ethnographies conducted in UK homes, which have drawn attention to disposal as an integral part of the consumption process, question the assumption that the act of throwing away is carefree and call disposal a social, anxiety-laden activity 'constitutive of and expressive of relations of care and concern' (Gregson, Metcalfe and Crewe 2007: 683).

This body of research has also highlighted the role storage devices play in complex, domestic processes of divestment. Kevin Hetherington, for example, argues that domestic ordering and sorting processes are fluid, and storage devices such as closets and chests, but also fridges and bins, are in-between spaces or so-called conduits of disposal where items are held until 'their uncertain value state is addressed' (Hetherington 2004: 166). Similarly, in an article that focuses on the storage of clothing, Gregson and Beale point out that wardrobes are not stable, bounded containers but 'temporary, transitory, spatial junctures, holding places in the lives of things' (Gregson and Beale 2004: 699).

The *kura* storehouse used by the Tokugawa elite, discussed above, offers a good example of a Japanese storage space that operated as a temporary holding place for domestic goods, in this case valuables such as heirlooms and seasonal items. Indeed, through the regular circulation of goods between the house and the storehouse people were able to create the iconic, minimal spaces that have become associated with the stereotype of the Japanese house. However, in contemporary Japan storehouses, like other storage devices, function primarily as final resting places for the surplus of goods kept in the home. In homes with insufficient storage, once storage devices are full and things start to leak out into the living space, inhabitants might feel pressed to evaluate their possessions. Those that have the option of creating extra storage space, on the other hand, can postpone assessment indefinitely.

Moreover, particular types of domestic objects are disposed of differently. In the UK context, Gregson has argued that the less tangential things are to people's everyday life the greater the frequency with which their worth is re-evaluated, and the greater their potential for being discarded. Thus, objects in flow that are regularly handled, such as clothing, or things that are frequently touched, such as domestic appliances, are more open to scrutiny and are therefore more rapidly replaced. These are the types of goods that may be influenced by fashion cycles, as referred to in

the start of this section by Clammer. By contrast, objects placed in storage devices, which are taken out of circulation, are rarely assessed (Gregson 2007: 160–4). However, the sheer volume of the surplus contained in many Japanese homes means that this difference in mobility might only be partially true. For example, in the case of textile objects, although many items of clothing, bedding and towels are regularly circulated inside the home, many more are stored away. Over time, these possessions are moved deeper inside storage furniture, and they become part of an indistinguishable category of unused goods (*fuyôhin*).

Finally, the usage of storage devices as conduits or containers is closely linked with the temporality of the dwelling. Whereas most dwellings in the UK tend to last for a long time with numerous people moving in and out over the years (Gregson 2007: 160), contemporary Japanese homes function more like containers that hold a particular group of inhabitants who during one generation fill the space with their possessions. As the original space starts to reach its capacity storage might be added, but eventually, after four decades, as the accumulation of stuff nears its absolute limits, the building reaches the end of its life and will be destroyed. In theory, the destruction of the house offers an unique opportunity to rid oneself of most of its contents. I was, therefore, surprised to find that people held on to a relatively large number of goods that were considered 'troublesome'. In the next chapter, I will investigate the widespread reluctance to dispose of certain things that need to be treated with special care.

Although the kimono ceased to be worn on an everyday basis before the mid-twentieth century, many Japanese women continue to possess large numbers of these garments. The prime kimono wearers in my 2003 sample were middle-aged and elderly women, who carefully stored a large number of them, folded and wrapped in rice paper covers, in special kimono closets. The majority of these kimonos (and their storage chests) were part of their dowry. As young brides they had brought kimonos in a variety of colours and patterns in tune with the seasons, the particular occasion and also the age of the wearer (Dalby [1993] 2001). Some, who study traditional arts such as the tea ceremony, regularly have the opportunity to wear a kimono, but most primarily don them for formal family occasions, such as weddings and funerals, or for important social events such as official dinner parties. Some of the younger married women, such as 37-year-old Mrs Matsui, told me that they started to wear kimonos when their children entered school and they regularly had to attend formal events such as entrance ceremonies.

Unmarried girls wear kimonos at life-cycle celebrations and festivals. Moreover, during the New Year period, many young women wear a winter kimono topped with fur, while *yukata*, kimono-like robes made from cotton with fashionable patterns and colours, are popular during summer festivals. At the Seven Five Three festival (*sichigosan*), held on 15 December, for example, seven- and three-year-old girls (as well as five-year-old boys) visit temples or shrines in traditional Japanese dress. During the coming of age ceremonies (*seijin no hi*), held on 15 January for 21-year-olds, as well as high school and university graduation ceremonies, men wear Western formal dress, while a large percentage of women choose to wear a kimono. Finally, during their wedding ceremony most women will wear a white silk kimono with wig, cap and full 'traditional' make-up, which may afterwards be covered with a colourful, patterned kimono (*uchikake*), while for the reception most will change into a Western-style wedding dress. Moreover, at weddings married female family members tend to wear a black formal kimono with an elaborate, multi-coloured design on the skirt (*tomesode*).

A dowry kimono was only supposed to last for one generation, and during a woman's lifetime her kimonos would be repeatedly dyed. Moreover, when the cloth could no longer be worn it would be put to other uses. However, in post-war Japan as kimonos ceased to be worn on a daily basis, when a woman passed away, her new or rarely worn dowry kimonos would be divided among maternal relatives (ishôwake). This said, many participants in my study argued that these days people prefer to 'return' money instead, and dowry kimonos are either thrown away or sold to antiques wholesalers. During the 1990s, many kimonos were sold to foreign tourists in special 'second-hand' kimono shops, and antique/temple markets. However, since the beginning of the millennium there has been an increased interest from Japanese customers in second-hand kimonos. This may be due, firstly, to the fact that during this time trendy urban women in their twenties and thirties have appropriated the kimono as a fashion statement. These consumers deliberately challenge established kimono-rules, such as wearing antique kimonos in colours or patterns 'inappropriate' to one's age.

A second reason for the increased popularity in second-hand kimonos is that many women recycle them into a range of other objects. Mrs Sakai, a housewife in Osaka, and her daughter Yuka are critical of 'people who live in mansions or so, who sell their kimono in a carton box for 5,000 yen, and all their dowry items …' Both women proudly showed me some handbags they made from a kimono and an obi they had saved from a friend's storehouse that was destined to be destroyed with all its contents inside. Moreover, Mrs Sakai used kimonos that had belonged to her own and her husband's parents to produce Western-style clothing such as dresses and blouses. These kinds of hybrid clothes are so popular that a professional industry has developed. Mrs Kagemori, the 63-year-old retired academic in Osaka, for example, paid professionals to turn most of her dowry kimonos into items of formal Western dress.

I came across many other examples of textile objects created from old kimonos. The cover of Mr Nakao's prayer book placed in the Buddhist home altar was made of an old kimono belonging to his mother. In the Iwaiis' Western-style guest room closet doors were covered with fabric from one of Mr Iwaii senior's grandmother's kimonos. Finally, the Matsuis, Wadas and Ms Kema possessed Ichimatsu display dolls dressed in kimonos made from fabric of their mothers' old kimono. This last example, clearly illustrates that kimonos, like the closets they are stored in, embody maternal family ties. However, whereas closets are only supposed to last one generation, kimonos can be made into a variety of other textile objects, and may thus be easily passed on across the generations.

SPREAD 8: REBUILDING THE FAMILY HOME; THE YANOS' PHOTO-DIARY

On 20 May 2003 – a day of great prosperity (*daian*) – a 'house-building ceremony' (*jichinsai*) took place on an empty plot of land in Kyoto – the spot where the Yanos' 40-year-old two-storey family house had stood and where their new house would be erected. In the preceding months, the whole family was involved in sorting through, packing and moving their possessions. This was a very slow process as in each cupboard, closet and drawer long-forgotten items were discovered.

One important category of goods (1) that could not be easily disposed of was items closely associated with their family history. These were (a) personal items that had belonged to deceased ancestors, (b) gifts given for life-cycle event such as *hina*-dolls belonging to their unmarried eldest daughter and, finally, (c) objects made by the Yanos' three children when they were little, such as drawings and school calligraphy. All these goods were thoroughly evaluated before the finally decision about whether to keep them or to throw them away was made. To speed things up, different members of the family were given the responsibility of deciding about the fate of things found in different storage spaces. However, this strategy proved unsuccessful because frequently things that one person decided to throw away were later rescued from the garbage pile by someone else. A second, larger group of stored away object (2) were decorative souvenirs and gifts. Some, such as a miniature scroll with views of famous tourist spots in Yokohama, were gifts from their children's school trips more than twenty years earlier. However, the majority of these items, such as two miniature lion masks could no longer be traced back to any particular person or event. Some of these souvenirs were disposed of, some I received as presents, but many resurfaced in a glass display case in the house the family occupied while their new house was build.

Once the Yanos had sorted through their possession the demolition crew moved in. They swiftly tore down the building and cleared the site of debris. Before the construction of the new house could start, a local Shinto priest conducted a house-building ceremony that consists of a number of

cleansing rituals to ensure that the building and its inhabitants will be spared from atrocities such as fires and earthquakes. The ceremony will also protect those working on the site against accidents, and across Japan similar rituals are held before construction work starts on any building, whether private or public. Mr Yano, paid for the ceremony, which cost ¥40,000 (about £200), but the head carpenter and his staff played a key role in the proceedings. Before the Shinto priest arrived at the site, they transformed the plot into a sacred space by raising four bamboo branches, each about 2.5 metres tall, at the four corners and tying them together with a sacred rope. On entering this space all participants washed their hands with a special set of wooden ceremonial tools. Another group of workers crafted a delicate earthen cone topped with rice plants, an edifice symbolizing a rice field that plays a central role in the proceedings. Towards the northern end of the site, the priest erected a table with offerings: a large, tiered pounded rice cake, an arrangement of fruits and vegetables and several bottles of sake. Most of these offerings were later collected by Mrs Yano who used them as the main ingredients for a soup that the family consumed on returning home.

The ritual blessings started with the priest facing the makeshift altar and reciting sacred texts to purify the ground (*harae*). All the participants stood behind him in quiet observance until each person (including the anthropologist) was invited to step forward and offer a sacred *sasaki* leaf to the deities. Then, Mr Yano 'symbolically' ploughed the 'rice field' with a wooden shovel in order to invite prosperity for all members of his family. The procedure continued with the priest blessing the four corners of the site, waving a sceptre decorated with white paper festoons, followed by Mr Yano, his wife and the head carpenter pouring sake and salt on each corner of the plot as well as over the 'rice field' cone. Finally, the priest placed a small wooden box with sacred earth from the local shrine on top of the earthen mount. The head carpenter buried this sacred box in the centre of the plot before construction work began. The ceremony officially ended with all those present sharing a cup of sake, while Mrs Yano distributed bags with sweets among the workers, and handed the head carpenter and the priest an envelope with money.

6
TROUBLESOME THINGS

Japanese homes are in domestic disarray … there is no unity according to a certain theme, colour, or shape. There is no aesthetic consciousness whatsoever

CDI & CORE (1993: 289–90)

DOMESTIC DISARRAY?

To accuse Japanese (women) of having 'no aesthetic consciousness whatsoever' is probably a bit too harsh. As I have pointed out in previous chapters, some of the interiors studied were decorated in accordance with a strict overall aesthetic scheme. Moreover, a majority of married women in my sample experimented with 'native' aesthetics in designated display areas in their homes. Still, I do agree that most seemed relatively unconcerned with creating any particular aesthetic effect in their everyday, lived-in environment. What the Communication and Design Institute (CDI) identified as 'domestic disarray' corresponds with what I have called the 'eclectic aesthetic' consisting of a blend of liked and disliked objects – souvenirs, handmade items and gifts. The ubiquity of this domestic aesthetic bears witness to the fact that taste is not purely an individual choice but that it is a practice embedded in a complex network of social and material relations (see Chapter 4). It also demonstrates that objects may 'create unintentional consequences to which agents have to respond' (Clarke 2002: 148).

One category of goods of which all those participating in my study possessed large quantities, whether on display on in storage, and which were frequently referred to as troublesome, is small decorative gifts. Many of these were souvenirs. In the literature, Japanese souvenirs are defined as inexpensive, easily recognizable commodities linked with a particular place that are bought home as gifts for others (Nitta 1992; Kanzaki 1997). My research (Daniels 2001a) confirms that souvenirs

play a key role in the consolidation of social relations and networks, as Japanese tourists are very conscientious of bringing home gifts for family, friends and colleagues. It is generally seen more as an obligation than a free choice. This said, souvenirs are also purchased as personal mementos (*kinenhin*) (Daniels 2001a: 130; see also Moeran 1983) and in the homes studied both types of souvenirs were on display.[1]

In Osaka, the Sakais offer a fascinating example because they turned their whole living room as well as their hallway into one large display space for souvenirs from all over the world. From the time of their marriage in 1971, more than thirty-two years before my study, the couple had been on a trip together at least once a year, and Mrs Sakai proudly claimed that she displayed 'something from each trip'. Many of the Sakais mementos were immediately recognizable as 'famous souvenirs' (*meibutsu*) from iconic tourist destinations throughout Japan.[2] Examples include Shisa lions from Okinawa, a fan from Gifu, Kokeshi dolls from Tohoku along with a pair of wooden Ainu dolls and a statue of a bear from Hokkaido. Japanese tourists of the Sakais' generation, so-called Silver Travellers, like to visit authorized, famous destinations that have established themselves as authentic places through association with famous products, commonly local food and craft (Clammer 1997: 144–5).[3] The success of this strategy is reflected in the frequency with which certain 'famous souvenirs' appeared in the domestic environments studied.

The Noguchis offer another example of a family that displays an array of souvenirs. Like the Sakais, this couple had travelled all over Japan, but instead of going on all-inclusive, organized group tours, they preferred to travel in a camper van that 70-year-old Mr Noguchi bought when he retired. Their many road trips are embodied in a large collection of brightly coloured paper lanterns that were attached all around the lintel of one of their Japanese-style rooms extending into their veranda. Each lantern was imprinted with the name of a tourist spot they had visited. Souvenirs with place names are popular travel mementos among participants of all ages, and they often become part of collections. Thirty-year-old post-doctoral student Sawai-san, who frequently travels abroad to attend conferences, for example, keeps a collection of stuffed animals with the names of the places he visited written on them in his home office.

International travel has steadily increased since the economic boom of the 1980s. In 2003, more than 13 million Japanese travelled abroad. The number one destination is the United States, followed by China, Korea and Thailand (AS 2004: 245).[4] The majority of these international travellers are under forty, but consumers of all ages are travelling further afield. The Sakais are again a case in point as apart from an array of famous Japanese souvenirs they also displayed decorative objects brought home from trips to China, Taiwan, Thailand, Singapore, Bali and Hawaii. Like domestic tourists, Japanese travelling abroad tend to buy famous products associated with specific countries. The Sakais' well-known foreign products included, for example, shadow dolls from Bali, a Hawaiian Hula doll and a Taiwanese mask.

The shopping section of any travel guide carries detailed information about must-have local products. Moreover, most travel agencies provide special catalogues from which souvenirs, associated with a particular destination may be ordered for delivery directly to one's home. The service is very popular because it enables tourists to enjoy their trip without having to spend precious time buying souvenirs or carrying the heavy load home. Foreign famous products listed are commonly foodstuffs such as Hawaiian Macadamia nuts, Belgian chocolates or Canadian Maple Syrup, but famous goods such as Venetian Glass, Dutch clogs or Russian dolls are also for sale.

SOUVENIR CABINETS: OBJECTS FROZEN IN TIME AND SPACE

The centrepiece in the Sakais' living room was a beautifully crafted wooden Chinese display cabinet that contained an array of famous souvenirs from China: copies of well-known Ming vases, incense burners and jade statues. The Sakais had purchased the cabinet complete with its entire contents on a recent trip to Beijing. In other homes, similar – albeit less elaborate – display cabinets, or 'glass cases', which are generally part of the dowry (see Chapter 5), were used to display souvenirs. The lower part of this piece of furniture consists of a number of drawers while the upper part contains a series of shelves that can be closed off with glass doors. Although a large section of the shelved area is used for displaying decorative things, some shelves may contain utilitarian items such as tableware or bottles of liquor, as well as paper documents.

Centrally placed against one wall of the Ebaras' living room, facing a sofa set arranged around a low coffee table, stood a large display cabinet. Mr Ebara is a manager at a large Japanese car company and, about twelve years before my study, he was transferred to a branch office in Frankfurt. As a result, the whole family spent four years in Germany. After their return to Japan the Ebaras bought a glass case to display their European souvenirs. One afternoon Mrs Ebara and her 24-year-old daughter Yu discussed the contents of this cabinet with me. At first Yu claimed that these objects were her mother's and she did not know anything about them. But Mrs Ebara repeatedly stressed that these were 'things belonging to the whole family'. Their stay abroad had clearly been a happy time and, as we went through the display, both women enthusiastically recalled memories triggered by specific objects. Some items were farewell presents from German friends, but the majority they had bought themselves while travelling in Germany and other European countries. A collection of miniature buildings – a Spanish villa, a Dutch windmill, an Italian palazzo, a Flemish Merchant house and a Swiss mountain chalet – embodied this 'once in a lifetime experience'.

As we made our way through the shelves it became clear that many of the items on display could no longer be traced back to their place of purchase. Over time, other decorative objects had been added to the original display of European souvenirs. A number of objects on display, such as some flowers and fruits made from silk, were handicrafts that Mrs Ebara had produced in local hobby classes for housewives. More than once mother and daughter quarrelled about the supposed origin of a particular object. Mrs Ebara, for example, linked a glass flute to a trip to Venice, while Yu claimed that she actually bought the flute on a school trip to Nagasaki. Two ceramic beer mugs, which Mrs Ebara classified as 'souvenirs from Germany', turned out to be local copies produced by the Japanese beer company Sapporo. The identity of many of the gifts' donors had also been forgotten and, on more than one occasion, Mrs Ebara answered rather vaguely, 'this is nothing particular, just a thing we received'. Soon their focus shifted to objects that needed no further explanation, such as a sign with 'Berlin Bahnhoff' written on it, or a piece of the Berlin wall.

Ms Kadonaga, the single lawyer in her mid-fifties, also displayed a large collection of souvenirs in a cabinet on the first floor of the house in Kobe that she shares with her elderly mother. After her father passed away, his collection of small mementos, brought home from frequent business trips, were placed in Ms Kadonaga's care. These objects subsequently formed the basis of her own souvenir collection. She talked vividly about some of her most treasured items, such as a family of stuffed Koala bears she bought on a trip to Australia, a wooden Kokeshi doll she received from a friend from elementary school and a jar filled with star sand collected on a beach in Okinawa. However, like many other participants in my study, she had forgotten where the majority of souvenirs originated from, whether or not they were gifts and, if so, who were the donors. The fact that she had merged her father's and her own collection made identification even more challenging, and a large number of souvenirs were just identified with the words 'father must have purchased them'. Like the content of the Ebaras' souvenir closet discussed above, many ornaments in Ms Kadonaga's cabinet were frozen in space and time, and their provenances were untraceable. Thus, the value of ornamental collections does not lie in personal meanings ascribed to each object, but the collection as a whole mediates a general sense of the past and family continuity.

Glass display cabinets generally contained a mixture of three types of decorative objects: personal souvenirs or *kinenhin*, gifts received from family and friends – among them souvenirs (*omiyage*) – and handmade objects. Interestingly, as we have seen in Chapter 4, contemporary decorative alcoves contain similar objects. Moreover, both glass cases and alcoves were primarily used by women over forty-five years old. Those of the under forty-fives who displayed similar ornaments tended to arrange them on open display racks. The Iwaiis junior provide an example. In their rented house in Kyoto, two large shelves stood against a wall in their dining-kitchen area; previously used to store Mr Iwaii junior's books they now contained a range of decorative objects. The two lower shelves were completely taken over by toys, a reference to their small baby; Mr Iwaii mused, 'Yes, our lives have basically become overflow[ing] with toys.' However, the majority of the things displayed were gifts the couple had exchanged between themselves. A statue of Snow White, for example, was her first gift from him from a trip to Disneyland, while he had received a stuffed gorilla from her. Some items they had made themselves. For example, a vase and two tea cups had been made by Mrs Iwaii junior while studying ceramics and there was a piece of textile he had dyed. Souvenirs included two wooden dolls she had received from friends who had been to Bali, and two small animal statues from a trip Mr Iwaii junior had made with his parents to Egypt. Finally, one wedding present – a vase and a letter Mrs Iwaii junior had received from her pottery teacher in Aichi prefecture – was on display. Mrs Iwaii junior called a number of other objects on display 'zakka', or 'miscellaneous things' that needed no further embellishment.

The example above shows that the displays put up in designated areas in the home of the younger generation closely resemble those of their parents.[5] In both instances, the aim is less to impress visitors than to commemorate social relations that are important for the inhabitants. However, the young tend to idealize the bond between the couple (see Chapter 1) rather than family and other relationships that are primarily driven by obligation. That said, over time, as the networks of social relationships in which the recently married are embedded become more complex, the items they choose to display may change.

THE TYRANNY OF ORNAMENTS

Display cabinets are ordering devices through which people try to assert some aesthetic control over ornaments that they have accumulated and that continue to flow into the home by confining them to a specific space. Some tried to prevent undesirable objects from entering the home altogether by starting a collection (Chevalier 1999: 510). Most souvenir collections consist of a mixture of both gifts and personal mementoes (Pearce 1995: 243–5). They are often a source of pride and admiration because they allow their owners to demonstrate that they possess an extended network of family and friends, that they have good taste and the time and money to travel widely. A number of souvenirs I came across have been produced especially with collectors in mind. Such, for example, was the case with Mrs Ebara's collection of souvenir teaspoons with images of a variety of European cities and Mr Noguchi's collections of lanterns, small paper kites and miniature animals. Miniature figurines seemed particularly popular among male collectors. Mr Sawai (born in 1974) and Mr Nakayama (born in 1970), for example, collected plastic figurines (anime fighter figures and Buddhist statues, respectively) that were token gifts inside chocolate eggs.

Over time some collections might spin out of control. As we saw earlier, Mrs Sakai liked to create eccentric displays of famous souvenirs, but her fondness for these kinds of gifts resulted in an eclectic mix of ornaments entering their home. In order to regain some aesthetic control, she started collecting owls. Collections of lucky shapes such as owls or frogs are popular. In theory, more lucky objects could result in more luck being accumulated, but, as I have pointed out in Chapter 3, the downside of this logic is that it is particularly difficult to rid oneself of these kinds of objects. Over the years the owls have steadily increased and, although Mrs Sakai 'officially' stopped collecting them a long time ago, 'everyone just keeps on giving them'. Eventually, the owls were ousted from their main living area but they found a new home in the hallway, where they currently occupy every available space. Similarly, Ms Kadonaga's souvenir collection, partly inherited from her father, has continued to grow. Although she manages to keep the mass of ornaments under control in a display case, in her view her collection has become increasingly oppressive as 'it is not about likes and dislikes, but about not being able to throw them away'.

The examples I have discussed above focused on those people participating in my study who, although they wanted some control over the volume and type of ornaments that entered their home, were fond of objects of this sort and used them to decorate their everyday living spaces. However, the majority expressed a strong dislike for decorative trinkets, and they were far less happy to receive them as gifts. Still, even if people did not like them or had no use for them, all felt reluctant to throw away ornamental gifts. In the anthropological literature about gifting, this reluctance to dispose of unwanted gifts is generally explained by referring to Mauss's (1967) well-known conceptualization of the gift as an inalienable object invested with part of the personality of the giver. This 'spirit in the gift' might turn against those who do not reciprocate appropriately. Based on Mauss's ideas, Carrier, for example, argues that many people in Europe and the United States feel reluctant to dispose of or recirculate disliked gifts, because gifts are intrinsically linked with the giver and they embody the reciprocal relationship between giver and receiver (Carrier 1995: 26–7).

The continuing focus on the obligation to reciprocate gifts (and the need to compare rules of reciprocity with models of economic exchange) has recently come under scrutiny by those who want to disconnect the research about the gift from the commodity. The aim is not to return to a supposed dualism between both but to avoid gifting practices being reduced to economic transactions (Gregson and Crewe 2003: 177). My research similarly argues that gifting is not only about the realization of reciprocity. In other words, the fact that something was once given as a gift does not mean that it continues to refer back to exchange, the giver and the relationship it embodied. Gifts, once reciprocated, become part of the diverse material culture of the home and the meanings and practices important in the previous phase of their lives may or may not matter (Attfield 2000). In the domestic sphere complex processes of appropriation and divestment are at work. As the following example illustrates, the mere presence of decorative gifts in the interior does not mean that the link with the donor continues to be acknowledged.

The Kagemoris, intellectuals who were living together with their 30-year-old daughter Shigeko, a PhD student, in the centre of Osaka, stored many of their possessions that were not continuously in use in two rented storage spaces. However, their 3DK apartment was still jam-packed with things. Against every wall in their living-dining area stood large bookshelves spilling over with books, while even more books, magazines and research papers were piled high on the floor. Scattered among their treasured collections of books they had an eclectic assortment of decorative trinkets. The majority of these ornaments had been received as gifts from their large circle of foreign acquaintances and work colleagues who they regularly invited to lavish parties in their home. The Kagemoris repeatedly stressed that they disliked these ornaments, but 'people keep on bringing them even if we assure them that this is not necessary'. Like the majority of my respondents, they felt reluctant to dispose of these unwanted gifts, at least right away. Because they had insufficient storage space, the Kagemoris stored these disliked ornaments 'randomly, wherever there is space' in their main living area. As is the case with collections of decorative objects, over time these trinkets had become part of an undistinguishable mass of similar things (see Chapter 5) that could not easily be disposed of or passed on to other people.[6] Paradoxically, the fact that the Kagemoris' array of disliked gifts was on display inside their crowded flat meant that they had habitually to review the value of these ornaments. Indeed, the arrival of each new ornament might prompt them to rid themselves of another one that had already spent some period of time in their home.

COMMEMORATIVE, DECORATIVE GIFTS AND UNIQUE RELATIONSHIPS

As we have seen in previous chapters, most home interiors do not adhere to a particular aesthetic scheme, and the widespread dislike for decorative gifts is generally not linked with particular tastes or fashions. The main complaint voiced against receiving ornaments was that 'their shape remains'. Japan is an advanced capitalist society with a thriving gift economy. This system involves the exchange of commodities and plays a crucial role in the creation and continuation of social relationships. Gift occasions follow each other up in quick succession and throughout the year a continuous flow of gifts enters the home. I was told that because of the sheer volume of gifts received, most preferred to give and receive gifts that 'do not remain'. Decorative gifts were only considered acceptable if they commemorated (kinen) special events. In the case of ornamental souvenirs this meant that they should embody special experiences such as a once-in-a-lifetime trip abroad. However, the fact that many Japanese regularly travel abroad and high quality foreign goods are readily available within Japan has somewhat diminished the unique value these goods might once have had.

Still, even decorative gifts that commemorate special events have the potential to become problematic. One particular ornamental gift that is displayed as well as stored away in most homes studied, and which may shed further light on the troublesome nature of commemorative gifts, is the display doll. Some dolls enter the home as business gifts or souvenirs from trips, but many are given to acknowledge *rites-de-passage*. Gifts for weddings or sixty-first birthdays are common, but the majority of the dolls on display are associated with the birth of children. In the Kansai region it is common for maternal grandparents to present infants with display dolls for their first Girls' (3 March) or Boys' Festival (5 May).[7] One type of doll given, known as an Ichimatsu doll, is a realistic representation of a female or male child dressed in a kimono. This is an effigy doll thought to protect children while they are growing up.[8] First-born daughters are also commonly given hina-dolls, which are sets of miniature dolls depicting a noble wedding during the Heian period (794–1192 CE).[9] Hina dolls are seasonal objects that are only displayed during the weeks leading up to the Girls' – or Dolls' – Festival (*hina matsuri*) on 3 March, when people pray for the health, happiness and reproductive capabilities of girls[10] (see Spread 9).

At the birth of a female child, when both types of dolls are given, the dolls are strongly associated with the giver(s), as they embody female family bonds across the generations. However, as children grow up, these objects become imbued with the personality of the recipient. In Japan, as in many

other cultures, there is a long history of dolls being employed as substitutes for people, and the Japanese word for doll – *ningyô* – literally means 'human shape'. During the Girls' Festival many religious centres, for example, organize ceremonies in which a pair of male and female paper dolls are rubbed against the body or breathed on before being set adrift on a river, taking the bad luck away with them. The effigy dolls for children mentioned earlier offer another example of the mimetic power of dolls, as people repeatedly remarked that, over time, the face of a particular Ichimatsu doll had begun to physically resemble the child who had the doll (see Daniels 2009c).[11] Most people in my sample thought that display dolls, which become inalienably linked with the recipient, needed to be treated with special care, otherwise they may acquire a harmful agency that is not reducible to the intentionality of people. During my fieldwork this concern manifested itself in the way dolls were stored and disposed of. A number of participants in my study covered the faces of their dolls before they were carefully wrapped in several layers of paper to make sure that 'they do not feel crushed' (*kurushii*) in their boxes. Moreover, many informed me that old or unwanted dolls needed to be brought to religious institutions for ritual disposal.[12]

The concern about the well-being of dolls, and also other ornaments, should be viewed within the context of the specific subject–object dialectic in Japan. In short, objects are thought to fulfil their potential through human consumption. As Ashkenazi puts it, 'the valuation of objects, is seen

in their utility, that is, in their direct and unmediated relationship to humans' (Ashkenazi 2000: 139). In the case of functional goods (*jitsuyôhin*) this means that they should actually be used, while decorative goods (*kazarimono*) are thought to reach their potential by being displayed in the home. If things are treated disrespectfully – such as throwing them away prematurely, before they have had a chance to fulfil their potential – then they might act against humans. Thus, although the decorative souvenirs discussed above are not thought to be imbued with the same powerful agency as dolls, because of their durability, these objects may also become closely linked with the recipient. Moreover, as the following example illustrates, some of the participants in my study thought that, if decorative objects were not properly used, they would have the potential to cause harm. Mrs Terayama, of Itami, for example, singled out three statues representing wise men; she did not like the statues but did not feel she could throw them away either because they might have a curse (*tatari*). Her husband brought these statues home from a business trip to China. When he saw them in a shop, it was obvious that they had been in there for a very long time and, because he thought they were pitiful (*kawaisô*), he decided to buy them.

Hetherington calls haunting 'an unacknowledged debt' that occurs when processes associated with disposal are unfinished or ineffective, and 'where questions of value are not properly honoured'

(Hetherington 2004: 170). As I have previously pointed out (Daniels 2003), within the Japanese context the belief that things that are treated without respect can act against humans is grounded in a particular attitude towards the inanimate world based on native folk beliefs and Buddhist thought. Buddhism teaches that all life forms, not only humans and animals but also plants and objects, should be treated with respect because they all have the potential to reach Buddhahood. As a further example, in Shinto, objects are believed to be endowed with spirits (Kretschmer 2000: 145–8). Moreover, the concern with the wellbeing of objects generally points at an awareness of the interrelatedness of human and non-human entities, and suggests that all living individuals have the obligation to care for others (ibid.: 333–4). This specific sensibility towards the inanimate world should not be understood as a timeless, essential component of Japanese culture, but as a dynamic, changing attitude grounded in a blurring of the boundary between people and things. Indeed, one of its most recent manifestations is what Ann Allison has called 'techno-animism', whereby people create intimate relationships with technological devices imbued with human characteristics (Allison 2006: 12–3).

EPHEMERAL GIFTS FOR THE RENEWAL OF VALUE

Decorative objects might be acceptable to commemorate specific, unique occasions[13] but, for frequently recurring gift occasions such as domestic travel and seasonal gifting (*oseibo-ochûgen*), food is considered to be the most appropriate item of exchange. First, food is liked for its social potential as the receiver can share these gifts with others in the home. Although ornaments may also be enjoyed by all the inhabitants of the home, they do not enable all to actively participate in creating family sociality (see Chapter 1). On the contrary, as we saw in Chapter 4, objects are often used to negate tensions between husbands and wives or adult women in the home. Second, food 'leaves no trace', and it was repeatedly pointed out that, by giving an item that can be consumed relatively quickly, the giver attests that he or she has taken the domestic situation of the receiver into consideration. It is the fact that, as food perishes, no one can be expected to keep it for long, and its potential for being shared makes it the perfect gift for the regular renewal and continuation of social relationships. Colloredo-Mansfeld has similarly demonstrated that, in the Andean community he studied, the using up of food is thought to 'replenish relationships, animating the life of a small, interwoven ecology of subjectivities, goods, and place' (Colloredo-Mansfeld 2003a: 282). In both contexts, the ephemeral quality of food is not associated with the negative value of depletion but with the generative value of renewal.

Depending on the gift occasion, subtle distinctions are made between types of foods. For example, fresh produce that needs to be consumed fast, such as fish and fruit, is a popular travel gift. However, fresh food is considered less appropriate during the twice-yearly seasonal gift periods in June and December when many people receive large quantities of food. During December 2002 the Kuwaharas in Itami, for example, received a surplus of fresh fish. Days such as 7 December, when they received a pre-roasted bonito fish from a former teacher of Mr Kuwahara, who lived in Koichi on Shikoku Island, a pack of smoked salmon from relatives in Kyushu in southern Japan, and a box of oysters from a friend in Hiroshima, are not unusual. Others also received a large amount of similar foods, such as beef, peaches or mandarins, so that instant, dried, canned or pickled foods were much appreciated.

Although Japanese gifts before the Second World War consisted almost solely of money or food (Yanagita [1940] 1962), in the post-war period the overall quantity of gifts exchanged as well as the number of durable items have both increased (Ito 1995: 95–6). The growth of the economy during the 1970s and 1980s led to a commercialization of gifting, with big supermarkets and department stores in charge of distributing large quantities of gifts.[14] Indeed, these businesses continue to operate special gift services that assist in choosing, wrapping and sending gifts using in-house delivery services.[15] Moreover, large food and drink companies have been the driving force in the creation of new forms of reciprocity such as Valentine's Day or Christmas (Moeran and Skov 1993; Ito 1995). These new types of gift occasions, associated with relationships of affection and love between individuals, which are especially popular with the younger generation, have been discussed briefly in the conclusion to Chapter 1. However, throughout this book my focus has been on practices that are considered essential for the production and reproduction of the social, economic and cosmic order of the family. In this chapter I am therefore primarily concerned with gift exchanges conducted between representatives of a particular group or so-called moral persons (Mauss 1967).

Importantly, my research does not suggest that socially prescribed gifting is an impersonal activity exclusively aimed at repaying debts (Befu 1983) or that the gifts concerned are chosen purely for their economic value in accordance with the status of the receiver. As the following example illustrates, in practice, the boundaries between formal and informal exchange are often blurred. Like many other people also in their late thirties, the Matsuis are not that involved in seasonal gifting yet. Still, they always make sure to present Mrs Matsui's parents with seasonal food gifts. Because Mrs Matsui knows that any foodstuff given will eventually end up back in her house she generally selects two items of the same food that she likes. This is an example of informal gifting linked with filial piety that is driven by obligation, but is also a genuine expression of gratitude and intimate care.

Interestingly, the majority of non-food gifts people receive for regularly occurring gift occasions are utilitarian things that can be used in the preparation or consumption of food, such as kitchen utensils, glasses or plates. As we saw earlier, the Kagemoris in Osaka disliked small decorative souvenirs but, as Mrs Kagemori proclaimed while pouring me another cup of tea, 'handy things that can be used every day, for example, this teapot Mrs Fujii brought back from her visit to the UK' are much appreciated. Others similarly considered functional objects that could easily be integrated into everyday routines, such as cushions or chopsticks, to be more appropriate.[16] However, utilitarian gifts may also become part of collections that are often in use. Mrs Kagemori, for example, had a collection of ceramic tableware, while Mr Kagemori collected lacquerware, the majority of which he purchased at antique markets.

Other examples were collections of teapots, teacups and glasses. Gregson and Crew suggest that, in confined spaces shared with others, collections may only be tolerated if they can both be displayed and used (Gregson and Crew 2003: 189). Some assumed that functionality cancelled out the ambiguities about likes or dislikes associated with ornaments but, in practice, there is no guarantee that usable gifts will be liked. Mrs Matsui in Nara, for example, who is 37 years old, regularly received functional souvenir gifts from her mother-in-law. However, she claims that, among these, 'there is not one thing that is really useful'. From a recent trip to Thailand, for example, her mother-in-law had brought home a silk shirt for her husband and an embroidered lipstick case for her; neither Mrs Matuis nor her husband has ever used either gift. She adds that durable souvenirs are generally not of very good quality and that she prefers to buy food.[17]

A final group of utilitarian gifts received during frequently occurring gift occasions, particularly seasonal gifting, are items employed in domestic cleaning routines such as washing powders, detergents or towels. Most referred to these goods with the term *shômôhin*, which is translated as 'expendables, supplies', but which literally means 'things that can be used up'.[18] These gifts have in common with other utilitarian items that their material form will eventually disappear through regular use. Although the various types of gift differ in the temporalities of wear and tear, so also in the nature of their eventual destruction – whether they are absorbed in other food, washed away by water, worn out while drying bodies or break while one is having a drink – their obliteration will eventually enable the creation and renewal of relationships among family members as well as with those outside the home. Of course, this process also supports an economy in which the notion of the gift is of paramount importance.

SURPLUS, DIVESTMENT AND INFORMAL SOCIALITY

In the previous section I showed that gifts that can be used up rapidly through shared, everyday use are most popular for regularly occurring gift occasions. I would like to stress that ideally these gifts should be consumed. However, the commodification and acceleration of the yearly gift cycle has resulted in such large quantities of gifts entering the home that most people are unable to use them up before the next load arrives.[19] This is especially true for gifts of a more durable nature, such as towels and tea sets. As a result, many Japanese people possess large quantities of these kinds of gifts, on top of the surplus of ornaments that I have discussed above.

Because of their durable, inalienable qualities it is virtually impossible to redistribute ornaments, but utilitarian gifts, particularly food, may be passed on through a number of informal networks. As Rupp (2003) has demonstrated, in the past, people belonged to extended, informal local support networks through which food and other stock was continuously divided and shared. In rural communities this practice is still common, as the Iwaiis senior, who live in a close-knit local community south of Nara, illustrate. When they receive seasonal gifts they only keep those things that they need themselves and the rest is recirculated (*mawashite ageru*) among neighbours. During summer gifting of 2003, for example, when gift boxes filled with fresh produce such as oranges or noodles arrived from family members living all over Japan, they kept about half the contents of each box and the rest was passed on. In turn, the Iwaiis senior frequently 'receive something we need from someone else'.

Urban participants also tried to redistribute unwanted food gifts among family, friends and neighbours. Examples are the Ebaras, who exchanged food with a sister who lived next door;

the Noguchis, who recirculated surplus food among two neighbours; and the Kagemoris, who shared unusual food stuff with their close friend Mrs Fujii. However, the scale and intensity of the redistribution of food gifts among urban dwellers differs considerably because most do not know their neighbours and their relatives live far away (Fujiwara 2003: 25–31). As I have argued in Chapter 2, the focus of urban social networks has shifted from the neighbourhood community to school and work relationships. Indeed, quite a few people told me that they resorted to taking disliked food gifts such as coffee or sweets to their offices, where they are then placed in a communal space with the message '*dôzo*' ('please take').

Like food, other unused utilitarian gifts such as towels or tea sets may move through several cycles of gifting and re-gifting. Some people passed these unwanted gifts to family and friends, but I was repeatedly told that it was important first to tell people that these were gifts, and to make sure that the potential recipients really wanted them. Everyone disapproved of people in positions of authority who dumped their disliked gifts on those lower in the social scale regardless of whether they actually wanted them. Typical in this are the Matsuis from Nara. Soon after their marriage, Mr Matsui received a gift set of ceramic plates from his teacher/mentor. Although this might have been a well-meant gesture, Mrs Matsui frowned upon this practice as follows:

> Well, this set of plates belonged to a former teacher of my husband who said that this was not his taste and he told my husband, 'Matsui-san what do you think, you just got married and you will probably need plates and so on.' Of course my husband was in no position to refuse and he replied, 'Yes, thank you very much' (she mimicked him), and then he brought it home with him, and of course I also felt like it was something that 'one would want to throw away but it is difficult to throw away'.

The phrase 'things that one would like to throw away but are difficult to throw away' was repeatedly used during my fieldwork to refer to unwanted gifts. Some disposed of these kinds of gifts through alternative channels such as bazaars and flea markets. I won't go into much detail here about practices enacted in these venues but I would stress that the bulk of gifts exchanged are 'unused goods' (*fuyôhin*). Interestingly, when discussing recycling, the notion of 'taking care of things' (*taisetsu ni suru*), discussed earlier, frequently surfaced. Most expressed a strong dislike for things that had been used and claimed they would never purchase goods of this kind. Further discussions revealed that their main reservation was that, because the previous users were strangers, they could not be sure how they had treated their possessions – in other words, whether or not they had taken care of them. This stream of thought also explains why used goods sold by professional traders are often in immaculate condition (see Spread 10).[20]

CONCLUSION: POSSIBILITIES AND CONSTRAINTS OF JAPANESE GIFT EXCHANGE

Unlike Maussian-based models of gift exchange, in Japan (as in Asia at large (Parry 1995; Yan 1996)) prestige is associated with receiving gifts. Those in my sample who occupy a high social position, such as teachers, doctors or company presidents, received comparatively large numbers of gifts as repayments for favours or services. This kind of upward gifting is asymmetric, as no return gift is expected. However, as the anthropologist Lebra has argued, even within unbalanced gift relationships, reciprocal gratification is possible as 'the superior can offer guidance, protection, and benevolence – material and non-material – which the inferior needs and is willing to take; whereas the inferior, in turn, can afford to give reliance, esteem, and loyalty which the superior wants' (Lebra 1975: 557). Still, unbalanced giving also reinforces a hierarchical structure and my ethnography clearly reveals the strong financial and social pressures placed on those at the giving end of the relationship.

One group compelled to express their gratitude for past and future favours by sending their superiors gifts are young people at the start of careers. It is common for parents to assist adult children in following proper gifting etiquette. In practice, gifting is largely a female affair as it is commonly women – wives or mothers – who are responsible for selecting and sending appropriate gifts to other women in order to facilitate and soften relationships between men. This is why, from a very early age, women are socialized into gifting practices and prepared for this important role (Ishii 1994: 192). A second group that is considerably burdened by the demands of gift culture are those 'white-collar workers' (*sarariiman*) who are on a low salary with few prospects for promotion but who have to continue sending gifts to superiors and colleagues throughout their career. The Matsunagas, a family of four who live in a small flat in the centre of Itami city, are in this situation. Mr Matsunaga, a 49-year-old *sarariiman*, has worked as a salesman for the same travel agency for the past twenty-five years, and Mrs Matsunaga does part-time work to make ends meet. During the seasonal gifting in June 2003, when I asked Mrs Matsunaga what kind of gifts they received, she remained silent for a while before replying, 'Well, you see, we are on the sending side.'

Large numbers of gifts entering a home attest to the inhabitants' success in creating and consolidating extended social networks. They may confirm social position and status, but they also embody family cohesion and continuity. Although most people asked felt that it was inappropriate to burden recipients – especially those of higher status – with gifts 'that remain', large quantities of decorative gifts, especially souvenirs, continue to enter Japanese homes. One explanation could be found in a clash between gift cultures, as my data suggests that the donors of many small, decorative gifts/souvenirs are foreigners who might not be aware that these trinkets will place a heavy burden on the recipients. More importantly, as Bourdieu has demonstrated, gifting is not just a disinterested obligatory act. Participants often engage in a 'confrontation of strategies' that can mark the particularity of the relationship or that may attempt to challenge or transform it' (Bourdieu [1979] 1984: 22–3).

The surplus of unwanted goods reveals the ambivalences and tensions associated with exchange. Some of those participating in my study strongly criticized gift exchange driven by obligation. Instead, they idealized a more disinterested type of gifting based on the European and North American notion of the 'pure' gift (see Carrier 1995: 157; Belk 1995: 69). However, as the following example illustrates, these people were also aware that, to paraphrase Smith, they were dealing with 'indebtedness and gratitude that the individual is hardly free to accept or refuse' (Smith 1974: 132). The Nakaos, a couple in their mid-fifties living in Osaka, tried in vain to withdraw from the endless cycle of gifting. Mrs Nakao has managed to come to an agreement with her close family members to at least stop exchanging seasonal gifts. However, other, more distant kin and business relations continued to send gifts and, in order to keep their relations in order, and both their businesses alive, the Nakaos felt they had to reciprocate. Therefore, only when drastic changes are implemented from above might one be able to escape the heavy demands associated with gifting without becoming a social pariah. During the economic crisis of the early 2000s, for example, the management of some workplaces prohibited gift exchange among their employees.

SPREAD 9: THE DOLLS' FESTIVAL

During the Dolls', or Girls', Festival (*hina matsuri*), held on 3 March, Japanese families pray for the health and happiness of unmarried daughters by displaying hina-dolls (*hina ningyô* or *ohinasan*) inside their homes. This celebration originated during the Tokugawa period (1603–1868) and draws on two different traditions, the first of which is a Taoist purification ceremony that originated in China, in which human shapes made out of straw and paper were invested with illness and misfortune and set adrift on rivers (Kawasaki and Moteki 2002: 58–61). A second influence is two effigy dolls employed since the fourteenth century to protect infants against evil. The first of these, the 'heavenly child' (*amagatsu*), was a stick figure that was placed next to newborn babies, mainly boys, to absorb illness and ward of evil (Baten 2000: 13). The second, 'lowly child' (*hôko*), was an X-shaped, textile doll, associated with girls, which was considered to capture evil spirits who would mistake the doll for the baby (ibid.: 37).

From mid-February until early March most participants in my study with unmarried daughters displayed sets of miniature dolls. Some families, such as the Matsuis, the Kuwaharas and the Takahashis, set up a tiered platform (*hina dana*) covered with a velvet cloth on which they arranged an elaborate display of dolls depicting a royal wedding from the Heian period (794–1185). The married couple is placed prominently on the top shelf, while the other shelves contain an extended entourage of court ladies, pages, soldiers and musicians, each with their appropriate tools, as well as a miniature version of a 'traditional' bride's trousseau. It is significant that the dolls depict a wedding, as marriage was – and still is – considered to be the wished-for, and often the only acceptable, path for girls in Japan (see Chapters 3 and 4).

These seasonal dolls are yet another type of domestic object that embodies female family bonds as they are generally given by maternal grandparents to first-born daughters for their first Dolls' Festival. Ornate sets of dolls are expensive purchases that take up a lot of space in the home, and during my fieldwork displays consisting only of the married couple were most common. Moreover,

over time, as girls grow older, those families who possess ornate displays felt less inclined to go through the trouble of putting them up. Still, all families with unmarried daughters continued to display at least a pair of miniature hina-dolls, while many referred to the widespread belief that if one does not display any dolls (or if one forgets to the take display down at the end of the festival) girls might remain single forever.

Because the display is thought to assist women in finding a husband, upon marriage the dolls may be left behind in the parental home where they quickly become part of the surplus of unused, stored away goods. However, about half the married women in my sample had kept their dolls and displayed them once they had children of their own. Indeed, some doll displays consisted of a collection of dolls and accessories belonging to several generations of women. For her 4-year-old daughter Nao's Dolls' Festival in 2003, for example, Mrs Matsui put up her own complete set of dolls as well as a series of miniature tools that had belonged to her mother and grandmother. When Nao was born, she did not receive hina-dolls, but her grandmother bought her an Ichimatsu doll, a realistic female doll dressed in traditional attire that is kept in a glass display case and which generally stays with and protects girls until they marry (see Chapter 6). During the Dolls' Festival this doll is given a prominent place next to the tiered display platform with the miniature dolls.

Interestingly, single women were most eager to show me their hina-dolls. Ms Kadonaga, the 55-year-old, single lawyer in Kobe, for example, considered her dolls to be among her most treasured possessions. She stored them away very carefully, each doll individually wrapped in its own box. She is particularly fond of a clay pair of hina-dolls and an Ichimatsu doll, which belonged to her mother, and whose kimono was made by her grandmother. Ms Kadonaga, like the four other single women in my sample, continued to put up hina-displays throughout their lives, and some even went as far as to refer to their hina-dolls as their children. These examples illustrate that some material excess in the home may be caused by blockages in the circulation of women, as single women are unable to pass on their dolls to the next generation, while over time they will become inalienable possessions the disposal of which would be inconceivable.

> I had this toaster for 6 years but I have not used it once. It turned old all by its self. Isn't
> that sad. Please cherish it while you use it.

The text above is the farewell note attached to a toaster that I acquired for ¥100 (about 50 pence) in
March 2003 at a bazaar held for incoming students at Kyoto University. It sums up two key issues
surrounding the disposal and recycling of goods in Japan. Firstly, a large percentage of goods that
are traded at temporary retail-sites such as bazaars and flea markets are functional items that are
either new or in pristine condition and, secondly, many people express concern about the wellbeing
of things.

Bazaars are fund-raising events held by organizations such as schools or churches, but also
more informal groups such as clubs for the elderly or housewives associations. The majority of
the goods that change hands at local bazaars are unused domestic goods, mainly unwanted gifts.
Most participants in my study donated functional gifts still wrapped in cellophane boxes; towels
were most common, but some gave boxes of washing powder or sets of plates. The divestment of
decorative goods through the second-hand arena also occurs, but this is more challenging because
ornaments cannot be used up quickly through shared consumption and will remain in the new
owner's home for a considerable period of time (see Chapter 6).

Gregson and Crewe single out charity as one reason why their UK informants try to dispose of
goods in the second-hand arena (Gregson and Crewe 2003: 123–4). The City Recycle Committee,
a voluntary organization that collects and repairs goods for recycling within the Kyoto area, yearly
supplies the goods for the Kyoto University bazaar. However, in Japan philanthropy towards people
outside one's immediate social networks is unusual (Befu 1983: 454). The focus of social life is on
specific relationships, driven by both obligation and sentiment, as opposed to a more universal
orientation driven by the ideology of disinterested giving that is common in Europe and North

America (Parry 1985: 467). Most people I worked with saw 'donating' goods to bazaars as an obligation, and the pressures involved can be considerable for those who do not possess large stocks of 'unused goods' (*fuyôhin*). Indeed, although it is also acceptable to donate handmade goods, some younger housewives feel pressured into buying new goods to donate.

Making money has been defined as another major impetus for trading in second-hand goods (Gregson and Crewe 2003). At Japanese flea markets, unused gifts are indeed exchanged for money, but the amount asked tends to be minute. Takahashi Yasuko's most popular merchandise was washing powders and bath salts. The latter, for example, only cost ¥100 (about 50 pence) for three packs. Mrs Matsui, who has enjoyed frequenting flea markets since her university days (see Chapter 1), sells unused gifts sets for ¥500 (about £2.50) each, which is about one-tenth of their original price. The Japanese sociologist Tatsumi argues that recycling is about 'the circulation of feelings and things'. Because objects are thought to be able to reach their potential through human consumption, those divesting of their own things in temporary retail environments are pleased that 'there seem to be people who think they would like to use them and are willing to even pay a bit of money to do so' (Tatsumi 2002: 150). Both Mrs Matsui and Takahashi Yasuko expressed their joy because people actually wanted to pay a little bit of money for their unused gifts.

I am cautious about overstating this concern with the inanimate world as the main incentive to dispose of unused gifts at flea markets is sociality. Flea markets, modelled after garage sales held in the United States, have been organized in Japan since the end of the 1970s. From the start they were popular among young people who saw them as a form of 'recreation' and 'communication'(CDI & CORE 1987: 97–9). In October 2003, Mrs Matsui persuaded two housewives she met through her daughter's kindergarten to set up stall at a local flea market. Once the three women had arranged their merchandise on plastic sheets, they sat in portable chairs and spend the next four hours chatting, drinking tea and eating snacks, only occasionally interrupted by the performance of selling things.

CONCLUSIONS: FRICTIONS, GAPS AND BLOCKAGES

DOMESTIC FRICTIONS: BETWEEN DUTY AND DESIRE

This book argues for the need to examine the messiness, ambiguity and frictions of everyday domestic practices in order to understand more fully the complex networks of social, material, spatial and spiritual interactions that produce and reproduce human life.[1] Domestic frictions or tensions between inhabitants of the Japanese homes studied are the result of the coexistence of two conflicting domestic ideologies. Like most contemporary Japanese, many seek to sustain a domestic ideal that prioritizes patrilinear blood ties with an emphasis on filial piety and the obligation to care for parents and ancestors. However, this family ideology coexists and overlaps with a newer model, strongly influenced by 'Western' ideals of domesticity, that stresses the importance of the bond between the marital couple and values informal personal relationships driven by affection and spontaneous sentiment (Chapter 1).

Most studies of family life assume that processes of urbanization and industrialization, and the spread of capitalist relationships, generally defined as 'modernity', will lead to a transition from one family model to the other (Bell and Coleman 1999: 7–8). In other words, it is thought that as people become 'more modern', affective relationships between autonomous individuals, preferably enacted in a private environment, become valued more highly. Such a progressive view is, in turn, grounded in European Enlightenment thinking that presumes that modern life is characterized by series of dichotomies, whether the individual versus the collective, the private versus the public

or sentiment versus obligation.[2] However, my Japanese case study has shown that, in practice, the two family models discussed above and the two ideologies on which they are based are in constant dialogue with each other. Indeed, it is at the intersection between social expectation and obligation and individual hopes and desires that generational and gender conflicts are rife.

The young (in particular women) in their quest for romantic love and conjugal intimacy clash with parents eager to establish formal ties between families and secure the birth of a dutiful successor; breaking with one's family altogether remains an inconceivable alternative for most, and many decide to remain single and childless if no compromise can be reached. Another, related, issue that causes conflict between parents and children is the gendered division of labour. In both family models, married women are held solely responsible for the management of the home, whether or not they are employed. The standard female domestic role does not only pertain to housework, children's education and care for the elderly; women are also expected to secure the wellbeing of all family members by creating beneficial ties with other people (Chapter 6) as well as with the spiritual world (Chapter 3). Thus, women in their twenties and thirties in my 2003 sample were not in a hurry to marry. Moreover, many had decided to go back to work after marriage and childbirth. By contrast, their mothers almost certainly remained full-time housewives throughout their adult lives.

Most middle-aged, married women happily complied with the stereotypical female domestic role, particularly if they have successfully immersed themselves in networks of intimate female relationships formed around their children's education or leisure pursuits (Chapter 4). Still, some dutiful wives and mothers also expressed dissatisfaction with their domestic situation. The use of ironic jokes directed at husbands and adult children allowed these women to reproduce the social system while momentarily entertaining at least the possibility of pursuing their individual dreams and desires. This said, because of the risk both of economic ruin and of social alienation very few put their own needs first and revolt. Nevertheless, I have provided two examples of elderly women who eventually revolt and decide to opt out of the system (Chapter 3). This topic would merit further investigation as it divulges the significance of individual desire within Japanese society.

Japanese men are, similarly, caught between these two contrasting family ideologies. On the one hand, they are expected to comply with the stereotype of the sole breadwinner/*sarariiman* who shows his commitment to his employer and works long hours to provide for his family. On the other hand, married men are pressured to spend quality time with their families, as their wives (and increasingly also the state) envision them as caring fathers. We saw in Chapter 1 that domestic friction occurs when husbands give in too easily to personal yearnings for relaxation at home. However, the fact that a large number of married men in my sample worked from home also questions the idea that the home is a 'haven' away from the competitive world of work. Still, few men engaged in any domestic labour – whether helping with cleaning, cooking and caring for children or improving the outlook of the home through DIY. This latter activity, for example, has enabled men in Europe and North America to make significant domestic contributions. Paradoxically, even if some younger men were eager to be more involved in domestic activities, many women in my sample felt reluctant to give up their exclusive reign of the domestic arena.

All human actions are influenced by both personal desires and social duties, and the supposed conflict between both rests on 'a subtle difference in concepts and practices people use for managing their presentations of self and for interpreting the actions of others' (Fishburne Collier 1997: 6). In other words, the various ways in which people conceptionalize personhood impacts on their understanding of the relationship between social obligation and individual freedom. Thus, Spanish families, studied by Fishburne Collier, operate within the European tradition that sees the person as

an autonomous private subject 'who has the freedom to act or refrain from acting out inner desires' (ibid.: 8). In Japan, by contrast, the boundaries between the self and the group are considered to be more blurred. Although an individual is held responsible for improving his or her own situation, individual actions are generally constructed and valued in relation to the group (Chapters 1 and 3). Throughout their life a Japanese person's sense of self is moulded and transcended by his or her membership of a variety of groups. The foremost inside, intimate group is the family, but other examples may range from age-related groups of classmates, people from the same native place and co-workers to the mothers of children attending the same class or members of a wine tasting club (Chapter 2). Because all Japanese relationships are based on these kinds of shared identities in order to maintain smooth social interactions one has to be conscious of the specific context one operates in and strategically adapt one's behaviour accordingly.

This strong strategic awareness has led both researchers and laymen to conclude wrongly that social interactions in Japan, as in China (Smart 1999), are primarily instrumental, formal and hierarchical. In this book I have challenged this assumption by showing that, in practice, all flourishing social connections, even the most formal ones, draw on a fusion between social obligation and sentiment (Chapter 6). Moreover, I have argued (Chapter 1) that relationships can be affective or intimate without being private. Thus, instead of the home being a private sanctuary where one is sheltered from the outside world of work, obligation and formality, in the domestic arena duty and desire, and the larger ideologies on which they are based, intertwine. In order for all to feel at home, individual desires for relaxation and personal freedom need to be continuously negotiated within the overarching communal, family interests.

SLIPPAGES BETWEEN PEOPLE AND THINGS: MATERIAL CULTURE AND THE MESSINESS OF EVERYDAY LIFE

In his ethnography of gift exchange in Indonesia, Webb Keane has pointed to 'the potential for alienation, slippage, or loss' involved in all social interactions (Keane 1997: 230). In his view, at the base of this risk, or hazard, is, firstly, the fact that 'interaction forces participants into mutual dependence, placing each, to an extent at the mercy of the other', and, secondly, the possibility that things can become totally detached from the subject (ibid.: 230–1). He further points out that both aspects have been largely overlooked by anthropologists because they tend to emphasize the intentionality and control of the subject's actions within a supposedly, ordered world (ibid.: 23–5). One of the goals of this book has been to stress the need to pay attention to the material world because it does not just function as a backdrop for human activity but crude, tactile contact with objects and physical environments also directs our day-to-day activities.

Once objects become part of the home they 'escape the boundaries of categorization, they become wild … and can be used to take on different values' (Attfield 2000: 74). In all the homes studied, domestic spaces and the material culture within were actively appropriated. I have, for example, revealed how participants successfully manipulated the material world in order to create a particular atmosphere inside their homes (Chapter 4). Women over the age of 45 preferred a 'native' aesthetic grounded in seasonality, while the younger generation opted for an overall aesthetic scheme created in accordance with a variety of ordering principles ranging from minimalism to colour-coordination. Importantly, both aesthetic ideals were adapted and moulded in order to deal with the messiness of social and material relationships. Thus, the 'native' aesthetic was only produced in designated spaces such as alcoves and hallways, while a more 'eclectic' aesthetic was allowed to flourish in informal spaces for everyday use. Those eager to craft a modern aesthetic scheme were only able to assert their control by relegating unwanted items, often gifts, to the back stages of the home. The examples above illustrate that aesthetic choices are embedded in complex social processes such as gifting and disposal. Moreover, it also shows that the material world directly influences – or, dare one suggest – monitors human actions.[3] The type of dwelling one is able to afford, for example, has a powerful impact on people's lives. The size of the house and the availability of sufficient storage, influences the speed by which everyday used domestic spaces fill up with possessions (Chapter 5). The effect of architectural structures and domestic layouts is particularly strong in Japan, where DIY is rare and structural reforms tend to be carried out by professionals and are therefore very expensive. Moreover, because it is common to destroy and rebuild houses at least once in every generation, inhabitants may allow their material contents to expand and part with the whole lot when the buildings reach the end of their life.

Importantly, those participating in my study did not dismiss the impact of the non-human world on their lives, and they extended the notion of care to spirits and ancestors (Chapter 3) as well as things. Many entertained the possibility that those objects that over time become inalienable linked with a particular person may affect the wellbeing of all living under the same roof. Initially, the specific human relationships these things – often gifts – embody may be acknowledged and remembered, but over time they become absorbed in the messiness of human and non-human worlds that make up the home. Most defined these objects as 'things one would like to dispose of but which are difficult to throw away' (Daniels 2009c). A large percentage are gifts that embody matrilineal ties. Examples I discussed are dowry items such as kimonos and storage furniture (Chapter 5), and, further, dolls that are given by maternal grandparents upon the birth of girls (Chapter 6). A second group consists of unwanted and generally unused goods, again mainly gifts, of which people receive a surplus that they are unable to recirculate through informal channels. In both cases, the specific material qualities of the things concerned, such as their shape or the temporality associated with their use, are linked with their ability to cause malevolent effects (Chapter 6).

As Bruno Latour (1993) has famously argued, the need to divided the human and non-human world is characteristic of the 'modern attitude' influenced by European philosophical ideas. Anthropology, a discipline that has developed out of 'Western' Enlightenment thinking, has been implicit in the development of these ideas as for much of the twentieth century anthropologists have artificially isolated people from their things in order to create an ordered, sanitized world.[4] Thus, until the 1980s, the focus has been on explaining the 'traditional' customs and beliefs of 'non-Western' societies that were thought to be less rational and that therefore blurred the relationship between people and things. Furthermore, among the huge variety of possible human actions, those based on blood ties (kinship) have been singled out as most deserving of attention when studying the 'other'. By contrast, as I have pointed out in the previous section, relationships that are considered to be based on sentiment, such as friendship, have been almost solely associated with European/North American societies.[5]

Since the late 1980s anthropologists working in a variety of cultural contexts have successfully challenged many of these Eurocentric, essentialist assumptions. Japan offers a particularly interesting ethnographic example because it is a modern capitalist society where people and things are

thought to be mixed. It forces us not only to reconsider the supposed distinction between reason and ritual (Chapter 3), but also to allow for the possibility that discourses and practices surrounding spirits and magic may actually be fundamental to the production of modernity.[6] Indeed, as the historian Figal has brilliantly argued, at the end of the nineteenth century, the Japanese actually turned to their rich folk mythology about spirit worlds (*yôkai*) to explain the changes wrought by modern life. In his words, 'under particular historical circumstances, a discourse on the fantastic – in its negativity and positivity – fundamentally shaped modernity in Japan ... ancient monsters bred in twilight do not vanish in modern times – they merely change their shape' (1999: 222).[7] Science and rational thinking inform the lives of contemporary Japanese, but, as we saw in Chapter 3 and Chapter 6, most also recognize the limits of reason and continue to fill the gap between the known and the unknown with myth and magic.

STATE INTERFERENCE, RELIGIOUS INTERVENTIONS AND THE CREATIVE POSSIBILITIES OF CONSTRAINTS

Throughout this volume I have argued that the Japanese state played a crucial role in the development of the ideal notion of the contemporary Japanese house and home. Since the 1880s, as part of an ongoing modernization project, consecutive governments have endorsed housing reforms based

on both native and foreign models of domesticity. However, it was more than one hundred years after this, following a sustained period of economic growth after the Second World War, driven by controversial state investments in the economy instead of social welfare and public housing, that the majority of the population was actually able to experience the sanctioned vision of 'modern living'. Indeed, in 2003 all Japanese live in LDK homes, whether designed as such or refashioned within a structure from an earlier period, that are furnished with sofas and dining tables – objects that were thought to facilitate sociality among family members. However, in practice sofas may just as easily be used for a 'selfish', lazy nap, while dining tables, although they occupy a central place in the domestic arena, are rarely used to share family meals. Similarly, in contemporary usage individual rooms such as bedrooms and children's rooms, first introduced through the LDK design, may diverge from their planned functions. Most children's rooms, for example, are solely used for study, while children continue to sleep with their parents until they reach their early teens (Chapter 1).

Another policy that was successfully implemented in the domestic world in the post-war period and still resonates powerfully today is the division of roles according to gender. Thus, married women, typecast as full-time housewives, were expected to have sole management of the home. Although I have shown that in 2003 domestic gender roles are contested (Chapter 4), huge expectations and pressures continue to be placed on married women as representatives of their families. Apart from caring for husbands, children and elderly relatives, one of their main responsibilities is to keep the domestic arena clean and tidy. The domestic ideology of tidiness draws not only on foreign models of domesticity that strongly link cleanliness with the respectability of the family but also on native philosophical and moral ideals that underlay the empty interiors of the homes of the pre-modern Tokugawa elite that the post-war generation aspired to emulate. During my fieldwork, domestic ordering devices played an important role in the management of the material culture of everyday life. Ideally, storage spaces such as closets, sheds and garages, but also the domestic infrastructure of display such as photo-albums, bookshelves and glass display cases (Chapter 5), operate as in-between areas that facilitate the movement of things in, through and out of the home. However, the majority of inhabitants did not use these spaces as conduits but as containers in which possessions could be stored indefinitely.

Growing affluence since the 1970s and 1980s led to an increase in the consumption of domestic goods and an acceleration of the scale of the gift economy. Although both these changes have resulted in a surplus of goods entering the domestic arena, in this publication I have argued that to come to a fuller understanding of why many Japanese homes are 'overflowing with things' (*mono darake*) we also need to consider changes in divestment practices. Surplus used to be divided and shared among the local community, but, although networks of neighbours that stress mutual cooperation organized around local temples or shrines continue to exist, the majority of those participating in my fieldwork were not native to the place where they lived and many did not even know their neighbours. Their lives continue to be embedded in a series of social relationships but they were centred around activities such as education, work and consumption/leisure practices that are not necessary linked with a particular place (Chapter 2).

Tensions between newcomers and locals with strong roots in a specific neighbourhood are played out in a number of public sites that connect individual homes with their immediate locality, and by extension with the state. Examples I have discussed are street gardens (Spread 3) and garbage disposal sites (Spread 4). Domestic garbage needs to be prepared and presented according to complex rules that are propounded in official pamphlets and posters. Because garbage bags are collected at communal pick-up spots, neighbourhood representatives will reprimand those who fail to live up to the high standards of trash preparation. Street gardens also push the boundaries between inside and outside relationships. Governmental policies that link car ownership with private parking space have resulted in space being used to build garages at the front of the home at the expense of rear gardens. However, many have creatively turned the patches of public space in front of their homes into street gardens. Because these in-between spaces are thought to add value to a particular neighbourhood they are generally tolerated by locals as well as by the state, upon whose property they tend to infringe.

The domestic entrance hall is another space where the inside and outside intertwine (Chapter 2). The hallway is considered to be hazardous because it is located at the intersection between human

and spiritual worlds. Most participants in my study displayed an array of lucky objects to avert the risk of malevolent spirits entering the home and causing misfortune to its inhabitants. Because over time charms are thought to absorb bad luck they need to be regularly renewed at temples and shrines.[8] However, because of the loosening (or even the breaking of ties) between local religious centres and people's homes, but also more general time pressures and constraints associated with urban life, the flow of material culture of luck has become blocked (Chapter 3). As a result, used-up lucky charms, potent with negative power, have accumulated in many Japanese homes. These objects, which have the potential to cause misfortune for those concerned, are a third type of domestic good that people feel reluctant to dispose of.

Evidence of the blockages in the exchange of goods and services between temples and house-holds can also be found at cemeteries across Japan in the form of 'graves without ties' (Chapter 3). In theory, the family of male descendants is responsible for tending to ancestors at the family grave by making offerings of food, incense and flowers. However, many descendants feel unable to fulfil this duty of care because family graves tend to be located in rural areas far removed from their urban residence. Moreover, many families are unable to find successors altogether as increasing numbers of daughters remain single. Still, it is all too easy only to blame the younger generation: some elderly women are 'behaving badly' and ridding themselves of social obligation Some, for example, insist on being buried separately from their husband and his family (Chapter 3), an action that places a heavy burden (financially, socially and materially) on dutiful descendants as they have to care for an additional family grave as well as a Buddhist home altar.

Importantly, material excess caused by blockages such as those discussed above tends to go hand in hand with new possibilities. In other words, when the circulation of goods and services becomes constipated new opportunities to create social, material and spiritual connections occur. Examples are the development of new burial practices that do not require descendants to take care of family graves, or new family models that also allow women to become successors. Another example of the creative possibilities associated with constraints are the various innovative ways people rid themselves of 'things one would like to dispose off, but are difficult to throw away' (Chapter 6). Unused, functional goods, for example, may be donated to bazaars or sold at flea markets. However, more hazardous domestic forms such as decorative trinkets, commemorative gifts and the used-up material culture of luck, are more likely to change hands at temple markets or specialized second-hand shops frequented by foreign tourists eager to bag cheap exotic souvenirs. Paradoxically, exchanges with foreigners are also to blame for some of the surplus kept in the homes studied, as foreign visitors, often in a well-meant attempt to respect Japanese gift culture, bring durable, decorative souvenirs for people to whom they are indebted. These kinds of gifts are strongly associated with certain places and people and are therefore particularly difficult for recipients to divest themselves of. Collections may enable some people to manage the flow of gifts into the home, but, we have seen that these goods might just as easily spin out of their control.

THE HOUSE: A MODEL FOR STUDYING 'COMMON CONSTRAINTS ACROSS DIVERSE CULTURAL ENVIRONMENTS'

> Anthropologists are meant to be professionally fascinated with cultural variation , but in fact they often dwell on aspects of human experience – such as birth, reproduction, and death – which *transcend*, at a fundamental level, cultural and historical variability, and which all human societies must deal with in some way. (Stafford 2000: 4)

I should like to end this book by making a larger claim for its potential to serve as a model for the study of the house and home worldwide, that simultaneously accounts for local specificity and common, cross-cultural human experiences. The quotation above is taken from Charles Stafford's ethnography about processes of separation in China in which he repeatedly calls for an anthropology that engages with 'common constraints across diverse cultural environments' (ibid.: 4) without resorting to new universals. Similar to Stafford, one of my main concerns in this publication has been with the cross-cultural tension between autonomy and dependency; desire and obligation (ibid.: 23). However, my approach differs in that I have focused on the house: a physical environment where 'shared human realities' are most profoundly experienced. Indeed, my Japanese case study has demonstrated that the domestic arena is a unique microcosm where everyday life, state control and religious intervention intertwine as abstractions and ideologies from the world of politics and religion may be transformed into personal, lived experiences, while individual and familial concerns can be elevated to a communal, national, but also otherworldly level.

Already during the mid-1990s a number of social anthropologists (Carsten and Hugh-Jones 1995; Carsten 1997; Hsu 1998) have proposed the use of the house as a 'heuristic device' to study human life across cultures. Carsten and Hugh-Jones, for example, have propagated 'a strong, ethnographically-based view of the house understood in holistic terms which takes account of processes of living that may be said to be universal' as the house consists of 'an ordinary group of people concerned with their day-to-day affairs, sharing consumption and living in the shared space of a domestic dwelling' (Carsten and Hugh-Jones 1995: 45). Similarly, Hsu has argued that this approach 'allows one to consider the house and its occupants within the same analytical framework' and 'reunites aspects of both *material culture and social structure*' (Hsu 1998: 71) (my emphasis). Although their objectives approximate those driving my research, in practice these anthropologists do not venture far beyond the well-established anthropological safe ground of kinship theory and lineage paradigms.[9] If domestic objects and physical environments (for example, the hearth) feature at all, they are considered, much in line with structuralist thought, to 'reflect' or 'represent' the social world; they are props or backdrops for human activity. One is left wondering how the inhabitants actually experience these spaces: What does it mean for them to feel at home? Why do things enter a particular home, and how are they displayed, stored and disposed of? Are some possessions treated with special care and why? What has been the impact of global trade, migration and the increased availability of consumer goods and communication technologies on everyday domestic life?

Importantly, while these anthropological studies about the house acknowledge 'kinship' to Levi-Strauss's ideas about house-based societies, there is an almost complete disregard for Bourdieu's earlier, more substantial legacy, which has spurred much of the anthropological/material culture literature about the domestic in the UK since the mid-1990s.[10] This state of affairs reminds us that any research agenda is always partial, driven by personal interests as well as larger academic

structures and power relations (Sangren 2007). Indeed, I grant that my own work is firmly embedded in British anthropological studies of things or 'material culture studies'. However, in this book I have also attempted to rekindle the dialogue between both anthropological research strands by stressing the importance of long-term ethnography inside the domestic environment that explores the interrelationship of people, things and spaces. At this point it is worth briefly returning to Stafford's ethnography (2000) because, although he never explicitly acknowledges the importance of the material world, his insightful discussions of doorways, beds, walls, windows, kitchens, food, newspapers, charms, ancestral altars and so forth and so on offer an rare example

of what may be achieved by conducting truly 'holistic' fieldwork (that transcends any artificial distinctions between social, spatial and material practices) inside the domestic arena.

Ethnography might have come under severe scrutiny because of its ambiguity. However, in my view, this is exactly the reason why it is such an appropriate tool to study the contradictions and complexities of mundane, domestic life. Indeed, 'ordinary people do not live their lives making simple consistent decisions in all situations. Cultural messages are multiple and conflicting, personal choices have consequences, meanings change, feelings may be ambivalent, and we can rarely stack our values into a consistent set of neatly ordered priorities' (Long 2005: 13). It is through messy exchanges that both researchers and those studied try to make sense of their lived worlds, while neither can make a claim for total truth. Some thing(s) escape the process of description altogether, and I have, therefore, argued that we should endeavour to transcend a narrow focus on representational practices and interviews by including the complexities and contradictions of the often taken-for-granted material world. Moreover, I firmly believe that through the innovative usage of images, characterized by their open-endedness, the incompleteness of the fieldwork experience may be carried through into the final research outcome.

This study of the house and home has critically explored the in-between: the domestic frictions, the messiness of things, but also the gap between the ideal and the ordinary. Hence, it aims to offer a template for comprehending how multiple versions of reality connect and/or clash and challenges persistent dichotomies such as desire versus obligation, things versus people but also, most importantly, Japan/the East versus the West. Above all, it is my hope that future 'holistic' ethnographies of mundane domestic routines, which account for local differences within shared realities, may lead to an engagement with, and understanding of 'the other' on an empathetic level beyond the exotic.

GLOSSARY: JAPANESE VOCABULARY

INTRODUCTION

tate-uri	a ready-built house
ikkodate	a detached house
manshon	an apartment
shûgô jûtaku	apartments (literally 'collective housing')
ikkodate jûtaku	detached house
chûmon jûtaku	made-to-order houses

tate-uri jûtaku	prefabricated houses on a developed plot
chûryû	mainstream
sarariimen	white-collar worker
shôji	paper sliding door
tokonoma	decorative alcove

CHAPTER 1

chirashi	advertisement pamphlet; flier
ie	the patriarchal family unit
ikka danran	the happy family together
yashiki	formal guest room
bunka jûtaku	Cultural Houses
america-ya	American bungalow
danchi	housing blocks of up to four to five storeys in height
kitanai	dirty
chabudai	a low table, a tray with legs (precursor of dining table)
zen	individual meal trays

yutori (suru)	to feel at ease
sawayakana	refreshing
yuttari (suru)	to relax
iyashite kuremasu	(from the verb *iyashu*) to heal
senmenshitsu	a lavatory; literally, a room for washing one's face
kotatsu	a low table with a heating element attached underneath
ochitsukimasu	(from the verb *ochitsuku*) to wind down
bôtto suru	being absent-minded, lost in thought

CHAPTER 2

machiya	traditional wooden townhouse	*getabako*	a shoe cupboard
jûtaku-shi	housing communities	*shôkayô*	for fire-fighting
gardeningu	gardening	*chônaikai*	a neighbourhood association
hômu sentâ	DIY store	*jizô-san*	neighbourhood
gareiji	private parking space		protection deities
tate-uri	a ready-built house	*tsukiai*	sociability
sudare	bamboo blinds	*puraibashii*	privacy
amado	storm shutters (literally, rain doors)	*mettani awanai*	we seldom meet
		amari shiranai	I don't know them very well
genkan	entrance hall		
nôka	farmhouse	*uchi*	inside
nagaya	tenement buildings	*soto*	outside

CHAPTER 3

butsudan	a family Buddhist altar	*ennichi*	a temple/shrine festival (literally 'day linked to a specific deity)
ihai	a (Buddhist) mortuary tablet		
shirei	a person's spirit	*kamidana*	a domestic Shinto altar (literally 'Shinto shelf')
senzo	guardian or ancestral diety		
		kami	a deity
omairi	visit ancestors at the family altar or grave	*ofuda*	a paper or wooden charm
		in	direct effect
mu-en botoke	wandering spirits (literally buddhas without attachments or bonds)	*en*	indirect cause
		yakuyoke	to ward off evil
		shûshin	self-cultivation, moral training
mu-en bôchi	graves without ties		
chi-en	territorial ties	*etomono*	(representations of) zodiac animals
danka	Buddhist parish system		
nenjû gyôji	annual events	*fukurô*	owl
hare no hi	festive days	*fu-kurô*	without trouble
kegare	pollution	*fuku ga kuru*	to invite luck
hare	sacred	*kaeru*	frog
ke	profane	*tanuki*	raccoon
fuku	good luck (as in good luck deities)	*hatsumôde*	to pay one's first visit of the year to a shrine
un	luck; fortune; fate	*shûtome*	mother-in-law
engi (ga ii)	auspiciousness	*butsuma*	an altar room; also used for a custom-made recess for the Buddhist family altar
sekku	auspicious days; seasonal festivals		

CHAPTER 4

tokonoma — decorative alcove

mitsugusoku — three objects (an incense burner, a vase and a candle stick) used in Buddhist ceremonies

chigai-dana — staggered wall shelves (usually built next to the decorative alcove)

toko-bashira — a wooden alcove post

ryôsai kenbo — 'good wife, wise mother' (a slogan used by the State to promote the division of work according to gender at the beginning of the twentieth century)

shufu — housewife, homemaker

paato — part-time employees

koto — a long Japanese zither with thirteen strings

okeiko — practice, training (often used to refer to traditional pursuits such as flower arranging or the tea ceremony)

yôfû — Western-style

washitsu — Japanese-style rooms

kakkoii — cool

oshare — smart

shumi — taste (aesthetic)

hako-iri musume — 'a daughter in a box' (term used to refer to daughters of the elite who were brought up sheltered from the outside world)

sodai gomi — large-size refuse (used as pejorative for retired men)

tanshin funin — work transfer (often forceful) to distant cities, leaving families behind

sensu — sense (aesthetic)

CHAPTER 5

nando — a storage room

oshi-ire — a built-in closet

shûnô — (inf. *suru*) to put things away

rifômu — re-form, make-over

kura — pre-modern, fire-resistant storehouse to protect valuable items from theft and natural disasters

nagamochi kuruma — chest on wheels that allowed for clothing and personal possessions could be wheeled off in case of a fire

muda — unnecessary, useless

tsubo — measurement (approx 3.3 m^2)

tansu — chest of drawers

kagu — furniture (literally 'domestic goods')

yôfukudansu — wardrobe (literally 'closet for Western clothing')

wadansu — Japanese-style closets

chadansu — cupboard for storing tea things

fuyôhin — unused goods

CHAPTER 6

kinenhin	memento, keepsake	*kawaisô*	pitiful, poor
meibutsu	famous souvenirs	*oseibo-ochûgen*	seasonal gifting
omiyage	souvenir	*oiwai no okaeshi*	return-gifts
zakka	miscellaneous goods	*shômôhin*	expendables,
kinen (suru)	to commemorate		supplies (literally 'things
hina matsuri	Dolls' Festival		that can be used up')
ningyô	doll	*mawashite ageru*	to rotate, recirculate
kurushii	crushed, having breathing		(from the verb *mawasu*)
	difficulty	*dôzo*	please take
jitsuyôhin	functional goods	*fuyôhin*	unused goods
kazarimono	decorative goods	*taisetsu ni suru*	to take care of things
tatari	a curse		

CONCLUSION

yôkai	a monstrous shape, ghastly apparition
monodarake	full of things

NOTES

INTRODUCTION

1. Influential books about traditional Japanese aesthetics were quickly translated into Japanese and many Japanese architects trained and learned to value their own heritage in architectural offices set up by foreigners.
2. Two hugely successful blockbusters from 2003, *The Last Samurai* and *Lost in Translation*, illustrate this dual fascination with Japan. The former draws on stereotypes about traditional Japanese aesthetic sensibilities while the latter is firmly embedded in the weird and wacky category.
3. Bourdieu's depiction of the Kabyle house is based on nostalgic stories about former village homes that he recorded among Kabyle living in new settlements, often after forced displacement (Silverstein 2004: 554).
4. This approach to the study of the home is epitomized by Levi-Strauss's influential concept of 'house-based societies' (Levi-Strauss 1983). Many anthropologists studying the home continue to be inspired by his view that the house, consisting of both material and immaterial wealth, plays an important role in the production of a particular type of kinship system (Carsten and Hugh-Jones 1995; Joyce and Gillespie 2000).
5. The first French publication of the Kabyle House which dates back to 1970 was translated into English in 1973, while Bourdieu's last reworked French version from 1980 only became available in English in 1990.
6. Bourdieu's essay(s) about the Kabyle house is not his only piece of research of interest to those studying the domestic as he was concerned with the quotidian throughout his career. In *Distinction* (Bourdieu [1979] 1984), his classic about class relationships in France, for example, he explores the link between class, *habitus* and taste within the domestic arena. He demonstrates that mundane choices about food, clothing and furnishings may have mental groundings, but they are foremost communicated through the body.
7. Although Bourdieu's work continues to attract critique whether he is said to possess an overly romantic view of the class struggle or to ignore the material qualities of the real world in which our bodies live (Csordas 1994).
8. Other important influences are the feminist literature that drew attention to the role of women in the domestic (Gullestad 1984; Moore 1986; 1994) and phenomenological studies that depicted the house as a living metaphor for social life (Blier-Preston 1987).
9. The launch of the journal *Home Cultures* in 2003, for example, confirms that this kind of research has firmly established itself as one of the most innovative areas of research within anthropology. Although the journal aims to be multidisciplinary, its three editors trained as anthropologists.

10. Kon and his research partner, Yoshida, first revealed the results of three years of research in Tokyo in a 1927 exhibition called *Kôgengaku*. This term is a neologism for *kôkogaku*, or archaeology, which was translated as 'modernologio', which is Esperanto for 'modernology' (Kawazone 2004: 45–9). I am unable to discuss this topic in any detail here, but it is worth noting that the 1980s revival of the anthropological study of material culture in the UK, similarly, owes much to ideas and methods that were first developed in archaeology (Hodder 1986).

11. This area, which covers the southern (or western) part of the main island of Honshu, has a total population of 18 million, or 14.4 per cent of the Japanese population. However, my study will primarily focus on those living in and around the three major urban cores of Osaka (2.6 million), Kobe (1.5 million) and Kyoto (1.4 million) (AS 2006: 86).

12. Exceptions are Ben-Ari's (1991) ethnography of two communities in Kyoto and Brumann's (2001) research into general housing issues, also in Kyoto.

13. A second type of urban ethnography, with an equally long history, but which includes more non-Tokyo sites, is studies about the workplace (Rohlen 1974; Ogasawara 1998; Graham 2003) and educational institutions (Singleton 1967; Rohlen 1983; Hendry 1986; Goodman 1990).

14. Two exceptions are Goldstein-Gidoni's (1997) fieldwork in a bridal company in Kobe, and Robertson's (1998) ethnography inside the all-female theatre company Takarazuka, located in the town of the same name between Osaka and Kobe.

15. The antipathy between inhabitants of the Kanto and Kansai areas surfaces, for example, during major sport events such as the yearly high school baseball tournament that is broadcast on national television.

16. Tokugawa Japan (1603–1867) already had a vibrant, urban consumer culture, but following abolishment of the feudal class system and the rapid development of new industries in the Meiji period (beginning in1868) there has been a continuous wave of immigration from the countryside to the cities. Before the Second World War only thirty per cent of the population lived in cities (Conrad and Saaler 2001: 25). In the post-war period, the urbanization process has intensified, and seventy-eight per cent of all Japanese were living in cities by 2003, with 43.9 per cent concentrated in the Tokyo, Nagoya and Osaka area (AS 2004: 32).

17. Although tatami mats have been largely replaced by wooden flooring it remains common practice to measure rooms in number of tatami instead of square metres. Historically, sizes of tatami mats differ by region, and even today a 6-mat room in Kyoto might be considerably bigger than a 6-mat room in Tokyo.

18. Several architects claimed that homes such as these are more popular in the Kanto than in the Kansai region. These statements corresponds with my own observations in both Osaka and Tokyo.

19. Although the 'mainstream' identity is broadly inclusive its all-pervading power has also created new categories of distinction. Apart from a few exceptions (see Dale 1986; De Vos 1982; De Vos and Wetherall 1983; Kondo 1990), the plight of those who are not part of the mainstream has been largely ignored in the literature, academic and other. It is only in recent years that a number of ethnographies have drawn attention to the others within, whether foreign migrant workers (Weiner 1997; Lie 2001; Roth 2002), the homeless (Gill 2001), homosexuals (Lunsing 2001) or people with disabilities (Nakamura 2006).

20. In 2000 about one-quarter of all households were single-person households, while 71.3 per cent were without children (AS 2006: 85).

21. These studies are strangely reminiscent of earlier psychological approaches to the material culture of the home by Csikszentmihalyi and Rochberg-Halton (1981) and Dittmar (1992).

22. The idea of adopting this dual strategy emerged when one family, whom I have known for more than ten years, suggested that, if I would like to study contemporary Japanese life at first hand I could live in their home. Two other friends made an equally generous offer, while two families with whom I had become acquainted in 2003 also agreed to *in situ* fieldwork.

23. Research collaborations can take a number of forms, but the most extreme example is the 'research partnership' in which participants set the research agenda and are actively involved in the writing-up

process (Park 1992). My aspirations are less radical, and my approach has been a loose combination of a narrative (Tedlock 1991) and a collaborative (Kuhlmann 1992) ethnography.

24. It is standard practice in anthropological texts to create pseudonyms not only to protect participants but also to guarantee the ethical grounding and scientific credentials of the discipline. However, how can this professional insistence on anonymity be reconciled with the wish on the part of those studied to receive due acknowledgement (Cook and Crang 2007: 166)? I became too aware of this issue after I send some of my publications to participants in my PhD research and received complaints that people had not been 'properly' named. One family even went as far as to send me a postcard with the solemn message: 'We are not the Moris but the Kuwaharas!' I admit that I have not found any easy solution, but because this is a multi-sited ethnography carried out over a large geographical area, and because about ten per cent of the participants in my study wanted to remain anonymous, I have to some extent been able to both protect the participants' identity and respect their desire for recognition.

25. This book is a translation of a hugely successful 1997 Japanese original.

26. Conversely, in the early days of the discipline anthropologists commonly drew on visual evidence to verify scientific ideas, whether in the form of anthropometric photographs or re-enactments (Edwards 1992). This said, since the 1930s, with the rising popularity of long-term ethnographic fieldwork based on immediate observation (Grimshaw 2001), there have been few anthropological studies that employ visual data, particularly in the final outcome. One notable exception is *Balinese Character*, from 1942, in which the anthropologists Mead and Bateson (1942) use a series of scientific, photographic essays to depict key aspects of social life in Bali. Although this study has a number of weaknesses, it successfully demonstrates how text and image can mutually inform each other. During the 1980s the potential for visuals in anthropological publications was further explored in some excellent collaborations between anthropologists and photographers (McAllister and McAllister 1980; Danforth and Tsiaras 1982), but these studies remain largely unknown in mainstream anthropology.

27. Although I have used an active, personal voice, I have also been eager to avoid the trappings of stylistic experiments that too easily become a pretext for self-absorbed explorations (Bourdieu 2003).

28. Academic publishers also place heavy restrictions on the number and kind of visuals in order to keep down the printing costs and therefore the eventual price of the published book.

29. Certain images, such as graphs, are tolerated either because they reveal the underlying, invisible structures of the human world or because they are created by machines such as telescopes or scanners and are, therefore, not thought to be mediated by human agency (Stafford 1998). Latour (2000), for example, has demonstrated how 'scientific' images are effective in creating objectivity by allying themselves with and referring to a series of other images. By the same token, aesthetically pleasing images are often singled out as examples of the worse artifice because of the obvious human interference in framing and composing them.

30. In 2006 I was awarded a British Academy Small Research Grant that enabled me to return to Japan with the British professional photographer Susan Andrews. During a two-week period, ten people who participated in my 2003 ethnography opened up their homes for us. Andrews took about 800 photographs that we reduced in regular meetings to 75 favourites that appear in the book. Andrews's photographs have been printed in a larger format than the other two types of images, not only because I consider their documentary and aesthetic quality to be complementary but also because the sheer detail of their content evokes the complexity of everyday life. Our collaboration has been very successful and we plan a joint-exhibition as well as a series of workshops to explore further the relationship between image and text.

CHAPTER 1. FEELING AT HOME

1. During a one-year period from November 2002 until October 2003, five participants in my study agreed to collect these pamphlets, called *chirashi*.

2. A similar arrangement is standard in apartments, but bedroom(s) are located on the same floor along a corridor

3. A number of recent studies that explore the role occidentalism played in the development of Japanese modernity have questioned any simple simulation or mimicry of the 'West'. Bonnett, for example, draws on Harootunian notion of coeval modernities in order to demonstrate how nineteenth-century Japanese thinkers such as Fukuzawa Yukichi 'actively created and deployed [the 'West'] within specific national debates and struggles' (Bonnett 2005: 522).

4. The openness of this side of the house meant that Tokugawa houses were surrounded by high fences with gates. These external features have also become characteristic of the exterior outlook of the contemporary urban dwellings, a point I will discuss in detail in Chapter 2.

5. See Teasley (2001) for a detailed description of cultural houses.

6. The exteriors of these houses were constructed in the 2 by 4 mode that is still most common today. They were modelled on American bungalows (*america-ya*), characterized by a wooden lower part and an upper part in mortar, that were imported to Japan as early as the 1910s (Uchida, Ogawa and Fujiya 2002).

7. During the 1920s, developers built a number of communities consisting of cultural houses in the suburbs of Tokyo. In Meijiro Bunkamura, for example, individual plots measured about 372 square metres. The fact that average dwellings at that time measured only 99 square metres shows that these dwellings were only affordable to the very affluent (Uchida, Ogawa and Fujiya 2002).

8. Etiquette textbooks for schoolgirls as well as women's magazines from this period were preoccupied with instructing middle-class women in the proper manner of receiving guests of various ranks (Sand 2003: 51).

9. In the living room (*i no ma*) tatami mats were covered with carpets on top of which were placed a sofa set, a television, a piano and other Western-style furniture (Aoki 2001: 28–9).

10. *Danchi*-living was not praised by all, and the media circulated negative reports about the cramped living conditions, the cost of living and feelings of loneliness among inhabitants (Partner 1999: 178).

11. For the majority of Japanese who lived in extreme poverty the homes of the American army personnel located in segregated towns represented a modern way of life that remained unattainable. Washington Heights in the suburbs of Tokyo, for example, was a self-sufficient town consisting of 827 houses and a number of schools, hospitals and shops. The smallest homes in the settlement measured 26 *tsubo* (86 square metres), while the average Japanese home would measure about 12 *tsubo* (40 square metres). (Uchida, Ogawa, Fujiya 2002: 122–3).

12. During the 1950s and 1960s these interiors and the furniture placed inside were copied by the Japanese housing industry. Uchida has argued that the main reason for this easy assimilation lies in the fact that the same Japanese carpenters who produced furniture and everyday goods for the occupation forces applied their skills to create homes for the local population (Uchida, Ogawa and Fujiya 2002: 122).

13. All contemporary homes use the LDK or DK standard. A 3LDK home, for example, refers to a space with a central living-dining-kitchen area with three individual rooms, a toilet and a bathroom.

14. In his discussion of the appropriation of Victorian interior styles and tastes by the Meiji elite, Sand, similarly, argues that occidental furniture and ornaments that were integrated into eclectic domestic settings were 'not subsumable in any simple sense to an aesthetic order established in Europe' (Sand 2000: 664).

15. David Morgan has demonstrated how for contemporary Americans the living room is considered the heart of the home. The space commonly contains a fireplace with mantel, a television set, favourite images or heirlooms and a piano or an organ. The main activities taking place in this room are 'conversation, entertainment, relaxation, devotions, reading, napping and watching television' (Morgan 1998: 165).

16. The radio played an important role in spreading the idea of the 'happy family together' because family members would gather around the low table to eat while listening to the radio (Koizumi 2002: 100–2).

17. In 1963, sixty per cent of Japanese possessed a *chabudai*, but ten years later this figure had decreased to ten per cent. By comparison, in 1988, seventy per cent used a dining table (Koizumi 2002: 113).

18. This number is even fewer than the fifty-eight per cent of couples who claimed they shared the same bedroom in a national survey conducted in 2005 (AS 2006: 27).

19. Another key feature of the modern Chinese home is the central living room with sofa set and television for both family use and the reception of guests. As in Japan, both family socialising and the reception of guests are activities that were previously conducted in separate areas of the home (Yan 2005).

20. The foremost function of a children's room is study, and the main piece of furniture placed there is a desk, generally purchased when a child starts elementary school.

21. Srinivas (2002) has demonstrated that bathrooms are also seen as a status symbols inside the middle-class Hindu home.

22. In the literature it is said that the order of bathing reflects people's status in the home. In theory, the father should take the first bath after he returns home from work. However, in the five homes in which I stayed for several weeks the order of taking a bath turned out to be more flexible. Small children or elderly grandparents, for example, would take a bath in the late afternoon. The only constant seemed to be that the woman of the house was the last to enter the bath after all her housework was completed. In the beginning, the families insisted that I, as a guest, should enter the bath first, but as time passed by this special courtesy was no longer considered necessary, and I felt relieved to finally be allowed to bathe after the rest of the family.

23. This room, called *senmenshitsu*, literally room for washing one's face, generally contains a washing basin, a basket for leaving one's dirty clothes, a washing machine, drying racks and clean towels.

24. A timer enables the water to be (re-)heated at a designated time, and some participants used this setting to have their bath ready when they returned home from work

25. During the bathing ceremony, family members are asked to participate in the performance through symbolic acts such as sprinkling water over the body or drying the face of the deceased. Suzuki gives a detailed explanation of the whole ritual (Suzuki 2000: 75–83).

26. A survey conducted among 836 respondents in Tokyo in 1994 found that 67.9 per cent used Japanese-style rooms to sleep in, 49.7 per cent for folding washing and 43.7 per cent for watching TV (Uchida 2002: 117).

27. The cheapest apartments, often rented by students and young professionals, tend to consist of only one multifunctional tatami room. However, more recently, one-room apartments with wooden flooring throughout have become more popular.

28. By 2003 this space had been covered with a carpet and turned into a play/study area for their grandchildren.

29. There are two families in my sample that are called Iwaii. The Iwaiis senior are a couple in their early sixties who live in the countryside south of Nara City. Their eldest son, Mr Iwaii junior, lives with his wife and their one-year old son, in a rented house in Kyoto. Similarly, two other families, who live with three generations under one roof, the Nishikis and the Takahashis, will be referred to as being either senior or junior.

30. Research from the Communication and Design Institute in Kyoto shows that during the 1990s *kotatsu* were largely replaced by 'hot carpets' (CDI and Core 1993).

31. Central heating was briefly introduced in Japan during the 1970s, but it was considered to be too expensive.

CHAPTER 2. HOME AND THE COMMUNITY

1. In 2006, as a member of an organized tour around several traditional wooden townhouses (*machiya*) in Kyoto, I became aware of the extent of this problem. Every townhouse visited was surrounded by apartment blocks, some more than ten storeys high that blocked the sun and made the garden and the rooms dark and humid

2. Because Tokugawa sumptuary laws stated that entrance gates were the privilege of the upper classes they became powerful signs of the status of inhabitants to the outside world.

3. Several home-owners told me they choose not to purchase an individually designed house partly because of the extra cost but even more because this kind of house would certainly stick out in their locality. Dwellings in housing communities (*jûtaku-shi*), developed by large national building cooperations, look identical, in accordance with the fashion of the time. However, in city centres exteriors are more varied as houses built in different periods line the streets.

4. The average size of the detached dwellings in my study was 100 square metres, while their plots measured about 150 square metres.

5. The size of parking areas is usually indicated by drawing one or two cars in front of the house.

6. These regulations raise questions about how private and public realms are defined in Japanese law, and how Japanese citizenship is created within the context of overwhelming respect for public authority. I am unable to discuss this topic in any detail here, but Patricia Boling (1990) offers an insightful discussion.

7. Just how much the Yanos valued each centimetre of their land became clear when they tore down their old house. One of their neighbours, who had built a new house a few years earlier, had erected a separation wall ten centimetres inside their property without asking the Yanos for permission. Because no amicable solution could be reached, the family went to court and received ¥1,000,000 (about £5,000) in compensation.

8. In *In Praise of Shadows*, Junichiro Tanizaki (1991), for example, eloquently describes the intricate play of light and shadow created by these windows.

9. These devices resemble in form and function the large wooden blinds (*amado*, literally, rain doors) that were traditionally situated in front of windows to protect the house against storms and provide extra security.

10. Nishiyama further argues that *nagaya* are the predecessors of the cheap wooden terraced houses as well as the two-storey apartment blocks that have been rented to blue-collar urban dwellers since the 1950s (Nishiyama 1989: 350–3).

11. The size of the hallway and the height of the elevation of the step can differ considerable, but all Japanese homes have this interior feature in common.

12. In some homes a bell attached to the sliding door rings when it is opened or closed.

13. The steel pivoting doors were first introduced in apartments during the 1950s and have been standard ever since.

14. I was repeatedly told that since my previous stay in 1999 Japan had become less safe. The media play an important role in increasing public anxiety about crime as audiences are bombarded twenty-four hours a day with news and detailed analyses of child murderers, newly discovered deadly bowel cancers, Chinese identity-theft gangs and so on and so forth. Nakano, similarly, argues that although actual crime levels remained relatively low, the media headlines about sensational crimes during the 1990s generated anxiety (Nakano 2005: 92).

15. These banners have a white plaque with the name of the neighbourhood and the number of the specific association (for example, group 4) attached to them.

16. In their decorative alcove Mr Yano also displays a certificate he received for his services to the local community as a volunteer on a school baseball team.

17. Although Ozaki and Rees Lewis recognize the importance of in-between-ness embodied in the entrance hall, the main drawback of their research is that they tend to base their discussions about inside–outside categories on outdated rituals and rehearsed stereotypes mentioned in the essentialist literature about Japan from the 1980s.

CHAPTER 3. DOMESTIC SPIRITUALITY

1. When a person passes away, seven seventh-day ceremonies are held. On the forty-ninth day, when it is thought the deceased has finished his or her time in an intermediate existence preparatory to rebirth, the temporary tablets carrying his or her posthumous Buddhist name that have been placed at the grave are replaced by a more permanent tablet called *ihai* that is enshrined in the domestic altar. These memorial tablets, thus, embody the individual dead of the house. Smith, for example, describes how during the Second World War people went to great length to save their ancestral tablets from the raging fires that followed air raids (1974: 84–5).

2. Official photographs of the recently deceased may be hung on a lintel above the altar, while in some homes less formal photos are displayed inside or around the altar.

3. Martinez argues that young wives are responsible for the daily offerings to the Shinto deities and older women in the household tend to the ancestors in the Buddhist altar (Martinez 1995: 189). Only five families in my sample possessed both, but in all these cases, if an older women was present, she would take care of both.

4. 'Graves without ties' are the focus of many folktales about angry spirits causing havoc. Waves of migration to urban centres since the end of the nineteenth century have resulted in large numbers of people being unable to care for relatives after death. As early as 1887, a *Jodo sect* temple in centre of Osaka, for example, began to create a Buddha statue every ten years from the cremated remains of people who had been abandoned. Thus, people praying at the temple automatically paid their respect to 'wandering spirits'.

5. The dead are also honoured on the two equinoxes and at the New Year, but since the Meiji period, *Obon*, held in August, is primarily associated with death and the commemoration of the ancestors. At the start of *Obon* incense and small horses made out of eggplant or straw are used to guide the spirits home to the altar, which is decorated with lanterns and special offerings of foods, drink and flowers, while large stacks of gifts are displayed and lavish family parties are held. At the end of *Obon* the spirits of the ancestors are sent back on small boats lit by lanterns that carry them away on rivers.

6. Between 1975 and 1985 there was a slight increase in co-residence because the majority of women born during the 1950s had a maximum of two children and in theory each child could either become a successor or marry one. This was possible because of the widespread practice called *muko yôshi* whereby a husband could be adopted into his wives family as the main successor. However, since the 1990s there has been a steady decline as one in four families, especially those with only daughters, cannot find a co-residing successor (Ochiai 1996: 149–51) while the number of single member households has also increased. In 2000, thirty-three per cent of households consisted of people over sixty-five years old, nineteen per cent of whom lived in three-generation homes, nine per cent of whom were elderly couples living on their own and five per cent of whom were living in single people households (AS 2006: 85).

7. Shinto, literally 'the way of the gods', is an ambiguous term used to refer to a diverse range of religious experiences throughout Japanese history such as pre-Buddhist ancient folk beliefs, medieval localized religious cults that mixed elements of Buddhism and Shinto as well as post-1868 state-led Shinto.

8. This syncretism has been periodically disrupted by waves of intolerance instigated by political leaders who exploited religion to control the population. During the Tokugawa period (1603–1867), for example, the military government used the nationwide Buddhist parish system (*danka*), which forced each household to register at a specific Buddhist temple, to suppress Christianity. At the end of the nineteenth century, on the other hand, the nationalist, military regime elevated Shinto to the status of sole state religion, and Shinto shrines were used to advocate a national ideology based around the worship of the emperor.

9. My focus in this study is on Shinto and sectarian Buddhism, and some Taoist concepts that have influenced both. However, the Japanese religious landscape is more diverse: a small Christian community (1 per cent) exists and numerous new religions (4.7 per cent) are thriving (AS 2006).

10. In his seminal 'Folklore Dictionary', Yanagita Kunio, the founder of Japanese Folklore Studies, defines 'annual events' as: 'festive days (*hare no hi*) that annul pollution (*kegare*)' through 'offerings made to the deities that are afterwards consumed among the community' (Yanagita 1951: 449). In other words, on specific days of the year a group of people, whether the household, the local community or the whole nation, hold purification rituals to increase spiritual energy. Japanese folklorists such as Yanagita and Wakamori equated these cycles of regeneration at the base of Japanese traditional cosmology with the Durkheimean sacred (*hare*) versus profane (*ke*) model. However, more recently, Japanese anthropologists have questioned this approach by pointing out that *hare* and *ke* but also the third concept of *kegare*, often left out of the discussion altogether, are 'inter-relative and supplementary' (Ito 1995: 126).

11. The English term 'luck' does not capture the richness of nuances that surround the concept within the Japanese context. For a discussion of the three most commonly used terms, *fuku*, *un* and *engi*, see Daniels 2003.

12. The adoption of the Gregorian calendar in 1872 meant that the date for each ritual occurrence has become fixed, and as a consequence many of the events no longer correspond with actual seasonal changes in nature.

13. Both ancestors and household deities are thought to reside among the living (Smith 1974: 86), and although both altars are the focal point for many domestic ritual practices celebrations can also take place without referencing them. During specific 'festive days', for example, parts of the home (as for the temporary displays erected for the girls and boys days) or the whole domestic arena (for example, during the New Year when a sacred rope is hung from the front gate) may be temporarily activated and transformed into ritual space (Ito 1999: 131).

14. All five families also possess a *butsudan*, which further proves that Shinto and Buddhism have successfully amalgamated in Japan

15. According to folk beliefs, because the god of fire and water spirits might bring destruction and decease, to prevent harm coming to the inhabitants the kitchen, traditionally situated in the back area of the home, needs to be protected (Yanagita 1951).

16. Buddhism stresses the agency of the individual in averting his or her destiny. Through their actions individuals can have a direct effect (*in*) on phenomena that occur in the world, while divine assistance may indirectly cause (*en*) good results

17. The decrease of *kamidana* in urban areas started during the 1950s, and in 1964–5, for example, only forty-five per cent of white-collar workers in Tokyo area possessed a shelf (Smith 1974: 88).

18. Unlucky ages for women are 18, 33 and 37 years, and for men 25, 41 and 61 years. During the year leading up to these birthdays, as well as the year after, most people visit religious centres to pray for their protection, and many bring home lucky charms. The fact that Mr Ebara's lucky charm was still on display nine years after he purchased it demonstrates that many people fail to return used-up charms to religious centres.

19. Sawada has eloquently described how during the nineteenth century Japanese scholars engaged in fierce debates about self-cultivation (*shûshin*), defined as 'the moral, ritual, psychological, and/or educational processes by which individuals were believed to attain well-being' (Sawada 2004: 3).

20. People with a Japanese-style room who had young children used this space to erected elaborate displays for the Dolls' Festival on 3 March or the Boys' Festival on 5 May. Those without *tatami* rooms displayed miniature dolls in their hallways.

21. Two arrows were placed in the kitchen and one in the hallway.

22. Discussions about seasonality in the Japanese home tend to centre on the complex rules that regulate the display of flower arrangements and hanging scrolls in traditional alcoves. However, during my fieldwork degrees of seasonal awareness varied greatly, and in practice expressions of domestic seasonality were often reduced to replacing zodiac animals at the start of the New Year (Daniels 2009b).

23. Zodiac animals are commonly given at the beginning of the New Year, but collectors such as Mrs Kadonaga received them as souvenirs throughout the year.

24. Indeed, by far the largest numbers of zodiac animal shapes in the home were those printed on New Year's cards. The efficacy of lucky objects is linked with their shape, irrespective of whether it is a two- or three-dimensional form.

25. In the garden leading up to their front door, the Takahashis placed two large frog statues together with a gigantic raccoon (*tanuki*) figurine. Raccoons are auspicious animals through their association with the phallic cult of fertility and virility (Inoue 1998: 231). They are typically depicted in anthropomorphized form; standing up with exposed male genitalia while holding a sake bottle. It is common to place them at the entrance of restaurants and bars to entice customers inside.

26. In domestic entrance halls lucky cats have their left paw raised while cats placed in business environments invite luck with their right paw. Statues representing beckoning cats that invite luck (*maneki neko*) can these days be found in businesses worldwide ranging from Chinese restaurants in London, to clothing shops in Italy.

27. The feeling of starting the year anew was most strongly associated with carefully attending to any outstanding business. This often meant sending seasonal gifts to people to whom one was indebted, but many were also anxious literally to pay off debt in terms of the amount owed on their credit cards before the end of the year.

28. In 2003 households with one child made up 11.9 per cent of the population, 12.2 per cent had two children, while 72.1 per cent were childless (AS 2006: 85).

29. This type of housing is barrier free; the apartments have buttons to call staff and are close to local amenities. There are places available for rent but service charges are very expensive and a large deposit has to be paid in advance; in order to secure a place one has to pay at least ¥8,000,000 (about £40,000) in advance (NHK 2003).

30. This decision was also influenced by the fact that Mr Matsui, who is a professional photographer, would be able to generate more work in the Nara area.

31. In 2000, 26.6 per cent of women aged between thirty and thirty-four years old remained single (AS 2004: 13). Single motherhood remains a taboo in contemporary Japan. Divorce is on the increase, but a family court lawyer told me that he tends to advise his female clients to stay with their partners because aliment payment evasion is common and they will have to face an unstable economic future.

32. This situation is only made worse by the fact that these days all parents are eager to find a successor and men are generally reluctant to adopt their wife's family name.

33. Japan has the fastest aging population in the world. It is estimated that by 2010, 33.2 per cent of the population will be over sixty-five years old (AS 2004: 15). There is a pressing need for more barrier-free homes, but the government and private companies are slow to react because these homes are not economically beneficial.

34. Since the 1950s there have been a number of grave-reform movements that criticize the Buddhist grave system and fight for the right for those without successors to have a grave. Examples are war widows, childless couples, families with only daughters and single people (Murakami 2000: 345).

CHAPTER 4. TATAMI TASTES

1. In 1955, fifty-seven per cent of women were in full-time employment, but this number had decreased to forty-six per cent by 1975 (Bishop 2005).

2. This policy resulted in institutionalized discrimination against women in the workplace for many years to come. Until the end of the 1960s it was, for example, legal to require women to terminate their job upon marriage

3. Three women aged forty-five and older over had never married. These were Ms Nishimura, Ms Kadonaga and Ms Kema.

4. Recent research shows that all Japanese women have to juggle the demands of both housework and activities outside the home (Matsunaga 2000).

5. Statistics show that since the 1980s dual income households have steadily increased. In 1980, there were 614,000 dual income households as opposed to 1,114,000 households with a male salaried worker and unemployed wife. By 1991, the former overtook the latter for the first time, and in 2002, 939,000 households consisted of dual earners while in 893,000 cases the man remained the sole breadwinner (AS 2003: 10).

6. Women are often excluded from after work male-bonding rituals characteristic of Japanese corporate culture (see Allison 1994).

7. The Iwaiis in Nara were the only family in my sample who actually possessed a special room in which to perform the formalized tea ceremony.

8. The tea ceremony embodies an ideal of beauty called *wabi* that is influenced by Zen and Confucianism, and which 'sets simple and unpretentious expression above the complex and striking. It abhors excess; it admires restraint. It sees a higher dimension of beauty in the imperfect than in the flawless' (Haga 1989: 201).

9. Jordan Sand offers an in-depth study of the ideal domestic aesthetic during the 1920s and 1930s based on guidebooks for decorating the home that targeted bourgeoise women (Sand 2003).

10. In a 2002 survey about women's art and cultural activities music came top (sixty-four per cent), followed by painting (sixty-one per cent) while the traditional arts occupied the bottom of the list: flower arrangement (twenty-one per cent), calligraphy (nineteen per cent) and the Japanese tea ceremony (fifteen per cent) (AS 2004: 13).

11. I actually came across nine alcoves, but the one I have left out of my discussion was situated in the Japanese-style bedroom in a rented apartment and the inhabitants had placed a mirror and a fax machine inside.

12. The presence of a small television in the Yanos' alcove in Kyoto seems to confirm this. However, this example could also suggest that in contemporary Japan new technologies such as televisions are treasured more than antiques or heirlooms. Kelly (1992) has demonstrated how, during the 1970s, people in the countryside placed televisions in their alcoves, while Udea reveals how electric fans graced the alcoves in farmhouses (Ueda 1998: 91).

13. I will discuss the contents of these hallway displays in more detail in Chapter 6.

14. Ethnographic data I collected in the UK in 2004–5 similarly suggests that some men in creative professions, in particular architects, desire to exercise control over the aesthetics of their homes.

15. Statistics show that only fifty-five per cent of women and twenty-two per cent of men thought that men should do any housework (Kawasaki 1996b: 34).

16. Most married men's active involvement in the home was limited to decision making with regard to structural issues or buying expensive fittings such as kitchens and baths (see Chapter 1).

17. Nakano lists a number of popular terms used to mock the alienation of retired men, among them the widely cited *sodai gomi*, literally 'a large-size piece of trash' (Nakano 2005: 52).

18. The term *tanshin fujin* refers to the often forceful work transfers to distant branches of a company that may separate men from their families for long periods of time.

19. Mrs Terayama proudly mentioned that her husband is fluent in English because of his frequent foreign trips, but added that he never takes her anywhere.

20. In many jokes a daughter's inability to marry is linked with the maltreatment of her dolls, given in the hope that she would find a good husband. Misfortune in marriage was often blamed on the fact that they either did not display their hina-dolls at all – or displayed them for too long.

21. In comics, films and other forms of popular culture the *sarariiman* is either depicted as a victim or a figure of fun (Matsunaga 1990: 152).

22. Moreover, as a recent collection of essays edited by Roberson and Suzuki (2003) demonstrates, many Japanese men are also exploring alternative masculine identities. Examples range from queer men and single male construction workers to fathers sharing childcare.

23. Most men do not engage in housework. However, Nakano has argued that some retired men have appropriate the feminine role of carers through engaging in community volunteer projects. These men

will clean tables, do dishes and vacuum floors in public, but they would not engage in this kind of activity in private (Nakano 2005).

24. For larger, structural work, such as resurfacing their balcony, the Nakaos hired professionals.
25. Most married women continue to be economically dependent on their husbands, and as a consequence when marital relationships break down the situation tends to be more dire for them.

CHAPTER 5. STUFF AND STORAGE

1. The Misawa company has been producing the 'kura-house' since the beginning of the 1990s and, in 1996, it won the 'Good Design Grand Prize'.
2. Another unexpected benefit of the storage room mentioned in the catalogue is its positive effect on children. First, it is a dark, mysterious space where they can play with friends, and, second, it is claimed that when children see family treasures kept in these spaces 'they will become conscious of the existence of their ancestors and the way people are linked, and they will start to treat things with respect' (Misawa Homes 2003: 81). By contrast, in folk tales old storehouses are often depicted as uncanny places where troublesome objects such as dolls may come alive. The *kura* evoked particularly unpleasant memories for one of my participants who during his childhood was often locked into the *kura* as punishment for naughty behaviour.
3. I have no data about whether or not kura-houses actually help to reduce the number of things people keep in their everyday living spaces.
4. Repeated destructive fires also led to the development of a chest on wheels (*nagamochi kuruma*) that was placed close to the entrance so that clothing and personal possessions could be wheeled off in case of a fire (Hanley 1997: 44).
5. *Kura* are still a common sight in places that have preserved a 'traditional' housing stock, such as some parts of contemporary Kyoto; most continue to be used as storehouse, but some have also been put to new, often commercial uses such as craft shops or art galleries.
6. After her parents passed away, they turned the second floor of her family home into two rental apartments.
7. The creation of new storage methods during the eighteenth century has been linked with the drastic increase in consumer goods, especially clothing, in the home (Hanley 1997: 43–4). Portable storage tools such as containers and chests of drawers (*tansu*) were previously used, but the variety of storage chests increased and new storage solutions such as storage rooms developed (Koizumi 1980: 110–1).
8. The word *kagu*, literally household goods, referred to all the movable articles in the home. Only after the introduction of Western-style furniture has the term been primarily linked with furniture (Sand 1996: 177).
9. Unlike Western clothing, kimonos are stored away folded into flat packs placed in special covers made of rice paper that protect garments against humidity and insects.
10. Rural Japan participated equally in this new consumer culture. Television played a crucial role in the dissemination of a 'mainstream' lifestyle all over Japan, as ownership jumped from fifty-five per cent in 1960 to ninety-five per cent in 1964 (Partner 1999: 140).
11. The 'three sacred containers' is a slogan framed during the 1950s that refers to the television, the washing machine and the refrigerator. There was mass consumption of these domestic goods during the post-war affluence, but since the beginning of the twenty-first century the three must-have treasures have become the wide-screen television, the DVD player and the digital camera (AS 2004: 45).
12. For example, beds were passed on as heirlooms because of their intrinsic worth and connection with family history (on the practice in eighteenth-century France, see Auslander 1996: 274).
13. Some smaller dowry items such as tiered, lacquered boxes and beautifully decorated plates destined for disposal ended up in my possession.
14. In the Kansai region the man's family gives betrothal gifts consisting of a sum of money equivalent to three months wages (or approximately ¥1,000,000 (about £5,000)). The woman's family will reciprocates

ten percent of this money to the groom's family, while in the Kantô region (from Nagoya northwards) the woman's family is expected to return about half the value of the initial gift.

15. After four years of university education most women will return home to live with their parents until they marry.

16. Employees at Misawa Homes argued that because land is so expensive only large conglomerates of developers are able to buy large-size properties. To maximize profit they will either built high-rises or divide the property into tiny lots.

17. In 1998 sixty per cent of all homes in Japan were owned (AS 2004: 189). The ideal of home ownership only became widespread during the post-war period when the number of houses provided by the government was largely insufficient and in order to ease the housing crisis beneficial short-term loans were offered to home buyers (Yamashita 2003: 70–5; Uchida 2002: 75).

18. Those working for the army, civil servants and managers in the private sector are expected to move regularly because of job transfers. However, once a family home is purchased the family tends to stay put, while the breadwinner either commutes for long hours or lives away from home in rented accommodation.

CHAPTER 6. TROUBLESOME THINGS

1. Most Western literature about tourism assumes that souvenirs are primarily purchased for personal consumption and that they have a commemorative function (Littrell et al., 1993: 198, Shenhav-Keller, 1995: 149–51). A notable exception is the study by Mars and Mars (2000) of ceramic souvenirs from Blackpool, which were bought by working-class women between 1880 and the 1950s as gifts for their mothers (ibid.: 99–100).

2. *Meibutsu* literally means 'things (*butsu*) for which an area is famous (*mei*)'. The first famous durable souvenirs were crafts that were small, light and not too fragile to be transported on foot (Kanzaki 1997: 148).

3. As early as the seventeenth century a Japanese consumer culture developed around travel to famous places. Knowledge about these places was circulated through all strata of the population via travel diaries and collections of visual representations, such a woodblock prints (Shirahata 1995: 60).

4. In 2003 SARS had a negative impact on international travel. However, in the other years between 2000 and 2004 approximately 17 million Japanese travelled abroad. This said, this is still only seventeen per cent of the population, and for most Japanese foreign travel remains very expensive. A traveller spends on average ¥169,000 (about £850) to travel abroad, while average costs for a domestic trip are only ¥29,500 (about £150) (AS 2004: 244 and 2006: 255).

5. All families studied possessed a large number of photographs, but except from formal pictures taken at special events such as graduations, these were generally stored away in albums. The placing of informal snapshots in the domestic interior is a relatively new practice that is most common among the younger generation. This topic would merit further investigation.

6. By contrast, those decorative gifts that they appreciate were given a prominent space in their home. A colourful painting, 'by a famous artist', which they had received from a Mexican friend, for example, hung on the wall above their dining table, where they spent most of their time.

7. Although boys also receive dolls, the correlation between girls and dolls is much stronger.

8. Ichimatsu dolls have been produced since the eighteenth century. Their head consists of a mixture of sawdust and glue with a special coating and the body is made of papier-mâché or wood with textile joints. The hair is either real human hair or silk, and they have glass eyes. The dolls wear kimonos as they are realistic representations of children clothed in the outfits they traditionally wear to visit religious centres to celebrate their third, fifth and seventh birthdays (Baten 2000: 107). Initially Ichimatsu dolls were used as toys, but these days they are expensive crafts placed in glass cases and commonly displayed in Japanese-style rooms. During May 2003 an exhibition and sale of Kyoto Ichimatsu dolls was held at the Maruzen bookstore in Kyoto City. Prices for standard-size dolls started at ¥40,000 (about £200), but some dolls cost more than ¥100,000 (about £500).

9. The origin of the word *hina* is *hiina* or 'miniature objects'. Originally miniature dolls made of paper or clay were used as embodiments of the deities during religious ceremonies (Mingu Jiten 1997: 477).

10. Although in principle hina-dolls are not toys, in some homes sets had become damaged or incomplete through years of handling by children and grandchildren.

11. This focus on the mimetic quality of faces should be seen in the light of common associations between the face and personhood in Japan (see Schattschneider 2004: 148–9)

12. Temples all over Japan regularly organize special memorial services for dolls in which they are ritually burned. In recent years these photogenic ceremonies have become hugely popular tourist events.

13. For most lifecycle events money is the preferred gift. Because of its unambiguous exchange value, money can easily be assessed within a series of past gifts given and received (Brumann 2000: 238). Depending on the age of the giver and his/her relationship with the recipient clear rules exist about the appropriate amount of money given (Kuraishi et al. 2000: 148). The presentation of money adheres to strict rules: bills need to be brand new, given in an odd, auspicious, number and they have to be placed in an envelope appropriately decorated for the occasion.

14. The commodification and professionalization of Japanese gift exchange has been largely ignored in publications before 1985 (Befu 1966, 1983; Lebra 1975). One reason for this might be that this is a relatively new phenomenon that only occurred during the late 1970s (Ito 1995: 113–8; Ishii 1994: 190). However, another reason for the lack of interest in this important aspect of exchange is that Japanese research about gifting has been dominated by attempts to link contemporary gift exchange with the food-commensality model developed by folklorists during the first half of the twentieth century. We have to wait until 1995 for a concise study that places Japanese gifting within broader anthropological gift theories and critiques the strong focus on the exchange of food (Ito 1995). Finally, considering that Japan is an interesting example of a contemporary gift society, it is surprising that the first comprehensive English-language study about contemporary gift practices based on long-term fieldwork was only published in 2003 (Rupp 2003). Rupp's work offers an array of interesting ethnographic examples of how people negotiate the contradictions and pressures of gift exchange. However, her conclusions do not extend far beyond challenging the much-discussed gift/commodity distinction. Of course, many readers might recall Hendry's 1993 study about presentation in Japanese gift exchange. Although her work sheds light on the wrapping and circulation of utilitarian gifts such as towels, its overall focus differs considerably from my research as Hendry endeavours to demonstrate that 'wrapping' is a form of non-verbal communication characteristic of most aspects of Japanese life, such as the wrapping of space, thoughts and the body

15. During my fieldwork some gifts continued to be personally delivered. Most commonly these were from neighbours or friends who would drop by to hand over small gifts, primarily souvenirs, casually.

16. A large percentage of these kind of gifts are 'return-gifts' (*oiwai no okaeshi*) for money given at lifecycle events or important personal occasions. These goods are generally less ephemeral, but because they can easily be integrated into domestic routines their form will eventually disappear through use (Daniels 2009a).

17. During a previous ethnography about Japanese tourism (Daniels 2001a) I found that retailers sold certain souvenirs of less reputable quality because their main customers were schoolchildren with little money to spare.

18. The verb *shôhi* as well as *shômô* can be translated as 'consumption', but the former has the connotation of spending and refers to the act of purchase while the latter refers to the actual physicality of using up things.

19. Moeran and Skov have eloquently summarized the scale of the yearly Japanese gift cycle as follows

> Christmas leads to New Year, which itself is linked with the Coming of Age Day (15 January), which leads to Valentine's Day, which is inseparable from White Day (11 March) which harks back to Girl's Day (3 March) and forwards to Boy's Day (5 May), which themselves are part of Mother's Day (10 May), not to mention Father's Day (6 June), or Old People's Day (15 September), and so

on and so on. (1993: 123–4)

20. Most people were less resistant to buying second-hand durable goods that the previous owner had only had a short relationship with, such as books or childrens' clothes and toys. Gregson and Crewe have also pointed to the popularity of these three commodity types among the participants in their UK study who recycled them as a reaction against the wastefulness of the first cycle of consumption (2003: 126). By contrast, none of those participating in my study expressed a similar concern about the ethics of consumption, but the potential danger of objects that have been neglected for a long time was frequently highlighted.

CONCLUSIONS: FRICTIONS, GAPS AND BLOCKAGES

1. Tsing (2005) has argued that it is in the messy, heterogeneous, unequal encounters, that she calls 'frictions', that 'cultures are continuously co-produced' (2005: 3).
2. This view is by no means limited to 'Western' researchers. See Ochiai (1996) for a Japanese example.
3. Since the 1980s, with the publication of Appadurai's seminal work *The Social Life of Things* (1986), most anthropologists acknowledge that, like people, objects have life histories. As things move through time and space, people will engage with them through a variety of practices and thereby continuously invest them with new meanings. Although innovative at the time, this approach has also resulted in an avalanche of studies that tend to give sole primacy to the intentionality of people. Thomas (1999), for example, offers an interesting critique.
4. By contrast, anthropological research in Asia has centred on ethical codes and relationships of obligation (Smith 1974).
5. One of the direct consequences of the modern attitude and the divide between people and things is the artificial distinction between the academic disciplines, whereby anthropologists study people and ideas, while archaeologists focus on the material world.
6. A growing body of anthropological literature challenges the assumption that magic is the antithesis of modernity (Moore and Sanders 2001; Meyers and Pels 2003).
7. However, the Japanese case also warns against the danger of associating otherworldliness with superiority as this may result in both essentialism and exoticism. Indeed, while foreigners have used the importance of spirits to exoticize Japan, domestic essentialist researchers have drawn on the specificity of Japanese spirituality to prove cultural uniqueness.
8. In Japan the market and religion are not seen as opposed, and religious activities can have economic goals (see Chapter 3). Thus, temples and shrines as well as commercial companies, have successfully capitalized on the necessary renewal of lucky objects.
9. In all fairness to Carsten, in her 1997 monograph about Malay kinship, she includes one chapter entitled 'The House' which pays attention to the material world with sections about building, moving and enlarging houses, house-plans and functions of rooms, mundane practices such as cooking and sharing food, sleeping arrangements and receiving guests. She even includes some discussions about display cabinets, storage and kitchen utensils.
10. See Miller's 2001 edited volume for an overview of material culture studies approaches to the study of the home.

BIBLIOGRAPHY

Ackermann, P. (1997), 'The Four Seasons: One of Japanese Culture's Most Central Concepts', in A. Kalland and P. Asquith (eds), *Japanese Images of Nature*, Richmond: Curzon Press.

Allison, A. (1994), *Nightwork: Sexuality, Pleasure, and Corporate Masculinity in a Tokyo Hostess Club*, Chicago: University of Chicago Press.

Allison, A. (2006), *Millenial Monsters: Japanese Toys and the Global Imagination*, Berkeley, CA: University of California Press.

Aoki, T. (2001), *Danchi 2DK no kurashi: saigen-showa 30 nendai* (Life in a 2DK Danchi: The Re-appearance of the 1955s), Tokyo: Kawade shobo.

Aoyagi, H. (2005), *Islands of Eight Million Smiles: Idol Performance and Symbolic Production in Contemporary Japan*, Cambridge, MA: Harvard University Asia Center.

Appadurai, A. (ed.) (1986), *Social Life of Things*, Cambridge: Cambridge University Press.

Asad, T. (1993) *Genealogies of Religion*, Baltimore, MD: The John Hopkins University Press.

Asahi Shinbunsha (AS) (2002), *The Japan Almanac 2003*. Tokyo: Asahi Shinbunsha

Asahi Shinbunsha (AS) (2003), *The Japan Almanac 2004*. Tokyo: Asahi Shinbunsha

Asahi Shinbunsha (AS) (2005), *The Japan Almanac 2006*. Tokyo: Asahi Shinbunsha

Ashkenazi, M. (2000), 'Swords, Collectors and Kula Exchanges', in M. Ashkenazi and J. Clammer (eds), *Consumption and Material Culture in Contemporary Japan*, London: Kegan Paul International.

Attfield, J. (1999), 'Bringing Modernity Home: Open Plan in the British Domestic Interior', in I. Cieraad (ed.), *At Home. An Anthropology of Domestic Space*, Syracuse, NY: Syracuse University Press.

Attfield, J. (2000), *Wild Things: The Material Culture of Everyday Life*, Oxford: Berg.

Auslander, L. (1996), 'The Gendering of Consumer Practices in Nineteenth Century France', in V. de Grazia (ed.), *The Sex of Things*, Berkeley, CA: University of California Press

Bakewell, L. (1998), 'Image Acts', *American Anthropologist*, 100: 12–22.

Barthes, R. (1964), *Image, Music, Text*, New York: Hill and Wang.

Baten, L. (2000), *Identifying Japanese Dolls: Notes on Ningyô*, Leiden: Hotei Publications.

Beauchamp, E. (ed.) (1998), *Women and Women's Issues in Post-World War II Japan*, London: Garland Publishing Inc.

Becker, H. (1982), *Art Worlds*, Berkeley, CA: University of California Press.

Befu, H. (1983), 'Gift-Giving in a Modernizing Japan', *Monumenta Nipponica*, 23: 445–56.

Belk, R. (1995), *Collecting in a Consumer Society*, London: Routledge.

Bell, S. and Coleman, S. (eds) (1999), 'Enduring Themes and Future Possibilities', in *The Anthropology of Friendship*, Oxford: Berg.

Ben-Ari, E. (1991), *Changing Japanese Suburbia: A Study of Two Present-Day Localities*, London and New York: Kegan Paul International.

Bestor, T. (1989), *Neighborhood Tokyo*, Stanford, CA: Stanford University Press.

Bestor, T. (2004), *Tsukiji: The Fish Market at the Center of the World*, Berkeley, CA: University of California Press.

Bishop, B. (2005), *Globalization and Women in the Japanese Workforce*, London: RoutledgeCurzon.

Black. A. and Murata, N. (2000), *The Japanese House: Architecture and Interiors*, London: Tuttle Publishing

Blier-Preston, S. (1987), *The Anatomy of Architecture*, Cambridge: Cambridge University Press.

Blomley, N. (2005), 'Flowers in the Bathtub: Boundary Crossings at the Public–Private Divide', *Geoforum*, 36: 281–96.

Boling, P. (1990), 'Private Interest and the Public Good in Japan', *The Pacific Review*, 3: 138–50.

Bonnett, A. (2005), 'Occidentalism and Plural Modernities: Or How Fukuzawa and Tagore Invented the West', *Environment and Planning D: Society and Space*, 23: 505–25.

Bourdieu, P. [1970] (1973), 'The Berber House or the World Reversed', in M. Douglas (ed.), *Rules and Meanings*, Harmondsworth: Penguin.

Bourdieu, P. [1972] (1979), 'The Kabyle House or the World Reversed', in P. Bourdieu, *Algeria 1960*, Cambridge: Cambridge University Press.

Bourdieu, P. [1979] (1984), *Distinction*, Cambridge, MA: Harvard University Press.

Bourdieu, P. [1980] (1990), 'The Kabyle House or the World Reversed', in P. Bourdieu, *The Logic of Practice*, Stanford, CA: Stanford University Press.

Bourdieu, P. [1997] (2000), *Pascalian Meditations*, Stanford, CA: Stanford University Press.

Bourdieu, P. (2003), 'Participant Objectivation', *Journal of the Royal Anthropological Institute*, 9: 281–94.

Broadbent, K. (2003), *Women's Employment in Japan: The Experience of Part-Time Workers*, London: RoutledgeCurzon.

Brown, A. and Cali, J. (2001), *The Japanese Dream House: How Technology and Tradition are Shaping New Home Design*, Tokyo: Kodansha International.

Brown, M. (1996), 'On Resisting Resistance', *American Anthropologist*, 98: 729–35.

Brumann, C. (2000), 'Materialistic Culture: The Uses of Money in Tokyo Gift Exchanges', in M. Ashkenazi and J. Clammer (eds), *Consumption and Material Culture in Contemporary Japan*, London: Kegan Paul International.

Brumann, C. (2001), 'Machiya vs.manshion', *Japan Studien*, 13: 153–92.

Buchli, V. (1999), *An Archaeology of Socialism*, Oxford: Berg.

Buckley, S. (1996), 'A Guided Tour of the Kitchen: 7 Japanese Domestic Tales', *Environment and Planning D: Society and Space*, 14: 441–61.

Campbell, C. (1987), *The Romantic Ethic and The Spirit of Modern Consumerism*, Cambridge: Blackwell.

Carrier, J. (1995), *Gifts and Commodities*, London: Routledge.

Carsten, J. (1997), *The Heart of The Hearth: The Process of Kinship in a Malay Fishing Community*, Oxford: Clarendon

Carsten, J. and Hugh-Jones, S. (eds) (1995), *About the House*, Cambridge: Cambridge University Press.

CDI & CORE (1980), *Katei ni okeru shôhin kôsei kara mita raifusutairu no kenkyû* (Research that Investigates Lifestyle through Material Culture of the Home), Kyoto: CDI Publishing.

CDI & CORE (1983), *Mono kara mita raifu sutairu setaiza to jidai* henka (Material Culture and Life Style; Generational Change), Kyoto: CDI Publishing.

CDI & CORE (1987), *Seikatsuzai nohobun to sairyûtsû* (The Disposal and Recirculation of Possessions), Kyoto: CDI Publishing.

CDI & CORE (1993), *'Yutaka na seikatsu' he no resutora* (Towards 'A Better Way of Life'), Kyoto: CDI Publishing.

Chaplin, E. (1994), *Sociology and Visual Representation*, London: Routledge.

Chapman, T. and Hockey, J. (1999), *Ideal Homes? Social Change and Domestic Life*, London: Routledge.

Chevalier, S. (1998), 'From Woolen Carpet to Grass Carpet: Bridging House and Garden in an English Suburb', in D. Miller (ed.), *Material Cultures*, London: UCL Press.

Chevalier, S. (1999), 'Destins des cadeaux', *Ethnologie Francaise*, 28: 506–14.

Cieraad, I. (ed.) (1999), *At Home: An Anthropology of Domestic Space*, Syracuse, NY: Syracuse University Press.

Clammer, J. (1997), *Contemporary Urban Japan – A Sociology of Consumption*, Oxford: Blackwell.

Clammer, J. (2000), 'Received Dreams: Consumer Capitalism, Social Process, and the Management of the Emotions in Contemporary Japan', in H. Befu, J. Eades and T. Gill (eds), *Globalization and Social Change in Contemporary Japan*, Melbourne: Trans Pacific Press.

Clarke. A. (2001), 'The Aesthetics of Social Aspiration', in D. Miller (ed.), *Home Possessions*, Oxford: Berg.

Clarke. A. (2002), 'Taste Wars and Design Dilemmas: Aesthetic Practice in the Home', in C. Painter (ed.) *Contemporary Art and the Home*, Oxford: Berg.

Clifford, J. and Marcus, G. (ed.) (1986), *Writing Culture: The Poetics and Politics of Ethnography.* Berkeley, CA: University of California Press.

Cole, R. (1971), *Japanese Blue Collar: The Changing Tradition*, Berkeley, CA: University of California Press.

Colloredo-Mansfeld, R. (1998), *The Native Leisure Class: Consumption and Cultural Creativity in the Andes*, Chicago: University of Chicago Press.

Colloredo-Mansfeld, R. (2003a), 'Consuming: Andean Televisions', *Journal of Material Culture,* 8: 273–84.

Colloredo-Mansfeld, R. (2003b), 'Introduction: Matter Unbound', *Journal of Material Culture* 8: 245–54.

Conrad, H. and Saaler, S. (2001), 'Wohnen in Japan: Markt, Lebensformen, Wohnverhaltnisse', *Japan Studien*, 13: 17– 48.

Cook, I. and Crang, M. (2007), *Doing Ethnographies*, London: Sage.

Csikszentmihalyi, M. and Rochberg-Halton, E. (1981), *The Meaning of Things*, Cambridge: Cambridge University Press.

Csordas, T. (1994), *Embodiment and Experience*, Cambridge: Cambridge University Press.

Cwerner, S and Metcalfe, A. (2003), 'Storage and Clutter: Discourses and Practices of Order in the Domestic World', *Journal of Design History*, 16: 229–39.

Cwiertka, K. (1999), *The Making of Modern Culinary Tradition in Japan*, Leiden: Leiden University.

Dalby, L. [1993] (2001), *Kimono: Fashioning Culture*, London, Vintage Random House.

Dale, P. (1986), *The Myth of Japanese Uniqueness*, Oxford: Croom Helm and the Nissan Institute.

Danforth, L. and Tsiaras, A. (1982), *The Death Rituals in Rural Greece*, Princeton, NJ: Princeton University Press.

Daniels, I. (1994), 'Japan: nationalisme als disciplinering', in R. Detrez and J. Blommaert (eds), *Nationalisme: kritische opstellen*, EPO: Berchem.

Daniels, I. (1996), Shamoji wo tôshitemiru Nihonjin no seishin bunka (The rice scoop and the spiritual life of the Japanese), MA dissertation, Department of Cultural Geography, Nara Women's University, Japan.

Daniels, I. (2001a), The Fame of Miyajima: Spirituality,Commodification and the Tourist Trade of Souvenirs in Japan, PhD dissertation, Department of Anthropology, University College London, UK.

Daniels, I. (2001b), 'The "Untidy" Japanese House', in D. Miller (ed.), *Home Possessions*, Oxford: Berg.

Daniels, I. (2003), 'Scooping, Raking, Beckoning Luck: Luck, Agency and the Interdependence between People and Things in Japan', *Journal of the Royal Anthropological Institute*, 9(4): 619–38.

Daniels, I. (2005a), 'Empty Guest rooms: Intimacy in the Japanese Home', paper presented at V&A Privacy Conference, London, June 4–5.

Daniels, I. (2008), 'Japanese Homes Inside Out', *Home Cultures*, 5: 115–40.

Daniels, I. (2009a), 'The "Social Death" of Unused Gifts: Loss and Value in Contemporary Japan', *Journal of Material Culture*, 14(2).

Daniels, I. (2009b), 'The Commercial and Domestic Rhythms of Japanese Consumption', in E. Shove, F. Trentmann and R. Wilk (eds), *Time, Consumption and Everyday Life: Practice, Materiality and Culture*, London: Routledge.

Daniels, I. (2009c), '"Dolls are Scary": What Constitutes Japanese Religious Activity?', In D. Morgan (ed.), *Religion and Material Culture: A Matter of Belief*, London: Routledge.

DeCerteau, M. (1984), *The Practice of Everyday Life*, Berkeley, CA: University of California Press.

De Vos, G. (1982), *Ethnic Minority*, Chicago: Chicago University Press.

De Vos, G. and Wetherall, W. (1983), *Japan's Minorities*, London: Minority Rights Group.

Dittmar, H. (1992), *The Social Psychology of Material Possessions*, New York: St Martin's Press.

Dore, R. (1958), *City Life in Japan: A Study of a Tokyo Ward*, Berkeley, CA: University of California Press.

Douglas, M. (1975), *Implicit Meanings: Essays in Anthropology*, London: Kegan Paul.

Drummond, L. (2000), 'Street Scenes: Practices of Public and Private Space in Urban Vietnam', *Urban Studies*, 37(12): 2377–91.

Edwards, E. (1992), *Anthropology and Photography 1860–1920*, New Haven, CT and London: Yale University Press.

Enders, S. (1987), 'Wohntypen', in R. Herold (ed.), *Wohnen in Japan*, Berlin: Schmidt Verlag.

Engel, H. (1964), *The Japanese House*, Rutland: Charles & Tuttle Company.

Faier, L. (2007), 'Filipina Migrants in Rural Japan and their Professions of Love', *American Ethnologist*, 34: 148–62.

Farquhar, J. (2002), *Appetites: Food and Sex in Post-Socialist China*, Durham, NC: Duke University Press.

Fawcett, C. (1980), *The New Japanese House: Ritual and Anti-Ritual Patterns of Dwelling*, London: Granada Publishing.

Figal, G. (1999), *Civilization and Monsters: Spirits of Modernity in Meiji Japan*, Durham, NC and London: Duke University Press.

Fishburne Collier, J. (1997), *From Duty to Desire*, Princeton, NJ: Princeton University Press.

Fogelin, L. (2007), 'The Archaeology of Religious Ritual', *Annual Review of Anthropology*, 36: 55–71.

Freeman, M. (2004), *Space: Japanese Design Solutions*, London: Universe Publishing.

Friedman, S. (2005), 'The Intimacy of State Power', *American Ethnologist*, 32: 312–27.

Fujiwara, T. (2003), *Tatakau maihomu* (Fighting in 'My Home'), Tokyo: Kosaido.

Funo, S. (1997), *Sumai no yumei to yumei no sumai* (The Dream of Living and Living a Dream), Tokyo: Asahi Shinbunsha.

Garvey, P. (2005), 'Domestic Boundaries: Privacy, Visibility, and the Norwegian Window', *Journal of Material Culture*, 7: 157–76.

Giddens, A. (1991), *The Consequence of Modernity*, Cambridge: Polity Press.

Gill, T. (2001), *Men of Uncertainty: The Social Organization of Day Laborers in Contemporary Japan*, Albany, NY: SUNY Press.

Goldstein-Gidoni, O. (1997), *Packaged Japaneseness*, Richmond: Curzon Press.

Good, B. (1994), *Medicine, Rationality, and Experience: An Anthropological Perspective*, New York: Cambridge University Press.

Goodman, R. (1990), *Japan's 'International Youth': The Emergence of a New Class of School Children*, Oxford: Clarendon Press.

Graham, F. (2003), *Inside the Japanese Company*, London: Routledge/Curzon.

Gregson, N. (2007), *Living with Things: Ridding, Accommodation, Dwelling*, Wantage: Sean Kingston Publishing.

Gregson, N. and Beale, V. (2004), 'Wardrobe Matter: The Sorting, Displacement and Circulation of Women's Clothing', *Geoforum*, 35: 689–700.

Gregson, N. and Crewe, L. (2003), *Second-hand Cultures*, Oxford: Berg.

Gregson, N., Metcalfe, A. and Crewe, L. (2007), 'Identity, Mobility and the Throwaway Society', *Environment and Planning D*, 25: 682–700.

Grimshaw, A. (2001), *An Ethnographer's Eye: Ways of Seeing in Anthropology*, Cambridge: Cambridge University Press.

Gullestad, M. (1984), *Kitchen Table Society: A Case Study of the Family Life and Friendship of Young Working Class Mothers in Urban Norway*, Oslo: Universitetsforlaget.

Haga, K. (1989), 'The Wabi Aesthetic through the Ages', P. Varley and I. Kumakura (eds), *Tea in Japan*, Honolulu: University of Hawai'i Press.

Halle, D. (1993), *Inside Culture: Art and Class in the American Home*, Chicago: University of Chicago Press.

Hanley, S. (1997), *Everyday Things in Premodern Japan –The Hidden Legacy of Material Culture*, Berkeley, CA: University of California Press.

Harper, D. (2002), 'Talking about Pictures: A Case for Photo Elicitation', *Visual Studies*, 17: 13–26.

Hashidate, M. (1990), 'Kyukamidanimura seikatsuyôgu chôsajôho', Bunkazai *Kenkyu Kiyô* (Research Bulletin into Cultural Assets), 4: 118–40.

Hashidate, M. (2002), 'Mono kara miru nenjû gyôji sono 2', *Shizuokaken Minzokugakushi* (Shizuoka Prefecture Folklore Studies Journal), 23: 48–58.

Hayashi, M. (1996), 'Koyomi no hensen to rokuyô (The Changes in the Calendar and the Six Days)', in S. Shimazono and K. Ishii (eds), *Shôhi saren shûkyo* (The Consumption of Religion), Tokyo: Shunjusha.

Helliwell, C. (1996), 'Space and Sociality in a Dayak Longhouse', in M. Jackson (ed.), *Things as They Are: New Directions in Phenomenological Anthropology*, Bloomington, IN: University of Indiana Press.

Hendry, J. (1986), *Becoming Japanese: The World of the Pre-School Child*, Honolulu: University of Hawai'i Press.

Hendry, J. (1987), *Becoming Japanese: The World of the Pre-School Child*, Honolulu: University of Hawaii Press.

Hendry, J. (1997), 'Pine, Ponds and Pebbles: Gardens and Visual Culture', in M. Banks and H. Morphy (eds), *Rethinking Visual Anthropology*, New Haven, CT and London: Yale University Press.

Hendry, J. (2000), *The Orient Strikes Back: A Global View of Cultural Display*, Oxford: Berg.

Herold, R. (1987), *Wohnen in Japan*, Berlin: Eric Schmidt Verlag.

Hetherington, K. (2004), 'Secondhandness: Consumption, Disposal, and Absent Presence', *Environment and Planning D: Society and Space*, 22 (1): 152–73.

Hillier, J and Rooksby, E. (eds) (2002), *Habitus: A Sense of Place*, Surrey: Ashgate Publishing.

Hodder, I. (1986), *Reading the Past*, Cambridge: Cambridge University Press.

Hsu, Elizabeth (1998), 'Moso and Naxi: The House', in M. Oppitz and E. Hsu (eds), *Naxi and Moso Ethnography: Kin, Rites, Pictographs*, Zurich: Volkerkundemuseum Zurich.

Hurdley, R. (2006), 'Dismantling Mantelpieces: Narrating Identities and Materializing Culture in the Home', *Sociology*, 40 (4): 717–33.

Imamura, A. (1987), *Urban Japanese Housewives: At Home in the Community*, Honolulu: University of Hawaii Press.

Inoue, M. (2003), 'Regendering Domestic Space', *Monumenta Nipponica*, 58: 79–102.

Ishii, K. (1994), *Toshi no nenjû gyôji* (Urban Annual Events), Tokyo: Shunkasha

Ishii-Kuntz, M. (2003), 'Balancing Fatherhood and Work: Emergence of Diverse Masculinities in Contemporary Japan', in J. Roberson and N. Suzuki (eds), *Men and Masculinities in Contemporary Japan: Dislocating the Salaryman Doxa*, London: RoutledgeCurzon.

Ishikawa, J. (2000), 'Nenjû gyôji kakusho', *Shizuokaken Minzokugakushi* (Shizuoka Prefecture Folklore Studies Journal), 21: 1–7.

Ishimoto, T. (1963), *The Japanese House: Its Interior and Exterior*, New York: Crown Publishers.

Ito, T. (1967), *The Essential Japanese House*, New York: Weatherhill.

Ito, T. (1969), *The Elegant Japanese House*, New York: Weatherhill.

Ito, M. (1995), *Zôyokôkan no jinruigaku* (An Anthropology of Gift Exchange), Tokyo: Chikuma

Ivy, M. (1995), *Discourses of the Vanishing: Modern, Modern Purpose Built or Refashioned Older-style City, Phantasm, Japan*, Chicago: University of Chicago Press.

Jeremy, M. and Robinson, M. (1989), *Ceremony and Symbolism in the Japanese Home*, Manchester: Manchester University Press.

Joyce, R. and Gillespie, S. (2000), *Beyond Kinship: Social and Material Reproduction in House Societies*, Philadelphia, PA: University of Pennsylvania Press.

Kanzaki, N. (1997), *Omiyage: Zôtô to tabi no nihon bunka* (Souvenir: Gift Giving and Travel in Japanese Culture), Tokyo: Aoyumisha.

Kaufmann, J. (1998), *Dirty Linen: Couples and their Laundry*, Middlesex: Middlesex University Press.

Kawano, S. (2005), *Ritual Practice in Modern Japan*, Honolulu: University of Hawai'i.

Kawasaki, E. (1996a), *Tsukiai wo tanoshimu sumai* (A Home in Which to Enjoy Sociality), Tokyo: Kagekunisha.

Kawasaki, E. (1996b), *Kaji to tatakau sumai* (Struggling with Domestic Duties), Tokyo: Kagekunisha.

Kawasaki, E. and Moteki, M. (2002), *Seikatsu bunka wo kangaeru* (Thoughts About the Culture of Everyday Life), Tokyo: Kanseikan.

Kawazone, N. (2004), *Kon wajirô: sono kôgengaku* (Kon Wajiro's Modernologio), Tokyo: Chikuma.

Keane, W. (1997), *Signs of Recognition*, Berkeley, CA: University of California Press.

Kelly, W. (1992), 'Tractors. Television and Telephone: Reach Out and Touch Someone in Rural Japan', in J. Tobin (ed.), *Re-made in Japan*, New Haven, CT: Yale University Press.

Kelly, W. (2002), 'At the Limits of New Middle Class Japan', in O. Zunz, L. Shoppa and N. Hiwatari (eds), *Social Contracts under Stress*, New York: Russell Sage Foundation.

Keyes, C. (1983), 'Introduction; The Study of Popular Ideas of Karma', in C. Keyes and V. Daniel (eds), *Karma: An Anthropological Inquiry*, Berkeley, CA: University of California Press.

Kiba, A. (1997), *Inyôgogyô* (Yin, Yang and the Five Elements), Tokyo: Tankosha.

Koizumi, K. (1980), *Kagu* (Furniture), Tokyo: Kinto shuppan.

Koizumi, K. (1995), *Shitsunai to kagu no rekishi* (A History of Home Interiors and Furniture), Tokyo: Chuo koronsha.

Koizumi, K. (2002), *Chabudai no showa* (The Low Dining Table during the Showa Period), Tokyo: Kawade shobo.

Kondo, D. (1990), *Crafting Selves: Power, Gender and Discourses of Identity in a Japanese Workplace*, Chicago: University of Chicago Press.

Kretschmer, A. (2000), *Kuyô in Contemporary Japan: Religious Rites in the Lives of Laypeople*, Gottingen: Cuvillier Verlag.

Kuhlmann, A. (1992), 'Collaborative Research Among the KIckapoo Tribe of Oklahoma', *Human Organization*, 51: 274–83.

Kuraishi, A., Komatsu, K. and Noboru, M. (eds) 2000. *Jinseigirei jiten* (Dictionary of Life Cycle Events). Tokyo: Shogakukan

Latour, B. (1993), *We Have Never Been Modern*, London: Harvester Wheatheaf

Latour, B. (2000), *Pandora's Hope: Essays on the Reality of Science,* Cambridge, MA: Harvard University Press.

Lebra, T. (1975), 'An Alternative Approach to Reciprocity', *American Anthropologist*, 77: 550–65.

Levi-Strauss, C. (1983), *The Way of the Mask*, London, Jonathan Cape.

Lie, J. (2001), *Multiethnic Japan*, Cambridge, MA: Harvard University Press.

Lipset, D. (2004), 'Modernity without Romance?', *American Ethnologist, 31*: 205–24.

Littrell, M., Anderson, L. and Brown. P. (1993), 'What Makes a Craft Souvenir Authentic?', *Annals of Tourism Research*, 20: 197–215.

Long, S. (2005), *Final Days: Japanese Culture and Choice at the End of Life*, Honolulu: University of Hawai'i.

Lozanovska, M. (2002), 'Architectural Frontier/Spatial Story', *Space and Culture*, 5: 140–51.

Lunsing, W. (2001), *Beyond Common Sense: Negotiating Constructions of Sexuality and Gender in Contemporary Japan*, London: Kegan Paul.

MacAllester, D and MacAllester, S. (1980), *Navajo Houses and Songs*, New York: Columbia University Press.

McCracken, G. (1989), 'Homeyness: A Cultural Account of One Constellation of Consumer Goods and Meanings', *Interpretive Consumer Research*, 168–83.

McCracken, G. (1990), *Culture and Consumption*, Bloomington, IN: Indiana University Press.

McDougall, D. (1998), *Transcultural Cinema*, Princeton, NJ: Princeton University Press

McDougall, D. (2005), *The Corporeal Image: Film, Ethnography, and the Senses*, Princeton, NJ: Princeton University Press.

McDougall, D. and Taylor, L. (eds) (1998), *Transcultural Cinema*, Princeton, NJ: Princeton University Press.

Mackenzie, M. (1992), *Androgynous Objects: String Bags and Gender in Central New Guinea*, Harwood Academic.

McVeigh, B. (2000), *Wearing Ideology: State, Schooling and Self-Presentation in Japan*, Oxford: Berg.

Marcoux, J.-S. (2004), 'Body Exchanges: Material Culture, Gender and Stereotypes in the Making', *Home Cultures*, 1: 51–60.

Marcus, G. (1995), 'Ethnography in/of the World System: Emergence of Multi-Sited Ethnography', *Annual Review of Anthropology*, 24: 95–117.

Mars, G. and Mars, V. (2000), 'Souvenir-gifts as Tokens of Filial Esteem: The Meanings of Blackpool Souvenirs', in M. Hitchcock and K. Teague (eds), *Souvenirs: The Material Culture of Tourism*, Farnham: Ashgate.

Martinez, D. (1995), 'Women and Ritual', in J. van Bremen and D. Martinez (eds), *Ceremony and ritual in Japan*, London: Routledge.

Matsunaga, L. (2000), *The Changing Face of Japanese Retail*, London, Routledge.

Mauss. M. (1967), *The Gift*, London: Cohen and West.

Mead, M. and Bateson, G. (1942) *Balinese Character*, New York: Academy of Sciences.

Meyer, B. and Pels, P. (eds) (2003), *Magic and Modernity*, Stanford, CA: Stanford University.

Miller, D. (1987), *Material Culture and Mass Consumption*, Oxford: Basil Blackwell.

Miller, D. (1988), 'Appropriating the Estate on the Council Estate', *Man*, 23: 353–72.

Miller, D. (1994), *Modernity: An Ethnographic Approach*, Oxford: Berg.

Miller, D. (1998a), *Material Cultures: Why Some Things Matter*, London: UCL Press.

Miller, D. (1998b), *A Theory of Shopping*, Cambridge: Polity Press.

Miller, D. (ed.) (2001), *Home Possessions*, Oxford: Berg.

Miller, D. (2008), *The Comfort of Things*, Cambridge: Polity Press.

Misawa Homes. (2003), *Misawa Homu no sumai* (Catalogue: Living in Misawa Homes), Tokyo: Misawa Publishing.

Miyawaki, M. (1998), *Miyawaki Mayumi no ii ie no hon -motto ie ni tsuite kangaete mimasen ka?* (Miyawaki Mayumi's Book About Good Houses – Let's Try and Think More About Homes?), Tokyo: PHP kenkyusho.

Moeran, B. (1983), 'The Language of Japanese Tourism', *Annals of Tourism Research*, 10: 93–108.

Moeran, B. (1996), *A Japanese Advertising Agency: An Anthropology of Media and Markets*, Richmond: Curzon Press.

Moeran, B. and Skov, L. (1993), 'Cinderella Christmas: Kitsch, Consumerism, and Youth in Japan', in D. Miller (ed.), *Unwrapping Christmas*, Oxford: Clarendon Press.

Moeran, B. and Skov, L. (1997), 'Mount Fuji and the Cherry Blossoms: A View from Afar,' in A. Kalland and P. Asquith (eds), *Japanese Images of Nature*, Richmond: Curzon Press.

Moore, H. (1986), *Space, Text, and Gender*, Cambridge: Cambridge University Press.

Moore, H. (1994), *A Passion for Difference: Essays in Anthropology and Gender*, Cambridge: Polity Press.

Moore, H. and Sanders, T. (eds) (2001), *Magical Interpretations, Material Realities*, London: Routledge.

Morgan, D. (1998), *Visual Piety: A history and Theory of Popular Religious Images*, Berkeley, CA: University of California Press.

Morse, E. (1886), *Japanese Homes and Their Surroundings*, London: Sampson Low.

Murakami, K. (2000), 'Changes in Japanese Urban Funeral Customs during the Twentieth Century', *Japanese Journal of Religious Studies*, 27: 335–52.

Murata, N. and Black, A. (2000), *The Japanese House: Architecture and Interiors*, London: Tuttle Publishing

Nakamura, K. (2006), *Deaf in Japan: Signing and the Politics of Identity*, London: Cornell University Press.

Nakano, L. (2005), *Community Volunteers in Japan: Everyday Stories of Social Change*, London: Routledge/Curzon.

National Institute of Population and Social Security Research, 1999, *National Survey on Singles in a Household 1996–1998*. Consulted at www.ipss.go.jp during January 2005.

Needham, R. (1972), *Belief, Language and Experience*, Oxford: Blackwell.

Nihon Mingu Jiten (Dictionary of Traditional Japanese Objects) (1997), Tokyo: Gyosei.

Nishiyama, U. (1942), *Jûtaku Mondai* (Dwelling Problems), Tokyo: Sagami Shobo.

Nishiyama, U. (1947), *Korekara no sumai* (Housing from Now On), Tokyo: Sagami Shobo.

Nishiyama, U. (1989), *Sumai kôgengaku–gendai nihonjûtakushi* (Empirical Studies of Contemporary Dwellings – A Modern History of the Japanese House), Tokyo: Shokokusha.

Nitta, F. (1992), 'Shopping for Souvenirs in Hawai'i', in J. Tobin (ed.), *Re-made in Japan*, New Haven, CT: Yale University Press.

Nitta, T., Tanaka, Y. and Koyama. S. (2003), *Tokyo ryûkô seikatsu* (Fashionable Lives in Tokyo), Tokyo: Kawade.

Ochiai, E. (1996), *The Japanese Family System in Transition*, Tokyo: Yuhikaku Publishing.

Ogasawara, Y. (1998), *Office Ladies and Salaried Men: Power, Gender, and Work in Japanese Companies*, Berkeley, CA: University of California Press.

Ogino, A. (2000), 'Kattesuzukeru nenjû gyôji to sono zenshûdan', *Shizuokaken Minzokugakushi* (Shizuoka Prefecture Folklore Studies Journal), 21: 57–70.

Olsen, B. (2003), 'Material Culture after Text: Re-Membering Things', *Norwegian Archaeological Review*, 36: 87–104.

Ornatowski, G. (1998),'On the Boundary between "Religious" and "Secular": The Ideal and Practice of Neo-Confucian Self-Cultivation in Modern Japanese Economic Life', *Japanese Journal of Religious Studies*: 345–76.

Oshima, B. (2000), 'Wagashiya to nenjû gyôji', *Shizuokaken Minzokugakushi* (Shizuoka Prefecture Folklore Studies Journal), 21: 70–2.

Ozaki, R. and Rees Lewis, J. (2006), 'Boundaries and the Meaning of Space: A Study of Japanese House Plans', *Environment and Planning D*, 24(1): 91–104.

Pader, E. (1993), 'Spatiality and Social Change: Domestic Space Use in Mexico and the United States', *American Ethnologist*, 20: 114–37.

Park, J, (1992), 'Research Partnership', *Women's Studies International Forum*, 15: 581–91.

Parry, J. (1985), 'The Gift, The Indian Gift and the "Indian" Gift', *Man*, 21: 453–73.

Partner, S. (1999), *Assembled in Japan: Electrical Goods and the Making of the Japanese Consumer*, Berkeley, CA: University of California Press.

Pearce, S. (1995), *On Collecting*, London: Routledge.

Pertierra, A. (2006), Battles, Invesions and Acquisitions, The Struggle for Consumption in Urban Cuba, PhD Thesis. Department of Anthropology UCL, London.

Pink, S. (2006), *Doing Visual Anthropology*, London: Sage Publications.

Pollock, N. (2005), *Modern Japanese House*, London: Phaidon Press.

Rabinow, P. (1977), *Reflections on Fieldwork in Morocco*, Berkeley, CA: University of California Press.

Reader, I. (1991a), *Religion on Contemporary Japan*, London: Macmillan Press Ltd.

Reader, I. (1991b), 'Letters to the Gods', *Japanese Journal for Religious Studies*, 18/1: 23–50.

Reader, I. and Tanabe, G. (1998), *Practically Religious: Worldly Benefits and the Common Religion of Japan*, Honolulu: University of Hawai'i.

Reimer, S. and Leslie, D. (2004), 'Identity, Consumption, and the Home', *Home Cultures*, 1(2): 187–208.

Robertson, J. (1991), *Native and Newcomer: Making and Remaking a Japanese City*, Berkeley, CA: University of California Press

Robertson, J. (1998), *Takarazuka: Sexual Politics and Popular Culture in Modern Japan*, Berkeley and Los Angeles, CA: University of California Press.

Roberson, J. and Suzuki, N. (eds) (2003), *Men and Masculinities in Contemporary Japan: Dislocating the Salaryman Doxa*, London: RoutledgeCurzon.

Rohlen, T. (1974), *For Harmony and Strength: Japanese White-Collar Organization in Anthropological Perspective*, Berkeley, CA: University of California Press.

Rohlen, T. (1983), *Japan's High Schools*, Berkeley, CA: University of California Press.

Ronald, R. (2004), 'Home Ownership, Ideology and Diversity: Re-evaluating Concepts of Housing Ideology in the Case of Japan', *Housing, Theory and Society*, 21: 49–64.

Roth, J. (2002), *Brokered Homeland: Japanese Brazilian Migrants in Japan*, Ithaca, NY and London: Cornell University Press.

Rowe, M. (2003), 'Grave Changes: Scattering Ashes in Contemporary Japan', *Japanese Journal of Religious Studies*, 30: 85–118.

Ruel, M. (1982) 'Christians as Believers', in John Davis (ed.), *Religious Organization and Religious Experience*, London: Academic Press.

Rupp, K. (2003), *Gift-giving in Japan*, Stanford, CA: Stanford University Press.

Sand, J. (1996), House and Home in Modern Japan, PhD dissertation, Columbia University.

Sand, J. (2000), 'Was Meiji Taste in Interiors "Orientalist"?', *Positions*, 8: 637–73.

Sand, J. (2003), *House and Home in Modern Japan*, Cambridge, MA: Harvard University Press.

Sangren, S. (2000), *Chinese Sociologics: An Anthropological Account of the Role of Alienation in Social Reproduction*, London: Athlone Press.

Sasaki, H. (1970), *The Modern Japanese House: Inside and Outside*, Tokyo: Japan Pub.

Sato, K. and Asakura, Y. (2002), *2002nen Souru sutairu* (Seoul Style 2002), Osaka: Kokuritsu minzoku hakubutsukan.

Sato, K. and Yamashita, R. (2002), *Futsûno seikatsu: Iisan ikka no 3200ten* (An Insight into Ordinary Lives – with the Lee Family), Tokyo: INAX.

Sawada, J. (2004), *Practical Pursuits: Religion, Politics, and Personal Cultivation in Nineteenth-Century Japan*, Honolulu: University of Hawai'i Press.

Schattschneider, E. (2004), 'Family Resemblances: Memorial Images and the Face of Kinship', *Japanese Journal of Religious Studies*, 31: 141–62.

Scheper-Hughes, N. (1995), 'The Primacy of the Ethical: Propositions for a Militant Anthropology', *Current Anthropology*, 36.

Schneider, A. and Wright, C. (eds) (2005), *Contemporary Art and Anthropology*, Oxford: Berg.

Shenhav-Keller, S. (1995), 'The Jewish Pilgrim and the Purchase of a Souvenir in Israel', In M. Lanfant and J. Allcock (eds), *International Tourism: Identity and Change*, London: Sage Publications.

Shirahata, Y. (1995), 'Information Studies of Tourist Resources', *Senri Ethnological Studies*, 38: 51–64.

Shove, E. (2003), *Comfort, Cleanliness and Convenience: The Social Organization of Normality*, Oxford: Berg.

Shove, E., Watson, M., Ingram, J. and Hand, M. (2008), *The Design of Everyday Life*, Oxford: Berg.

Singleton, J. (1967), *Nichu: A Japanese School*, New York: Holt, Rinehart and Winston.

Silverstein, P. (2004), 'Of Rooting and Uprooting: Kabyle Habitus, Domesticity, and Structural Nostalgia', *Ethnography*, 5: 553–78.

Skov, L. and Moeran, B. (1995), 'Introduction: Hiding in the Light: From Oshin to Yoshimoto Banana', in L. Skov and B. Moeran (eds), *Women, Media and Consumption in Japan*, Surrey: Curzon Press.

Smart, A. (1999), 'Expressions of Interest: Friendship and Guanxi in Chinese Societies', in S. Bell and S. Coleman (eds), *The Anthropology of Friendship*, Oxford: Berg.

Smith, R. (1974), *Ancestor Worship in Contemporary Japan*, Stanford, CA: Stanford University Press.

Smith, R. (1987), 'Gender Inequality in Contemporary Japan', *Journal of Japanese Studies*, 13: 1–25.

Sôgô josei rekishi kenkyûkai (Comprehensive women's history study group) 1993. *Nihon josei no rekishi – onna no hataraki* (A History of Japanese Women – A Woman's Labour), Tokyo: Kadakawa shoten.

Spielvogel, L. (2003), *Working Out in Japan: Shaping the Female Body in Tokyo Fitness Clubs*, Durham, NC: Duke University Press.

Srinivas, T. (2002), 'Flush with Success: Bathing, Defecation, Worship, and Social Change in South India', *Space and Culture*, 5: 368–86.

Stafford, B. (1998), *Good Looking: Essays on the Virtue of Images*, Cambridge, MA: MIT Press.

Stafford, C. (2000), *Separation and Reunion in Modern China*, Cambridge: Cambridge University Press.

Stasz, C. (1979), 'The Early History of Visual Sociology', in J. Wagner (ed.), *Images of Information: Still Photography in the Social Sciences*, Beverly Hills, CA and London; Sage.

Strathern, M. (1990), *The Gender of the Gift*, Berkeley, CA: University of California Press.

Suzuki, H. (2000), *The Price of Death: The Funerary Industry in Contemporary Japan*, Stanford, CA: Stanford University Press.

Suzuki, S.(2002a), *Sumai wo yomu – gendai nihon jûkyoron* (Examining Homes – A Theory of Contemporary Japanese Housing), Tokyo: Kenchiku shiryo kenkyusha.

Suzuki, S.(2002b), *Sumai wo mongataru* (Talking About Living), Tokyo: Kenchiku shiryo kenkyusha.

Taira, K. (1993), 'Dialectics of Economic Growth, National Power, and Distributive Struggles', in A. Gordon (ed.), *Postwar Japan as History*, Berkeley, CA: University of California Press.

Tambiah, S. (1985), 'A Performative Approach to Ritual', in S. Tambiah, *Culture, Thought and Social Action: An Anthropological Approach*, Cambridge, MA: Harvard University Press.

Tanazaki, J. 1977 (1933), *In Praise of Shadows*, London: Leete's Island Books.

Tanuma, S. (2007), 'Post-Utopian Irony', *Political and Legal Anthropology Review*, 30: 46–66.

Tatsumi, N. (2002), *Mooichido 'suteru' gijutsu–'mentenansu' no hôhô* (Disposal Skills Once Again – Maintenance), Tokyo: Takarajimasha

Taussig, M. (1993. *Mimesis and Alterity*, London: Routledge.

Taut, B. 1938 (1937). *Houses and People of Japan*, Tokyo: Sanseido. English translation.

Teasley, S. (2001), 'Nation Modernity and Interioir Decoration', *Japanstudien*, 13: 49–87.

Tedlock, B. (1991), 'From Participant Observation to the Participation of Observation', *Journal of Anthropological Research*, 47: 69–94.

Thang, L. (2001), *Generations in Touch: Linking the Old and Young in a Tokyo Neighborhood*, Ithaca, NY and London: Cornell University Press.

Thomas, N. (1999), 'The Case of the Misplaced Ponchoes', *Journal of Material Culture*, 4: 5–20.

Tilley, C. (2001), 'Ethnography and Material Culture', in P. Atkinson, A. Coffey et al. (eds), *The Handbook of Ethnography*, London: Sage.

Torres, G. (1997), *The Force of Irony: Power in the Everyday Life of Mexican Tomato Workers*, Oxford: Berg.

Traphagan, J. (2004), *The Practice of Concern: Ritual, Well-Being, and Aging in Rural Japan*, New York: Carolina Academic Press.

Tsing, A. (2005), *Friction: An Ethnography of Global Connection*, Princeton, NJ: Princeton University Press.

Tsuzuki, K. (1999), *Tokyo: A Certain Style*, San Francisco: Chronicle Books.

Uberoi, P. (1999), 'Times Past: Gender and the Nation in Calendar Art', *Indian Horizons*, 46: 24–39.

Uchida, S. (2002), *Kieta modan tokyo* (Modern City Tokyo), Tokyo: Awade Shobo.

Uchida, S., Ogawa, M. and Fujiya, Y. (eds) (2002), *Kindai nihon jûtakushi* (A History of Modern Japanese Dwellings), Tokyo: Kajima Publishing.

Ueda, A. (1998), *The Inner Harmony of the Japanese House*, Tokyo: Kodansh International.

Urushibana, H. (1999), Housing Policy and Design: The Role of Housing Policy and its Effects on Design in Japan and Britain, DPhil thesis, York.

Van der Horst, H. and Messing, J. (2006), 'It's Not Dutch to Close the Curtains', *Home Cultures*, 3: 21–37.

Vom Buck, G. (1997), 'A House Turned Inside Out: Inhabiting Space in a Yemeni City', *Journal of Material Culture*, 2: 139–72.

Waswo, A. (2002), *Housing in Postwar Japan: A Social History*, London: Routledge.

Watanabe, M. (2002), 'Datsuryokuka Shisutemu/Chirashi no machi (Incapacitated System/Noise City)', *10+1*, 26: 66–75.

Weiner, M. (1997), *Japan's Minorities: The Illusion of Homogeneity*, London: New York: Routledge.

Wiltshire, R. (1996), *Relocating the Japanese Worker*, Folkstone: Curzon Press.

Worth, S. (1972), *Through Navajo Eyes*. Bloomington, IN: Indiana University Press.

Wu, Y. (2004), *The Care of the Elderly in Japan*, London: Routledge.

Yagi, K. (1992), *A Japanese Touch for Your Home*, Tokyo: Kodansha International.

Yamashita, K. (2003), *Mochiie shinwa no susume* (The Popularity of the Home Ownership Myth), Tokyo: Heibonsha.

Yan, Y. (1996), *The Flow of Gifts: Reciprocity and Social Networks in a Chinese Village*, Stanford, CA: Stanford University Press.

Yan, Y. (2005), 'Making Room for Intimacy: Domestic Space and Conjugal Privacy in Rural North China', in R. Knapp and K. Lo (eds), *House, Home, Family: Living and Being Chinese*, Honolulu: University of Hawai'i Press.

Yanagita, K. (1951), *Minzokugaku Jiten* (Folklore Dictionary), Tokyo: Tôyôdo.

Yanagita, K. [1940] (1962), *Teihon Yanagita Kunioshû* (Collected Works of Yanagita Kunio), Tokyo: Chikuma Shobo.

Yasuda, A. (2002), 'Kôdan chintai seikatsu (Life in a Municipal Housing Development)', *10+1*, (26): 85–101.

Yoshida, T. (1935), *Das Japanische Wohnhaus,* Berlin: Ernst Wasmuth.

Young, D. (2004), 'The Material Value of Colour: The Estate Agent's Tale', *Home Cultures*, 1: 5–22.

FIGURES

INTRODUCTION

CHAPTER 1

CHAPTER 2

CHAPTER 3

CHAPTER 4

CHAPTER 5

CHAPTER 6

SUSAN ANDREWS'S PHOTOGRAPHS (2006)

CHAPTER 3

CHAPTER 4

CHAPTER 5

CHAPTER 6

CONCLUSION

INDEX

food
    consumption of, 35–6
    gifts of, 170–1
    preparation of, 35
footwear, slippers, 50–1
France, decorative style, 116–17
friendships, 74
frogs, lucky charms, 91–2, 164, 209n25
Fujin no tomo (Housewife's Friend) magazine, 142
Fujiwara, T., 146
Fukuzawa Yukichi, 204n3
funeral rituals, 41, 205n25
furniture
    dowries, 26, 142–6
    for storage, 26, 137–42, 211nn7–8
    Westernized, 31
futons, 37, 78–9

garages, 57–60, 74
garbage disposal, 78–9, 190
gardens, 56–7, 74
    street gardens, 76–7, 190
Garvey, P., 60, 63
gates, 54–5, 74
gender divisions
    domestic roles, 17, 20, 106, 120–4, 184–5, 190
    stereotypes, 125–6
    see also men; women
generational relations, 94–5, 99, 121–2, 184
gifts
    commemorative, 165–9
    commercialization, 170
    culture of, 26, 174–6, 192
    display of, 128, 161–2
    dolls, 166–9, 187
    food, 170–1
    impacts of, 187
    money, 213n13
    redistribution, 172–4, 180–1
    seasonal cycle, 172, 213n19
    souvenirs, 158–61, 212nn1–3
    spirituality, 164, 187
    studies of, 213n14
    unwanted, 26, 164–5, 173–4
    utilitarian, 171–2, 213nn16,18
Girls' (Dolls') Festival (*hina matsuri*), 85, 166, 167, 178–9, 208n20

god shelves (*kamidana*), 86–91, 208nn15,17
Goldstein-Gidoni, O., 202n14
graves, of relatives, 82–3, 98–9, 191–2, 207n4
Gregson, N., 149
guests, entertainment of, 28–9, 30–1, 33, 53–4, 204n8

habitus, 5, 201n6
hallway, 61–3, 190–1, 206n11
    displays, 113
Hashidate Masumi, 7
haunting, 168–9
heating, 46, 205nn30–31
Hendry, J., 213n14
Hetherington, Kevin, 149
hina-dolls, 154, 166, 178–9, 213nn9–10
Home Cultures, 201n9
homes
    anthropology of, 4–5, 192–5, 201n4
    chûroka-style layout, 30–1, 32
    ideal, 27–9
    imachûshin-style layout, 31, 32
    modern style, 24, 30–1
    ownership, 17, 148, 212n17
    pre-modern, 28–9
    size of, 187
'hot carpets', 46, 205n30
house building
    architect-designed, 15
    conglomerates, 10, 14
    family businesses, 15
    regional styles, 15
households, *see* families
housing communities (*jûtaku-shi*), 54–5, 206n3
Hsu, E., 193
Hugh-Jones, S., 192–3
humour, 120–2, 126, 210n20

Ichimatsu dolls, 166, 167, 179, 212n8
identity, Japanese, 9–10, 186
images, use of, 22–4, 203n26
Indonesia, gift exchange, 186
inside–outside dichotomy, 25, 61–3, 75, 78–9
Interia (Interior) magazine, 117, 131
international travel, 160–1, 212n4
intimacy, 25, 37–8, 47–8, 186
    see also privacy